THE PERSISTENCE OF PRESENCE

The Persistence of Presence analyses the relationship between emblem books, containing combinations of pictures and texts, and Spanish literature in the early modern period. As representations of ideas and ideals, emblems are allegories produced in a particular place and time, and their study can shed light on the central cultural and political activities of an era.

Bradley J. Nelson argues that the emblem was a primary indicator of the social and political functions of diverse literary practices in early modern Spain, from theatre to epic prose. Furthermore, the disintegration of a unified medieval world view left many seeking the kinds of deep knowledge that could be accessed through symbolic pictures, increasing their cultural significance. In this detailed examination of emblem books, sacred and secular theatre, and Cervantes' critique of baroque allegory in *Los trabajos de Persiles y Sigismunda*, Nelson connects the early history of emblematics with the drive towards cultural and political hegemony in Counter-Reformation Spain.

(University of Toronto Romance Series)

BRADLEY J. NELSON is an associate professor and chair in the Department of Classics, Modern Languages and Linguistics at Concordia University.

BRADLEY J. NELSON

The Persistence of Presence

Emblem and Ritual in Baroque Spain

UNIVERSITY OF TORONTO PRESS
Toronto Buffalo London

Toronto Buffalo London
utorontopress.com

Reprinted in paperback 2021

ISBN 978-0-8020-9977-8 (cloth)
ISBN 978-1-4875-2621-4 (paper)

University of Toronto Romance Series

Library and Archives Canada Cataloguing in Publication

Title: The persistence of presence : emblem and ritual in Baroque Spain / Bradley J. Nelson.
Names: Nelson, Bradley J., 1963– author.
Series: University of Toronto romance series.
Description: Series statement: University of Toronto romance series | Paperback reprint. Originally published 2010. | Includes bibliographical references and index.
Identifiers: Canadiana 20210285443 | ISBN 9781487526214 (softcover)
Subjects: LCSH: Spanish literature – Classical period, 1500–1700 – History and criticism. | LCSH: Emblem books, Spanish.
Classification: LCC PQ6066 .B73 2021 | DDC 860.9/003–dc23

This book has been published with the help of a grant from the Canadian Federation for the Humanities and Social Sciences, through the Aid to Scholarly Publications Program, using funds provided by the Social Sciences and Humanities Research Council of Canada.

University of Toronto Press acknowledges the financial assistance to its publishing program of the Canada Council for the Arts and the Ontario Arts Council, an agency of the Government of Ontario.

Canada Council for the Arts
Conseil des Arts du Canada

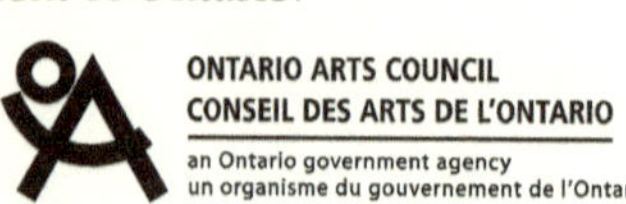

Funded by the Government of Canada
Financé par le gouvernement du Canada

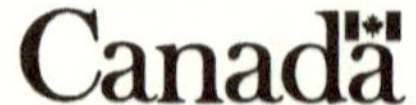

Contents

PART TWO: APPLIED EMBLEMATICS

PART THREE: BODIES AND SIGNS

Illustrations

Acknowledgments

I would like to express my deepest appreciation to my mentors Nicholas Spadaccini and the recently deceased René Jara, as well as to Luis Ramos-García, without whose enthusiastic support I would have never even gone to graduate school. I also want to thank the talented group of Golden Age scholars from Minnesota, especially David and Moisés Castillo, whose ongoing support and critiques have been invaluable to this project in particular and my intellectual growth in general. Ed Friedman's unwavering support of my development as a scholar since my early days as a PhD candidate has been an unending source of inspiration. Tom Conry deserves a special nod for guiding me to Ritual Studies, which was the turning point in converting this project from a PhD dissertation into a book. Charles Ganelin, David Hildner, William Childers, José Antonio Giménez-Micó, Sean Gurd, Bruce Burningham, Susan Paun García, and Bob Blue have read or listened to various versions of some of the ideas presented here, and their comments and suggestions have been extremely helpful. I have had many warm, funny, and productive encounters with friends and colleagues in El Paso at the annual *AHCT* conference. Special thanks go to the University of Minnesota for providing a generous dissertation fellowship at the beginning of the project as well as the Program for Cultural Cooperation between Spain's Ministry of Culture and United States Universities for a generous travel grant. Special thanks also go to Concordia University for providing me with a generous start-up grant, and the Social Sciences and Humanities Research Council of Canada for the research grant that helped bring this project to fruition.

I would like to express my heartfelt appreciation to the readers of the University of Toronto Press for their knowledgable questions and comments, and also to my managing editor, Barb Porter, who is mainly responsible for getting the book ready for the press.

Revised versions of the following previously published essays and articles are included here, by permission: 'A Ritual Practice for Modernity: Baltasar Gracián's Organized Body of Taste,' *Reason and Its Others in Early Modern Times (Spain/Italy 1500s–1700s)*, ed. David R. Castillo and Massimo Lollini, *Hispanic Issues* 32 (Nashville: Vanderbilt UP, 2006), 79–100; 'From Hieroglyphic Presence to Representational Sign: An Other Point of View in the *Auto Sacramental*,' *Hispanic Baroques: Reading Cultures in Context*, ed. Nicholas Spadaccini and Luis Martín-Estudillo, *Hispanic Issues* 31 (Nashville: Vanderbilt UP, 2005), 107–36; '*Los trabajos de Persiles y Sigismunda*: Una crítica cervantina de la alegoresis emblemática' in *Cervantes* 24.2 (2004): 43–69; 'Emblematic Representation and Guided Culture in Baroque Spain: Juan de Horozco y Covarrubias,' *Culture and the State in Spain: 1550–1850*, ed. Tom Lewis and Francisco Sánchez, *Hispanic Issues* 20 (Minneapolis: U Minnesota P, 1999), 157–95; '*El Alcalde de Zalamea*: Pedro Crespo's Marvelous Game of Emblematic Wit' in *Bulletin of the Comediantes* 50.1 (1998): 35–57.

I owe a huge debt of gratitude to my family and friends, in particular my wife Mary, without whose support and patience I would not have been able to dedicate myself to such an enterprise.

For many of us there is a dedicated educator without whose presence and persistence we would never have come so far. Such is the case with my high school Spanish teacher and dear friend, Bill Kreie, who passed away while I was finishing my PhD. It is not easy to teach a foreign language in a small town in rural America, and I dedicate this book to him and all the other foreign language teachers who fight the good fight.

THE PERSISTENCE OF PRESENCE

Introduction

> At least if it does not happen to Alciato with his *Emblemas* as occurred to Erasmus with his *Chiliadas,* having twice promised not to add to them, in the end, he altered and amplified them such that whoever had the first *Chiliadas* didn't have the *Chiliadas.*
>
> [A lo menos si no acaeçe a Alciato con sus *Emblemas* lo que à Erasmo con sus *Chiliadas* que aviendo dos vezes prometido de no las aumentar, al fin làs mudò y añadiò de tal manera que quien tenìa de las primeras *Chiliadas* no tenìa *Chiliadas.*]
>
> Bernardo Daza Pinciano, *Los emblemas*[1]

> The laws of compulsory obedience oblige one to many things, but the powers of pleasure to many more.
>
> [A mucho obligan las leyes de la obediencia forzosa, pero a mucho más las fuerzas del gusto.]
>
> Miguel de Cervantes, *Los trabajos de Persiles y Sigismunda*

This is a book about *presence,* its creation and reception. By presence I mean the way in which certain encounters or events compel us to transcend our mundane existence and to contemplate what appears to be a higher, more universal – more *real* – experience of meaning and being. Such experiences and objects are perceived as possessing an *aura,* an indescribable but almost palpable surplus of meaning, which holds the promise of something that is otherwise lacking. The main hypothesis of the discussions to come is that the emblem, in its many cultural and social contexts and mutations, is best understood as a medium in which conflicting models of presence and aura are articulated and questioned in baroque Spain. In a recent study of the visual image, W.J.T. Mitchell defines a *medium* as 'just ... a "middle," an in-between or go-between, a space or pathway or messenger that connects two things – a sender to a receiver, a writer to a reader, an artist to a beholder, or (in the case of the spiritualist medium) this world to the next' (*What Do Pictures Want?* 204). Following the lead of art historian and iconologist Erwin Panofsky (*Meaning*), Mitchell stresses that a *medium* includes not just the object of contemplation and the technologies deployed in its representation but also the sender and receiver of the communicative act. He advocates a materialist approach for understanding the persistent power of the image in late modernity and so, too, will I propose that the emblem and its role in the production of presence in baroque Spain is best understood as a modern social practice of the first order. For this reason I have placed the religious concept of *presence* in dialogue with the materialist echoes of *aura* (Benjamin): in the emblem, these two metaphysical modes will meet and struggle for dominance.

The central claim of this book is that emblematic structures are powerful tools for the creation of presence effects and, as such, a primary indicator of the social and political functions of literary practices in early modern Spain. This thesis rests on three suppositions: 1) that what is most often at stake in both the theoretical definition and concrete deployment of emblematic structures is the performance of presence; 2) that the performance of presence comes into play in early modernity when power is both articulated and questioned; and 3) that the best way to study the historical force and functions of literature is by focusing on those strategies that most efficiently and consistently realize – or block – the performance of presence. This understanding of presence is grounded in Hans Ulrich Gumbrecht's definition of power, which he offers as an alternative to the Foucauldian insistence on institutional and discursive power structures: 'Unlike Foucault, I think that we miss what is distinctive about power as long as we use this notion within the Cartesian limits of the structures, production, and uses of knowledge. My counterproposal is to define power as the potential of occupying or blocking spaces with bodies' (*Powers* 5). Gumbrecht's groundbreaking work on the ritual performance of presence in the Middle Ages informs his 'anti-Cartesian' understanding of power, which makes it very useful for studying the ritualistic use of words and images in early modernity. Following the distinction posited by Jan Assmann between the semantic and the material sides of the linguistic sign – a distinction also found in early modern emblem theory in the division between a verbal *soul* and hieroglyphic *body* – I argue that the way in which emblematic structures block access to the material circumstances of their articulation represents a particularly potent form of power. This argument necessitates a certain rapprochement between Gumbrecht and Foucault in that the visual or emblematic sign is equated with Gumbrecht's *body*, a move permitted by the aforementioned emblem theory. Walter Benjamin's identification of the corpse as the baroque signifier par excellence in his study of baroque allegory and drama provides a useful trope for this theoretical accommodation (*Origins of German Tragic Drama* 217).

Emblem, Iconology, Emblematic Iconology

If Marx is right in stating that the 'correct scientific method' is one 'whose goal is the recovery of its own origins, a "reproduction of the concrete situation" that it was devised to explain,' then a properly complex historical understanding of the emblem must revisit the origins of emblematics as well as some of the canonical readings of those origins (cited in Mitchell, *Iconology* 105). This shuttling back and forth between the visual-literary artefact and those philological and iconological approaches whose goal is the elucidation of the meaning and function of the emblem seeks to demonstrate, in the first instance, how Andreas Alciato, the author of the first emblem book, becomes the central object, or image, in what Gumbrecht calls 'the production of presence' (*Production* 8). In analysing how the 'form of the author' Alciato blocks our access to the material processes of production of the *Emblematum liber*, the goal is to inspect more closely the authorial forms wielded by literary critics as well as the literary field of baroque Spain. This analytical frame will then be brought to bear on the authors and texts viewed through the problematic optic of the emblem. The reader will have noticed that I have used both *early modernity* and *the baroque* to refer to the historical period and literary corpus which are the objects of study of this book. I will speak more about the baroque later on in this introduction, but for the time being, I will simply state that I am following the work of José Antonio Maravall and Fernando R. de la Flor in identifying the time period between 1580 and 1680 as corresponding to a tumultuous and conflictive temporal landscape that covers the late Renaissance to the end of the baroque. Although Renaissance thinkers and artists manifest the historical consciousness that we associate with a modern mentality, which is to say, the awareness that our contemporary moment is distinct from earlier, 'more perfect' times, it is the baroque which sees the full realization of the lack of epistemological and ontological certitudes characteristic of modernity. It also happens that this period covers the most prolific period of the production and publication of emblem books in Spain. In fact, the emblem and the baroque may be considered two names for the same phenomenon.

We begin with the canonical, tripartite definition of the emblem, in which an *inscriptio*, or titular motto (fragmentary soul), is combined with an equally fragmentary visual image (body), and followed by a *subscriptio* (commentary) that guides the reader towards the solution of a verbal-visual enigma. According to early modern emblem theorists, the meaning of the emblem is not found in any one component but rather in the combination of the three, wherein the whole is greater than the parts. In this way emblem theory effects a swerving of the reader's attention away from the individual, material parts of the emblem, each of which might otherwise serve as the object of an iconological or philological inquiry, towards a unifying and abstract meaning: emblem theory is thus allegorical. That being said, when Alciato publishes his collection of translated epigrams in 1531, there actually is no specific theory on which to base his literary enterprise. The reason most often given for the enormous success of the *Emblematum liber* is that 'Alciato brought about the union' of previously dispersed if widely disseminated discursive and cultural practices of the late Middle Ages and early Renaissance (Selig, *Studies on Alciato* 5). Although there were well established traditions in the creation and use of heraldic devices, manuscript illumination, the glossing of classical epigrams, and allegorical courtly and religious dramas and pageants, Alciato's epigrams are the first works to exhibit what Selig calls the 'perfect fusion of all the component parts of the emblem: motto, device and verse, together expressing the intent of the author' (5).

I would like to take a closer look at the moment and process of production of the first emblem book by questioning one of the critical assumptions underpinning Selig's statement concerning the foundational role of the *Emblematum liber* and its author. This presupposition can be glossed as follows: 'although the theoretical rationalization of the emblem's form lagged several decades behind the publication of his book, Alciato purposefully and self-consciously combined its elements with a clear vision of their meaning.' Setting aside the obvious temporal paradox, one problem with this statement is that this is not at all how the first emblem book came about. Sagrario López summarizes how the *Emblematum liber* came to publication: 'Inspired by the *Greek Anthology*, Andrea Alciato ... composed 99 epigrams, each one of which he gave a title. As luck [*fortuna*] would have it, thanks to the imperial adviser Peutinger, the work would end up in the hands of the printer Steyner, who, with commercial interest, considered how appropriate it would be to add an illustration to each epigram. This task was given to the engraver Breuil, and the book was published in 1531 in Augsburg with the title *Emblematum liber*' (Introducción 31). López's comments on Alciato's limited role in the production of the book demonstrate that he cannot really be considered the *father* of the emblem, a discursive form that requires a visual image as well as a formidable technological apparatus and social habitus in its production. The manuscript, which, as far as we know, contained no images, nor any mention of images, passes through the hands of an influential humanist and imperial advisor, Conrad Peutinger,[2] who makes sure that the work is well received by a printer in Augsburg, Steyner, who in turn determines that the epigrams would be more reader-friendly – sell more quickly? – if they were accompanied by visual images. So he hands the manuscript over to the engraver Breuil. Peutinger, Steyner, and Breuil are all fascinating figures in their own right, and all of them have much more experience with emblem-like composition than does Alciato. What is more, there is no evidence that Alciato was involved in the discussions concerning which images should go with which epigrams, nor in the actual making of the engravings; nor did he participate in the layout of the work. This situation will change with later editions, but according to Stephen Rawles, as late as 1534, by which time multiple editions and translations of the book had already appeared, 'there could be no generic expectation of a "tripartite emblem"' (68).

The meaning of the emblem as a discursive protagonist of the first order thus lagged far behind its invention, in which multiple and sometimes non-communicating agents had a direct hand. In another article, López stresses that 'the use of engraved illustrations made the production of this type of work much more difficult, because it required a complicated process in which the emblematist, the artist who drew the concepts that the author wished to represent, the engraver who carved the plates, the editor or publisher who financed the edition, and the printer were all implicated' ('Los libros' 178). It is readily apparent that the aura that surrounds the artist Alciato and his role as *inventore* is much more complex and, in fact, interesting than the direct paternal relationship between the artist and his or her creation as it is traditionally understood. It is probably more correct to consider Alciato the step-father of the emblem rather than its progenitor. What we are looking at in terms of both the literary and commercial markets is the complex process of production of what will become a highly prized commodity. In this materialist approach, one begins to appreciate how the authorial figure of 'Alciato' works to 'block the space' that would otherwise give us access to the material processes and contingencies involved in the publication of the *Emblematum liber* (Gumbrecht, *Powers* 5). The image of the self-conscious artist occupies what is better understood as an empty space, a lack at the centre of the complex interaction between diverse agents in the creation and dissemination of emblems. In emblematic terms, the relation between the figure of the artist, the inscription offered by the *Emblematum liber*, and Selig's philological commentary concerning Alciato's foundational role in later works obscures the problem of authorship as well as the historical contingencies that resulted in the publication of the work. Rather than allowing the complexity of the process of production, publication, and dissemination of the *Emblematum liber* to produce lines of inquiry into multiple fields, the authorial emblem channels our penetrating gaze into the void of authorial intent. What López's valuable observations make apparent is that the author and the text occupy distinct levels of both the creative and the critical enterprise.

One approach to this problem is offered by Carlos Gutiérrez's recent study of the baroque poet and courtly intriguer Francisco de Quevedo, in which Gutiérrez distinguishes between the '*microquevedo* (intra-textual position-takings) and the *macroquevedo* (the space of sociopolitical and literary possibilities; *habitus* and the all-embracing position-takings, definitively)' (20). Gutiérrez signals his references to the latter 'emblem' of authorial power, which he calls the 'macro-Quevedo,' with the uppercase QUEVEDO. In our case, the permutations and interventions that Alciato's manuscript undergoes on the road to publication place questions of authorial intentionality and generic definition in a purely hypothetical or mythical framework, one perhaps best represented by the upper-case ALCIATO. The historical foreshortening that paves the way for Selig's declaration concerning Alciato's central role in the invention of the emblem is itself emblematic in the way that an entire range of aesthetic, social, and technological possibilities is channeled into the timeless image of ALCIATO.[3]

Returning to López's Introducción, she uses the allegory *'fortuna'* to embody the historical agency, or lack thereof, behind the convergence of artistic, political, economic, and technological (self-) interests and circumstances in the publication of the first emblem book. According to this view, Peutinger, Steyner, and Breuil become unwitting and subrogated agents of an impersonal and overarching historical intentionality emanating from and around the author-figure ALCIATO. Would it not be more accurate, more philologically responsible, to recognize that the founding gesture of the tripartite, emblematic form is tentative, contingent, and multiple? Institutionally informed, commercially driven, and artistically imitative, it is better understood as a medium in which diverse and even contradictory discourses and forces come into contact and struggle with and against each other. Mitchell's aforementioned definition of *medium*, by which he means 'the whole set of material practices that brings an image together with an object to produce a picture' (*What Do Pictures Want?* 198), brings us closer to understanding the production as well as the modernity of the emblem. The intransigent questions concerning Alciato's actual role produced by López's narrative bear witness to the fact that the very attempt to elucidate the meaning of Alciato and his book inevitably produces what Deleuze and Guattari have called 'lines of escape,' once historical materialities are admitted entrance (*A Thousand Plateaus* 203–5). It could be stated that the science of philology unravels the integrity of the authorial fabric of meaning from the inside out when it turns its attention to the materiality of literary creation and dissemination.

My somewhat belabored point is that the occlusion of the messy materialities of emblem production should itself be read as emblematic, since the emblem and its ever-present theory do just this kind of work. According to Peter M. Daly, 'the emblematic mode of representation' becomes a dominant discourse at the onset of modernity, when the image began to vie with the sacred word for ontological and epistemological supremacy (*Literature* 25–32).[4] What Daniel Russell has called the 'age of the emblem' (*Emblematic Structures* 8) arises out of 'the crisis of representation, the collapse of the distance between representation and world … [which] brought back the desire for presence' (Gumbrecht, *Powers* 13). Thus, the emblem appears in a world that has become multiple and conflictive, and in which the traditional hierarchy between the word and the sign has become unstable. In the end, emblematics is a medium in which the desire for presence may convincingly compensate for symbolic, historical, and social instability by evoking a unified meaning from a constitutively hybrid form.

Nevertheless, if the emblem embodies a desire for presence in the face of a world of disintegrating certainties, it also embodies this same disintegration in the dispersed and confused nature of its material production. Even as the emblematist sets himself apart from the past in order to select and make present those signs deemed most communicative because of their residual iconicity, the emblem, in its multiple and contradictory materiality, points to the absence of certainty symptomatic of the increasing fragmentation and relativization of the unified worldview that characterized the Middle Ages. And just as the emblem attempts to anchor symbolic movement in allegorical structures linked to a visual image, so too does textual and literary criticism continue to anchor the semiotic instability of the literary artefact in the problematic ground of authorial intent.

According to Gumbrecht, philology is implicated in a search for epistemological certainty on which to ground its editorial practices and scientific legitimacy: '[A]ll philological practices generate desires for presence, desires for a physical and space-mediated relationship to the things of the world (including texts), and … such desire for presence is indeed the ground on which philology can produce effects of tangibility (and sometimes even the reality thereof)' (*Powers* 8). What Gumbrecht calls the 'presence effect' of allegorical and philological discourses both arises from and reproduces the void at the heart of modern symbolic edifices. As historians and philosophers from José Antonio Maravall to Slavoj Žižek have argued, the founding moment of modernity is not the affirmation of transcendental certitude based on rational categories of thought by self-present Cartesian subjects, but rather the experience of the abyss out of which reason, like the emblem, dramatically arises as a gesture of symbolic power, all the while harboring an unconscious symptom of its constitutive limitations. In the words of Lyle Massey, 'the tension produced by this seeming contradiction, which is present not only in Descartes but in much other seventeenth-century thought, is the result of a "genuine sense of contingency and limitation … in conflict with a tendency to regard the power of the rational mind as virtually limitless"' (1154). The role of the emblematic body in this disenchanted world is to block, or fill, this abyss with an ineffable and therefore transcendental presence of mysterious origins and meaning. Nowhere is this more evident than in the seriousness with which emblematics treats the question of reception.

Most of the early modern thinkers and writers studied here make a concerted effort to contain the reception of their emblems within strict moral and epistemological boundaries. That being said, the insurmountable problem in reception analysis is that 'only in exceptional circumstances do we have evidence for the acts of reception' (Gumbrecht, *Making Sense* 24). For example, Bruce Wardropper and Viviana Díaz Balsera have observed that it is difficult, if not impossible, to speculate on what might be going through the mind of a spectator who watches an *auto sacramental*. The problem is that theatrical production and reception represent two different levels, or faces, of the aesthetic event. Any attempt to move from the one to the other implies a shift in discursive form, a translation if you will, which always leaves traces of the critic's desire. One way to frame, if not solve, this problem is to focus on the analysis of staged acts, or performances, of emblematic reception as they appear in literary texts. Time and again, the authors studied here present contradictory or competing interpretations of 'emblematic moments,' performed in most cases under a staged gaze; these moments invariably have a direct bearing on the overall ideological possibilities of the work in question. Since these competing interpretations are often asymmetrically framed in terms of their correctness or legitimacy, we not only can arrive at a valid reading of the desired, or privileged, meaning; we can also study those 'incorrect' meanings that are used to dialectically frame the privileged intent and which open onto a social and historical space of multiple and contradictory meanings. In such moments, the emblem becomes what Walter Benjamin calls a 'dialectical image.' Mitchell explains: 'The essence of the dialectical image is its polyvalence – as object in the world, as representation, as analytic tool, as rhetorical device, as figure – most of all as a Janus-faced emblem of our predicament, a mirror of history, and a window beyond it' (*Iconology* 205). As we have seen in the case of Alciato, the moment we refuse to resolve the perspectival tension between image and meaning in an emblematic performance is when the emblem becomes most communicative of the historical predicament of early modern authors and readers.

When theoretical discussions concerning the correct or incorrect – orthodox or heterodox – interpretation of emblems are brought to bear on an emblematic moment as presented in a play, for example, the critic is able to construct a hermeneutical frame of sorts in order to explore early modern attempts to construct a mass of 'readers' that cuts across caste, class, and gender lines of differentiation and demarcation. The famous tripartite structure of the emblem itself, with its visual symbol, Latin motto, and vernacular commentary, represents both the unification and cultural differentiation of illiterate, erudite, and merely literate subjects. Both explicitly and implicitly we find prescribed and proscribed models and modes of production and reception in emblematic texts, which provide at least a partial view of the possible range of actual interpretations at the time of a work's publication and/or performance. By focusing on the staging of tension-filled moments of emblematic reception, the goal is to 'translat[e] a historical knowledge embedded in monothetic structures into the polythetic structures of their appropriation' (Gumbrecht, *Making Sense* 37). This method is an exact inversion of how the emblem normally functions, in which multiple possibilities are channeled into a univalent allegorical relation. It also corresponds with Jacques Lezra's definition of 'eventful reading': 'Eventful reading can only succeed where it becomes the practical disposition toward an understanding of what will have occurred neither as what properly had to occur, nor as what took place adventitiously, but as what remains from or resists that distinction "before" it is aestheticized as an event that afflicts a subject whose advent it marks' (33). The result of an eventful reading, then, is not the resolution of material contingencies and aesthetic practices into a unified meaning or intent, but rather the recognition of a resistant kernel of Otherness to not only the meaning of a specific artefact but to the very structure of meaning which frames analysis from the moment one decides to resolve the enigma of authorial intention.

Ritual Origins and Materialities of Communication[5]

In the historical movement from the Renaissance to the baroque, emblems become a constitutive element of virtually every religious and political spectacle and discourse in Spain, where they largely serve the purpose of making present the universal and transcendental guarantees of Counter Reformation thought, while educating subjects in the reception and production of an allegorically-based knowledge.[6] This was not always so. In the confusing origins of modernity, emblematic devices often conveyed very individualistic and secular performances of genius (*inventio*). Whether we are talking about *empresas*, which aristocratic subjects displayed in courtly masques and contests, poetic devices like the enigmatic *invenciones*,[7] or the humanistic translation of classical epigrams, the impetus for these performances of visual and verbal wit is, in the words of Pierre Bourdieu, the accumulation of symbolic and cultural capital by courtly and/or humanist subjects (*Outline* chapter 4).[8] These strategic games and contests reveal that the phenomenon of presence is not completely contained within institutional boundaries, as ostensibly takes place in the dramatization of sacred events in medieval religious and political spaces; to the contrary, presence is negotiated through dialogic encounters between multiple players.[9] More to the point, these symbolic contests, which revolve around the creative play with the multiple denotations and connotations of inherited verbal and visual tropes, display an eminently theatrical view of the world, meaning that emblematic iconicity is produced in ontological and epistemological conditions that appear antithetical to the achievement of presence. The self-conscious donning of masks and playing of roles ought to work against the feeling that one is in the presence of the real thing; in fact, the impression that the sign is holding or hiding a more profound meaning behind its visual appearance is what motivates, not presence, but the desire for presence. Just as an empty tomb triggers the desire for the presence of a body, so, too, does the mysterious and reticent signifier spark the desire for the fullness of meaning.

Because of this destabilizing theatricality, the emblem becomes a key strategy for simultaneously exploiting and masking the theatrical nature of social and political hierarchies through the production of highly ritualized, intense moments of symbolic production. Whereas the ritual dramatizations of ecclesiastical and monarchical allegories of transubstantiation perform the active inscription of the unified cosmos with and within the symbolic trappings of earthly institutions of power, courtly and humanist expressions of individual genius and heroism open up and inhabit a breach in the universalist ontology, one that, like its institutional counterpart, misrecognizes and occludes its contingent moment of articulation.

The first translation of *Emblematum liber* into Spanish provides another instructive episode in the origins of emblematics.[10] Bernardino Daza Pinciano, a Spanish émigré, procures an edition of the book with marginal comments and additions by Alciato himself, which the author was going to amend 'so that the work would be finished for once and for all' [para ser la obra una vez cumplida] (Daza Pinciano 13). The year is 1549, eighteen years after the publication of the first edition and more than a decade after its first translation into French. Daza protests that his *Emblemas* are not an erudite or learned work written to impress the reader with his knowledge; rather, the entreaties of 'those Spaniards, not understanding the Latin Tongue, [were] enough to make me tarry on such a frivolous task' [para aquellos Españoles que no entendiendo la lengua Latina fuere esto bastante para hazerme gastar algun tiempo en tan excusado trabajo] (7–9). According to Daza's words, the translation was done in great haste and rather carelessly. In the 'Preface to his friends,' however, his false humility becomes apparent, and we see just how laborious the translation proved to be.

At first, Daza attempts to translate the emblems into Italianate verse forms 'verse by verse and word for word' (14). He soon finds this attempt at safeguarding semantic rigor and poetic form counterproductive, for several reasons: the rhythm of his native Castilian, the harmony of the verses, as well as the meaning of the emblems themselves all prove too difficult to overcome in a simultaneously literal and poetic translation. Embodying his own *empresa* with the verbal emblem of a ship whose captain must throw out cargo to ease a difficult passage, Daza rationalizes his subsequent and frequent decisions to add and subtract verses, notwithstanding the addition of the occasional proverb from his own cultural repertoire. The *licencias* he self-consciously takes in working and reworking the translation result in a completely new creation. In a Borgesian structure, our primary source is the Spanish translation of an appended edition of a Latin translation of Greek epigrams.

Daza's earlier comment concerning the Alciato edition he is translating is also noteworthy, because he is evidently working from a version that had not yet been published. Put another way, and echoing the epigraph at the beginning of this introduction, Daza's source is a work that does not officially exist. Moreover, were such an edition to come into existence, the status of the first edition as the ultimate expression of the author's intent would come into question, setting the conventional temporal structure of authorial intention on its head. For Daza, not only is the source book a work in progress, the translation itself cannot be said to be a faithful reproduction of this original, but instead a rather free interpretation of an unfinished Urtext. Two markedly different translations will follow: a 1573 translation by the esteemed humanist Francisco Sánchez, El Brocense, and a 1615 version by the humanist cleric Diego López. In the case of Sánchez, we find a translation that takes Alciato back to his classical roots, while López produces what R. de la Flor terms 'an Alciato "in the divine mode"' (cited in Fernández López 354). In conclusion, when we talk about Alciato in Spain, we are not referring to any one author but rather to a multiple and variable entity who mediates an entire range of institutional interests and material practices, all of which surround, reveal, and occlude the mythical moment of genesis of the book and its progeny.[11] To cite Julio Baena's tour de force deconstruction of the four-century-long effort to 'correct' and 'fix' a definitive version of *Don Quixote*: 'by having multiple modes of existence that are equally valid, it cannot, strictly speaking, exist as something unequivocal or definable' (*Discordancias* 96). In order to make Alciato become present as a transhistorical figure, a primordial act of demarcation and mystification is required, which, according to Catherine Bell, places not only the social deployment of emblematics but also the early modern philological effort to define and legitimate emblematic theories and precepts within the purvey of ritual practice (*Ritual Theory* 89–92).

Ritual Theory, Emblem Practice

In *Ritual Perspectives and Dimensions*, Bell observes that during the first half of the twentieth century, ritual scholars, anthropologists, and sociologists invested their scientific energies and practices either in the narrative (mythological) motifs of ritual *content*, or the basic (universal) schematizations of ritual *form*. In the first instance, anthropologists such as James George Frazer and Mircea Eliade sought to establish a transhistorical collection of Urmyths capable of placing modern man in contact with his primitive and collective origins by documenting the persistence of primordial motifs and structures of human thought in the cultural performances of so-called primitive societies. As Bell points out, this communication of a central and collective series of myths by an elite cadre of ritual specialists also happens to be one of the functions and goals of religious ritual itself (*Ritual Perspectives* 31). Rather than bring science closer to understanding the status and function of ritualized narratives in so-called primitive cultures, Bell argues that the scientific theories and practices informing these studies acted instead to legitimize the modern 'objectivity' of the scientists and their enterprise by projecting a positivistic scheme of human evolution onto the societies whose cultures they were studying. The end result of this labour was the conflation of the ritual content they were seeking with a preconceived notion of universal myth. As Mitchell reminds us, 'history and anthropology are not just descriptions of events and practices but of *representations* of events and practices ... "ways of world-*making*," not just mirroring' (*Iconology* xiv).

Scholars of ritual structure, such as Claude Lévi-Strauss and Arthur Van Gennep, focused on the basic structures of human cognitive activity, which they then analysed within the more modern and 'rational' structures of their scientific method. As in the case of Frazier and his followers, the modern vs. primitive dichotomy is rarely questioned in this paradigm, functioning instead as a kind of limit, or 'unthought,' of the structuralist study of ritual in the way it protects both theoretical assumptions and the conclusions they support concerning human culture and human thought from further inquiry. To paraphrase the words of Daniel Russell in his studies of the emblem, their theoretical discourse and scientific practice affected the object of their inquiry more than the object of inquiry affected their theory and practice.[12]

The field of emblem studies has seen a similar dichotomization of research practices, although the situation, as I see it, is exactly reversed in comparison to the field of ritual studies. Many historical studies, such as those of Mario Praz and Robert Clements, work towards a more or less precise set of definitions and borders, i.e., *structures*, of not only the emblem but of many of its sub-genres as well. Their goal is to map the taxonomy of emblematic practices in order to guide the analysis of its 'products.' Many shorter studies, in the meanwhile, focus on the meaning, or content, of individual emblems, or a series of related emblematic motifs, tracking down their medieval and classical sources as well as comparing them to a wide array of literary correspondences. In both cases, rather than impose an external, scientific model onto the data, emblem scholars often attempt to unveil and imitate the theories and practices found in early modern texts in the effort to make present a more or less authentic meaning. In Daly's words, 'I have assumed that my reception equals early modern intention' ('Digitizing' 51).

A fundamental problem with this approach is that the decision to mimetically reproduce early modern emblematics prevents scholars from looking at the 'unthought' of emblematic practice itself. There have been comparatively few attempts to analyse the practices of emblematists in a way that would reinsert them into their socio-cultural relations by focusing on what Bell terms the 'misrecognition' of the social and political implications of their own activity (R. de la Flor, *Barroco*; Pinkus).[13] Several of the most ambitious research projects in emblem research today seek to reinforce those approaches that concentrate on the establishment of emblematic meaning by linking digitized emblem books to on-line reference libraries. These projects increase and 'democratize' access to the cultural repertoire that informs emblem production, but the stratification of knowledge that accompanies such projects produces an eerie likeness to the invention of reference tables and indexes in the early modern printing press, without necessarily considering how technology and technological decisions affect, not the access to, but the reception and interpretation of knowledge.[14] Such a turn can only be accomplished by shifting our gaze away from meaning and towards the material processes and social matrices implicated in the composition and dissemination of emblems and the institutions that support and promote them. The emblem does not merely signify an idea or concept, nor can it be limited to Gracián's definition of the metaphysical conceit: 'an act of understanding, which expresses the correspondence found between objects' [un acto de entendimiento, que exprime la correspondencia que se halla entre los objetos] (*Agudeza* 32). The emblem also *does* something beyond the ingenious communication of an idea, and this activity is best understood by exploring its role in ritualistic social practices, and vice-versa.

In his well-known *Culture of the Baroque*, Maravall describes not only the persuasive effects of the multifarious manifestations of 'baroque guided culture' but also the creation of a wider cultural sphere of *competencias* in which subjects become active participants in their own (re)formation: 'Rather than letting themselves be persuaded, therefore, it is a matter of making themselves persuaded, which seems to offer a more active nuance. That is, they possess a cultivated predisposition to be persuaded' (74). Unlike Foucault's notion of the modern 'subject-effect,' Maravall's model focuses on the individual encounter between artists and writers and the crisis-attuned mentality of the sixteenth and seventeenth centuries. In the conflictive cultural and social space of the Spanish baroque, the emblem configures 'a more independent and active role' for the emergent subject of language (Russell, *Emblematic Structures* 15). This discursive independence is the new requisite for political power in a world in which instability and mobility have become the norm. It is also where ritual theory and practice step in to help move independent subjects toward choosing, or at least consenting to, that which is most compatible with the reconstituted 'monarchical-seigniorial segments' of Spanish Counter Reformation society.

One solution to the oft-cited contradiction between the 'free' humanist subject and Maravall's concept of baroque guided culture can be found in the efficacy with which discursive practices cultivate social and cultural empowerment in their creators as well as their readers.[15] Where Bell posits the existence of a cultural competence she terms *ritual mastery* to help explain the persistence and proliferation of ritualistic practices in modern society, I offer the term *allegorical mastery* as a first step toward understanding the cultural and ideological significance of emblematic production and reception in early modern Spain.

The main point of contact between Bell and Maravall that I would like to explore is the confluence between Bell's concept of 'redemptive hegemony' and Maravall's notion of 'a dynamic guidance through activity.' In the same way that Gumbrecht's definition of power provides a more materialist understanding of the way that spaces are opened or blocked by 'bodies,' Bell's notion of redemptive hegemony emphasizes how subjects can negotiate legitimate spaces for themselves from an inferior position. Her basic point, which will be developed later on, is that a subject does not have to be in a position of power to exercise ritual mastery; rather, ritual mastery is a strategy for creating legitimate spaces for heretofore excluded or inferior subjects by aligning their material and political desires with those of the dominant hegemony, and vice-versa. A subject's ability to wield ritual structures and tropes gives it a measure of self-determination as long as that determination can be seen to redeem the hegemonic field, however obliquely. This may include the subtle or not-so-subtle alteration of this field, as we will see in the discussions of Juan de Horozco y Covarrubias's *Emblemas Morales* and Calderón's *El alcalde de Zalamea*. Ritual mastery adds an important quotient of self-determination to Maravall's subject of control in the sense that both the subject and the social or political hegemony are 'redeemed' by the activity of the previously excluded or marginalized subjects. Many current readings of Spanish baroque culture take a critical line where Maravall's concept of 'guided culture' is concerned due to what critics see as Maravall's overly deterministic characterization of the relationship between literature, especially theater, and attempts by the nascent Spanish state to form an ethnic, cultural, and political hegemony (Kallendorf, '¿Qué he de hacer?'). Without unnecessarily belaboring a point that will be dealt with in more complexity in later chapters, it is worth pointing out that at no time does Maravall posit a monolithic understanding of a caste-oriented Spanish state in seventeenth-century Spain. Rather, the so-called monarchical-seigniorial segments of Spanish society is a term that refers to uneasy and constantly shifting alliances between a residual aristocratic *organicism* and an emergent bourgeois *animism*, within the framework of an aspiring monarchical absolutism (Juan Carlos Rodríguez, *Theory and History*). The usefulness of Bell's concept of redemptive hegemony lies in its ability to frame an analysis of how previously excluded subjects can simultaneously redeem their own social and cultural identity and that of a dominant if unstable ideology in a single move, thus showing how an event which seems to challenge the status quo may serve to strengthen and expand existing political institutions through subtle alterations. By tying semiotic innovation to the maintenance of social and cultural hierarchies, the emblem provides many privileged moments for understanding how this negotiation of power functions.

As evidenced by the marked differences between the many editions of Alciato, 'any reader of emblems is … potentially a maker of emblems since the deciphering of an emblem entails the realization that the emblem motif could have been used differently' (Russell, *Emblematic Structures* 167). It is not merely the emblematic motifs that vary from emblem to emblem; emblem theory is also an inexhaustible source of Derridean *différance*. What we see in the emblem is not so much the separation of the theoretical from the practical but rather, in the words of Bourdieu, the creation of an interpretative *habitus* in which a symbolic activity makes sense (*Field of Cultural Production* 110). To borrow a term from Godzich and Spadaccini, the emerging history and theory of the emblem become the *instrumentality* of the emblematists' search for cultural and social legitimacy ('Popular Culture' 44). One of the most effective traits of an emblematic moment is the way in which it sets itself apart from the plot as a particularly intense symbolic event and, in many cases, an important key to understanding the meaning of the work in which it appears (Russell, *Emblematic Structures* 92). In this way, the emblem is homologous to Bell's characterization of ritual as 'a matter of various culturally specific strategies for setting some activities off from others, for creating and privileging a qualitative distinction between the "sacred" and the "profane," and for ascribing such distinctions to realities thought to transcend the powers of human actors' (*Ritual Theory* 74). We are once again talking about the production of presence.

Corpus

In *Making Sense in Life and Literature*, Gumbrecht states that 'the greatest ambition of reception aesthetics [is the] reconstruction of literature's influence on history' (26). According to this model, literary creation and reception are social acts and not mere reflections of a more profound, historical base: in short, there is a fundamentally literary component to modern subjectivity. Nevertheless, even the most advanced theories of reception recognize that the ways in which literature engages social actors and institutions are largely indirect. In Iser's words, 'no literary text relates to contingent reality as such, but to models or concepts of reality, in which contingencies and complexities are reduced to meaningful structure' (70). Similar to the way Mitchell argues in his statement concerning the representational status of anthropological narratives, Gumbrecht states that 'texts mediate not historical knowledge but historical consciousness' (*Making Sense* 37). What makes the emblem so interesting in light of these assertions is that not only do emblem theorists invest a lot of energy into the question of reception, but the emblem itself becomes the medium of exchange between medieval conceptions of the sacred meaning of words and the infinite abyss that opens up between the sign and its meaning in modernity. Erwin Panofsky's comments on the epistemological and ontological discoveries and limitations of Renaissance perspective shed light on this development: 'Perspective subjects the artistic phenomenon to stable and even mathematically exact rules, but on the other hand, makes the phenomenon contingent upon human beings, indeed upon the individual: for these rules refer to the psychological and physical conditions of the visual impression, and the way they take effect is determined by the freely chosen position of a subjective "point of view"' (*Perspective* 67). Like Renaissance painting, in the movement from schematized aspects of texts to acts of concretization by the reader/spectator there is plenty of room for interpretative slippage (Iser 21). For this reason, as I stated earlier, the methodology of this study focuses on acts of reception organized and realized within literary texts themselves; which is to say, that the emblematic moment includes both actors and spectators in the diegetical medium of the text.

These staged performances can be analysed, on the one hand, as images of the intended or ideal reception through which statements concerning the ideological posture of the works can be considered and either substantiated or questioned. More often than not, however, at the same time as an idealized reception-image is inscribed within the text, deviant or incorrect interpretations are deployed either to privilege (dialectically) or subvert (dialogically) the ostensibly 'correct interpretation.' I would argue that no text can be considered either conservative or subversive until the relationship between deviance and correctness inscribed in the text itself is unraveled, and even then only according to the theoretical model brought to bear on the text. The mere presence of deviance has no meaning in itself but only in relation to the internal dynamics of the text and, by extension, in relation to the distinct modes of historical consciousness both inscribed in these textual dynamics and brought to bear on them by readers. If we include the contemporary theoretical-analytical approach as an inalienable aspect of the determination of said meaning, then we come to a more nuanced historical appreciation for both the meanings of the text and the ways in which these meanings are identified and legitimated.

Rather than discard or substantiate these deviant interpretive inscriptions, they will be read here in light of two possible frames of reference, each one with its own limitations. On the one hand, they will be used to explore their possible relation to a diverse reading community, one whose potentially deviant interpretations motivate the desire of the author-figure to privilege allegorical as opposed to dialogical readings of the text, or vice-versa. On the other hand, we must recognize that these transgressive characters are themselves artistic creations and should be analysed with an eye toward their poetic function, first and foremost. Both interpretive frames offer indirect views of historical conflicts and tensions, as critics such as William Childers and Jaime Contreras have argued in their archival work on the *morisco* and *converso*, or crypto-judaic, communities in early modern Spain.

I. The Emblem

There are three main sections in this book, the first of which attempts to outline in very broad strokes a theory of emblematic reception specific to the historical situation of early modern Spain through an interconnected reading of Juan de Borja's *Empresas morales* and Juan de Horozco y Covarrubias's *Emblemas morales*. Chapter 1 takes up Borja's invention of what Rafael García Mahíques has called the 'empresa hispánica' (Introducción 47). For neoplatonists who first theorized and practiced the construction and interpretation of all sorts of *emblemata*, the ultimate goal was to discover a conduit to original or ideal knowledge through the construction of an ideogrammatical language unsusceptible to the inaccuracies and temporal shortcomings of alphabetic language. In the words of E.H. Gombrich, '[Ficino] thought that the numbers and proportions of a thing preserved in the image reflect the idea in the divine intellect and therefore impart to the image something of the power of the spiritual essence which it embodies' (174). According to García Mahíques, Borja's *Empresas morales* takes a more parochial view of the hieroglyphic image; in fact, nothing could be further from the Ignatian rendering of *desengaño* that informs Borja's collection than Ficino's search for ideal knowledge. Borja's text is almost aggressively anti-theoretical in its terse dismissal of Renaissance theories of the device (*empresa*), offering instead 'self-evident' and therefore unquestionable notions of reason and customs on which to base his emblematic program.

By analysing the Prologue and several of Borja's emblems in light of the *Spiritual Treatises* of his father, (San) Francisco de Borja, it becomes clear that Borja's denigration of emblem theory prepares the ground for a direct application of Ignatian meditative techniques to the hybrid structure of the emblem. This conceptual and iconological marriage configures, in turn, a baroque model of Catherine Bell's notion of redemptive hegemony. My intent here is not to conflate the Jesuit religious thought contained in these works with a specific definition of baroque culture, but rather to track how Spanish, Counter Reformation ideology responds to the more generalized baroque condition of *desengaño*, which I take to be consistent with the way in which '[h]uman minds were upset by the melancholic sensation that the Earth was deprived of its ancient centrality' (Battistini 22). Among the factors that contribute to this period of modernity in Spain, Fernando Ordóñez lists the following: 'the consolidation of the colonial system in America and other African and Asian enclaves; the implementation of the Counter-Reformation as action and reaction on the part of the Catholic Church to the Protestant Reform movement; and the transition to the mercantilist system as economic paradigm' (296). *Desengaño*, then, is a term that describes the way that a baroque mentality possesses, or responds to, not just the changes that have become synonymous with modernity but, more importantly, the consciousness of those changes and the crises, both real and imagined, that accompany the epochal shift.

Recent work on the baroque can be categorized according to two broad frames of analysis, as observed by Luis Martín Estudillo and Nicholas Spadaccini: 'there are those who were interested in historically oriented interpretations focusing on the Baroque's containment side (Maravall) ... while others highlight its transgressive or liberating aspects as evidenced by many Latin American voices on this subject (José Lezama Lima and Severo Sarduy)' (334–5). My understanding of the emblem strives to bring these two paradigms into productive dialogue by looking at emblematic moments from a dual perspective: first, as a dialectical *structure* erected in the interest of forestalling historical change; and second, as a dialogical *encounte*r that has the potential to reveal the lack of epistemological and ontological foundations of baroque edifices of power. In the case of Borja, his *Empresas morales* straddles the religious world of the Society of Jesus and the political world of the absolutist state, which accounts for the unique blend of religious, scientific, and political images and themes in its construction of a tightly controlled reading practice. Borja takes the most individualistic of the emblematic modes, the *empresa*, and converts it into a meditative method for curbing individual desire – for knowledge, for self-improvement, for social mobility, for social change, etc. In this way, the emblem is resituated at the centre of a 'self-help' program based on emergent technologies of self-repression. Presence in this scheme leads to the reification of an allegorical understanding of the world founded on the absence of material guarantees of meaning on which an epistemological or ontological project might be erected. All of which means that history, individual histories in particular, cannot be redeemed nor be made significantly present in this life but only serve as an imperfect vehicle for the journey to the next.

In chapter 2, I analyse how Juan de Horozco y Covarrubias privileges emblematic discourse above all other artistic and historical endeavors through the evocation of an allegorical theatre of the history of art. By employing the language of perspectival painting in what Karen Pinkus calls the 'return to the (mythical) origins of graphic characters,' Horozco attempts to evoke a signifying surplus on which to construct his version of Hispanic linguistic universalism (7). His iconological theory forges a link between diverse forms of artistic mimesis, the will to power of a declining Spanish Empire, and individual subjects by guiding the reader's desire for secret meaning towards the interests of the Spanish state. Santiago Sebastián's effort to open the field of Art History to the contributions of emblematics is the point of departure for my hypothesis concerning the fabrication of textual profundity – 'depth of meaning' – through the perspectival arrangement of historical sources and literary citations.

II. Applied Emblematics

Chapters 3, 4, and 5 deal with the intimate relation between emblematics, theatre, and the construction of modern subjectivities, as the role of mass spectacles has long been considered a key element in the construction of Spanish national consciousness. Emblem scholars agree that theatre is the most emblematic of all baroque literary genres, and my specific focus will be on the dramatic staging of emblematic moments. The goal is to demonstrate how the emblem is not only an inexhaustible source of allegorical motifs and allusions, but how it also serves as a powerful rhetorical tool whose potential as an artistic and ideological medium is realized in the festive atmosphere of the public plazas and *corrales.* In theatrical settings, the tendency of the emblematic artifice to vanish from the scene, once allegorical and historical meanings are established, is facilitated by the overwhelming influence of an emergent technology of spectacle. In his landmark study of the emblem in Spain, R. de la Flor reminds us that: 'The festival, fundamentally the "festival of State," is thus converted into a representational frame for these "achievements of ingenuity (wit)," through which the culture of the time celebrates itself to itself. Even in the case where [the emblem's] difficult meaning could not be deciphered by the multitudes, nor its transcriptions read by the common spectator, its very presence and utilization by the mechanisms of power, or those institutions that massively deployed them, manifests an active pedagogy and a project of adaptation of these icono-linguistic artefacts for mass society' (*Emblemas* 226). The cathartic effect created by the search for and discovery of meaning in the emblem is magnified on the stage, resulting – ideally – in the collective interpellation of the audience into foundational narratives of monarchical unity. As stated earlier, the guidance of the spectator towards a 'correct' interpretation necessitates his or her engagement in a conflict between deviant and correct discursive and moral models. In ritual terms, the enactment of a threat and the subsequent redemption of Spanish unity in the face of this threat are channeled through the recreation of the origins of the nation-race-family.

The ritualized performance of these origins is the main subject of chapter 3, which embarks on an excursion of sorts to the frontiers of temporal, geographical, and aesthetic terrain in an analysis of Lope de Vega's *El Nuevo mundo descubierto por Cristóbal Colón*. The baroque concepts of fragmentation, emptiness, and estrangement are brought to bear on Lope's staging of the first encounter between Europeans and a peculiar dramatic entity I call the 'emblematic *indio*.' The movement from the crisis caused by the appearance of the cross on the shores of *La Deseada* to the eventual acceptance, or recognition, of the *presence* of Christ in the image of the crucifixion by the *indio* displays how Spanish imperialism extends itself in time and space in order to construct and incorporate American Otherness into the symbolic economy and mystical body of Spanish national identity. What is discovered in this play is the universal presence of a Hispanic Catholic hegemony in both the geographical territory and the cosmological history of the Amerindians, as Lope's *indio* shows himself to be a very intuitive and gifted reader of allegorical meanings into the figures and symbols of Spanish conquest and colonization.

Representations of the Other are also the centre of the discussions in chapters 4 and 5, which focus on Pedro Calderón de la Barca. Walter Benjamin calls Calderón's honour plays an exemplary, even superior, model of baroque allegory in his *Allegory and Trauerspiel*. Thus it is no surprise that the playwright most recognized for his allegorical complexity and profundity can help us to understand the rhetorical strategies and ideological potential of the emblematic representation of presence. By comparing and contrasting the treatment of emblematic tropes in an *auto sacramental* (*El Gran Mercado del Mundo*) and a *comedia de villanos* (*El alcalde de Zalamea*), chapters 4 and 5 set out to show how the emblematic techniques of visual *admiratio* and conceptual difficulty lure the spectator, elite as well as *vulgo* (although these are not mutually exclusive terms), into participating in the pathos of the dramas as well as imagining and projecting possible solutions or endings onto the moral conflicts created by Calderón's labyrinthine plots.

Presence reasserts its religious character in the world of the *auto sacramental*. Nevertheless, as William Egginton points out in *How the World Became a Stage*, the translation of ritualistic dramatizations of divine presence from the 'full space' of the temple to the 'empty and homogeneous space' of the *corrales*, or the plaza, presents serious challenges for the playwright (37), the main question being: How does one create an experience of presence within the changeable space and deceptive game of wit characteristic of modern theatricality? My analysis of *El gran mercado del mundo* argues that Calderón responds to this challenge in two ways: first, by incorporating markedly ritualistic structures into his plays; and second, by constructing a perspectival game in which God's grace, embodied in the pleasing figure of *Gracia*, is made present through an unequal competition for her hand in marriage. In a dialectical operation analogous to Borja's *Empresas morales*, Calderón unequally juxtaposes two antithetical, emblematic modes of being in the world: the theatrical and individualistic model of the *empresa*; and the self-abasing, which is to say, Ignatian model of meditative emblematics. By opposing a narcissistic search for being in the world, embodied by *Mal Genio*, to the 'undeceived' and obedient search for meaning of his brother *Buen Genio*, Calderón bridges the liturgical world of religious ritual and the theatrical world of public festival through an asymmetrical assemblage of allegorical perspectives. In essence, the two protagonists represent the historical religious tension between iconophiles and iconoclasts. According to Mitchell, iconoclasm is 'a social structure grounded in the experience of otherness and especially in the collective representation of others as idolaters' (Mitchell, *Iconology* 19). The Other in this case becomes a mirror of all that is excluded yet necessary for the consolidation of a Spanish, ethno-religious hegemony. It is important to note that historiographical studies of seventeeth-century Spain have tended to downplay the actual presence of 'threats' to the ethnic purity and religious orthodoxy of Spanish elites. For this reason, Mitchell's theses on iconoclasm and iconophilia will be brought into dialogue with Bell's understanding of the *ritual motivation of bias* in order to work through the relationship between the theatrical presence and historical absence of terror-inducing threats to an as-yet-unrealized Spanish national project.

Chapter 5 continues the discussion of theatrical presence, beginning with John T. Cull's astute observation that the emblem is intimately connected to the production and interpretation of the 'discovery' scenes that are so vital to the world of the *comedia nueva* ('Hablan poco' 619–20). Cull's reading is enriched by John J. Allen's and José María Ruano de la Haza's work on the architecture and staging practices of the *corrales*, as all note that the most common 'discovery' in such scenes is a dead and often violently disfigured human corpse. This discussion is expanded and problematized by Egginton's concept for analysing the theatrical staging of presence: 'the crypt' (*How the World*

105–13). He argues that the representation of violence introduces a 'full space' on the stage, marking a moment when the indeterminacy of theatricality comes to a sudden halt (*How the World* 105–11). In my analysis of *El alcalde de Zalamea*, I contend that the discovery of the dead, garroted body of the military captain Don Álvaro serves as a test case for yet another unequal contest between devices and emblems, as Pedro Crespo ritualistically converts his personal and incredibly theatrical, vengeance device into an emblematic exemplum of justice. Crespo resurrects his moribund honour through a theatrical representation and performance, thus exemplifying Louis Marin's thesis concerning the central role of representation in the creation of absolutist power: 'Representation, in this curious story, is at once the imaginary return of the dead man, his resurrection in image, and the symbolic right of his presence, the law of his authority and the authority of his law' (232). In the narratives of Isabel's rape, told by both father and daughter, the aristocrat Don Álvaro is converted into a terrifying image of the Other whose gruesome death serves as the text of a new contract between the king and his subjects, one based on artistic control rather than purity of blood. Understood in this way, Crespo's appeal to a juridical tradition signals the arrival of a new subject of power, one whose manipulation of discourse breaks the monopoly of power of a decadent, aristocratic caste and opens a space for a subject of representation whose legitimacy is based on his literary and artistic abilities. By reading Crespo's juridical and moral immobilization of Felipe II as an example of what Bell calls *ritual agency*, Calderón's play can be understood as a modern emblem of how ideological fields of identity are created, not through interior belief but rather through a skeptical and hesitant nod of consent.

III. Bodies and Signs

In 'Bodies and Signs,' I take this study into the emptiness at the heart of emblematic representation in the Spanish baroque. This is the world of anamorphosis, in which truth becomes a question of individual perspective and where the 'natural' hierarchies of Aristotelian thought become just one more rhetorical effect. Christine Buci-Glucksmann characterizes this turn away from fullness of being as a '"germ of tranquil atheism" which marks the seventeenth-century Baroque, the figure is already subject to the order of accident, changeability, precariousness and mortality' (133). Thanks in large part to what R. de la Flor identifies as the nihilistic undertow of the philosophy of *desengaño*, the success or failure of symbolic constructions, i.e., their truth effects, becomes increasingly tied to the emerging concept of artistic taste (*Barroco* chapter 1). Baltasar Gracián's *Agudeza y arte de ingenio* is generally recognized as the first extensive articulation of the concept and social field of *taste*, and the goal of chapter 6 is to analyse Gracián's practical philosophy through the apparent dichotomy between reason- and faith-based paradigms of thought in Counter Reformation culture. In particular, I focus on the ritualistic aspects of Gracián's discursive construction and performance of the organized body of taste. As the title of the chapter suggests, ritual is not something that rationalism leaves behind in its move toward the secularization of knowledge and the transcendental subject. In Bell's deconstruction of twentieth-century, anthropological notions regarding 'primordial' ritual structures and their myth content, we have already seen that the dialectical tension between a primitive and ritualistic faith and scientific rationalism is at the heart of modernity's efforts to mark an ontological and epistemological break with the past – its Other – and, as such, plays a preeminent role in Gracián's oeuvre. A pointed analysis of modernity's simultaneous dependence on and resistance to ritualization breaks the stalemate between religious and rationalist approaches to Gracián by displaying how his texts stage the 'primordial,' ritualistic creation and rationalization of the modern, abstract subject of representation. Put another way, Gracián's modernity does not emerge by disentangling it from the ritual residue of the baroque; rather, ritualization is the only way we can approach the lessons that baroque culture holds for modernity.

In opposition to Gracián's disembodiment of the modern subject, and representing the most innovative and contestatory use of the emblem in baroque Spain, Miguel de Cervantes injects life and bodily matter into the macabre and cautionary corpses that occupy the meditative stages of baroque allegory. It is for this reason that chapter 7 breaks with the temporal chronology of the book by ending with the work of an author whose life and works are situated halfway between the invention of the hispanic *empresa* and its apotheosis in Gracián's ouevre. The challenge presented by Cervantes, as far as the emblem is concerned, arises from a split perspective concerning its aesthetic value and epistemological shortcomings. On the one hand, emblematic motifs are ubiquitous throughout his oeuvre; on the other, Cervantes' works cannot be said to reproduce emblematic presence in the same way that we find in Lope or Calderón, which means that we are looking at a radically distinct use of the emblematic relationship between the iconic *body* and the signifying *soul*. The cervantine critique of baroque allegory is channeled through a carnivalesque consideration of human bodies and their meaning in which the material specificity and 'otherness' of the body form the basis for an alternative symbolic practice, one which finds a way out of the marvelous labyrinths of emblematic chimeras. One need only cite such quixotic emblems as the Helmet of Mambrino, the *retablo de las maravillas*, or the Balsam of Fierabrás in order to recognize Cervantes' parodization of emblematically constructed presence-effects.

In chapter 7, *Los trabajos de Persiles y Sigismunda* is analysed with an eye towards the ways in which Cervantes assembles a discursive mode that contests the allegorical containment of the linguistic and libidinal energies released by baroque *desengaño*. My hypothesis is that by privileging and problematizing the relationship between language and the body, by refusing to discard the grotesque body and its socio-historical predicament as a barrier to knowledge and redemption, Cervantes reframes the incorrigible nature of the human body – its sensuality as well as its bestiality – in order to ground his discursive practices and moral vision in an earthly arena where other tongues must be learned and other bodies penetrated and received. Framed by Bakhtin's concept of *grotesque realism* and Gumbrecht's alternative notion of *material presence*, my analysis of the body in Cervantes encounters both a living organism and a medium in its own right, one that connects the subject to its historical and cultural circumstances as well as to other subjects (Gumbrecht, *Production* 17–20). This has serious consequences for the emblematic mode, and in the second half of this chapter I claim that Cervantes goes so far as to resuscitate the emblem itself by subrogating the meaning and function of the emblematic motifs *Ocasión* and *Fortuna* to the contingencies and accidents (and bodies) of the novel's protagonists, rather than allegorizing characters' lives according to a universalizing, providential vision of the end of history. If Gracián's organized body of taste represents the absolute emptying-out of the material signifier in the interest of a powerful, if empty, courtly subject, Cervantes' imperfect and scarred bodies turn our gaze back towards a material arena of desire-based interactions.

In closing this introductory section, I would like to suggest that the role reversal I am attempting with respect to the traditional analytical posture that brings the 'ornamental' emblem to bear on 'substantive' literature might serve as a model for future interdisciplinary considerations of Renaissance and baroque cultures. In the world of emblem studies, it is taken for granted that emblematic structures penetrate and structure virtually every aesthetic and discursive space of early modernity, much like the picaresque hero is able to penetrate distinct social and cultural fields. Homologous to Benjamin's understanding of the way in which photography transformed the very notion of artistic creation, the emblem 'is neither art nor nonart (mere technology): it is a new form of production that transforms the whole nature of art' (Mitchell, *Iconology* 183). Due to its cooptation by religious and monarchical authorities, the emblem also prods the modern reader to recognize the politically embedded nature of early modern art. It is often forgotten that poets like Lope de Vega and Calderón de la Barca, much like the painter Diego Velázquez, considered their art, at least publicly, to be a tangential activity whose ultimate goal was the public staging of their 'innate' nobility, and not an end in itself.[16] Much is to be learned by bringing that which seems ornamental, like the emblem, into the foreground and temporarily relocating that which we have traditionally taken to be the central artistic activities of the baroque to the margins. In like fashion, our rationalist prejudices concerning modernity give way to an understanding of the ritual practices at the heart of the rationalist 'revolution' once we invite the Other into meaningful dialogue.

PART ONE

The Emblem

1 Emblem Theory, Emblem Practice: A Consideration of Juan de Borja's Resistance to Theory[1]

Customs are second nature, and changing them feels like death.

[La costumbre es otra naturaleza, y el mudarla se siente como la muerte.]
Miguel de Cervantes, *Los trabajos de Persiles y Sigismunda*

Juan de Borja and 'El arte nuevo de hacer emblemas'

Unlike his Italian predecessor, Juan de Borja assembles his *Empresas morales* (1581, Prague) in the midst of the growing theoretical debate concerning the composition and function of the emblem. Both the Prologue, in which Borja lays out a new understanding of the *empresa*, and the devices themselves bear witness to an author who seeks to control the place and potential function of his enterprise in Counter Reformation Spain and Europe. Credited with the invention of the 'empresa hispánica,' Borja is the first Spanish author to write an original emblem book, and the changes he initiates are substantial enough to warrant his placement at the vanguard of Spanish emblematics.[2] Where Alciato takes a belated interest in the typographical and editorial materialities of his book, Borja's project is the result of several years of gestation and fruitful intercourse with a number of institutions and collaborators. In terms of the artistic, technical, and editorial processes of composition and dissemination, it is noteworthy that Borja is known to have brought into his diplomatic and aristocratic circles figures such as Francisco de Holanda, the painter and draftsman who composed *De Aetatibus Mundi Imagines*, and Luis Jorge Barbuda, a well known cartographer and draftsman. The influence of both *letrados* can be found in Borja's predilection for mathematical and geometrical images and metaphors (García Mahíques, Introducción 37). This marriage of an emergent scientific paradigm to Ignatian meditative practices is itself worthy of an extensive study, but unfortunately it lies beyond the purview of this book. Given the standardized format of the *Empresas morales*, which situates the motto and image of each emblem on the right hand page (recto) with the commentary on the left (verso), it is also likely that Borja supervised, or at least participated in the layout and printing of his work (García Mahíques, Introducción 47–8).

Readers who are familiar with the *Empresas morales* are probably wondering what type of theoretical reading can be done on a work that for all intents and purposes contains no theoretical program. In fact, no Spanish emblem book is more responsible for Selig's observation concerning the lack of theorists and preceptors in Spanish emblematics than Borja's (*Studies* 37). My response to this (rhetorical) question is that this is precisely what makes the work so interesting from a theoretical – and ritual – point of view. In spite, or perhaps because, of its theoretical reticence, Borja's sweeping alterations to emblem theory and practice have proven more influential than any other document concerning emblems produced in Spain. We can come to a better understanding of why this is so by considering an equally 'anti-theoretical' and influential work on aesthetic theory from another time and another genre.

In his essay on Lope de Vega's *Arte nuevo de hacer comedias*, Edward Friedman notes that Lope's theoretical treatise is rather closed-mouthed where dramatic theory is concerned: 'In his poetics, Lope departs from a consciousness of paradox: he offers an anti-theoretical statement which documents his knowledge of theory to a group versed in the literary issues of the day ('Resisting Theory' 90). This 'paradox,' as Friedman explains, arises from two disjunctions: first, the fact that Lope's theory is responding to a large corpus of already realized dramatic performances, thus inverting the relationship between theory and practice as it is generally understood; and second, the disparity between the author's source of authority, *el vulgo*, and the occasion and audience for which he has prepared the justification of his art: the Academy of Madrid ('Resisting Theory' 89). Another way to look at this apparent paradox is by framing Lope's theory within the philological paradigm of early modern emblematics, where the history of the theoretical debate would suggest that theory follows – and legitimizes – practice, and not vice-versa. This inversion of the theory-practice relationship is, in fact, what we will discover in Golden Age literature in general, much as occurs in the field of literary studies. What is recognized as literary practice depends as much or more on the critics who study literature as on the literary corpus itself. Whatever the actual intention(s) of Lope's performance (only partially reflected in the text), Friedman is most suggestive when he brings the work of Paul de Man to bear on the poet's 'resistance to theory.'

According to de Man, 'The resistance to theory is a resistance to the use of language about language. It is therefore a resistance to language itself, or to the possibility that language contains factors or functions that cannot be reduced to intuition' (138). Lope's public exposition of his ambiguous, untheoretical theory of drama becomes an occasion for dismissing the dominant understanding of Aristotelian precepts and replacing it with his own 'self-evidently' superior practice. Lope bases the legitimation of his theory on the popular success of his plays, which has the effect of making his formula seem natural, arising from a pragmatic and arguably intuitive understanding of *gusto*. His plays exemplify this theoretical resistance by channeling conservative discourses of honour through 'organic' stock characters, such as the *campesino*, the *mujer varonil*, or the *gracioso*, thus making elitist dogma appear natural and universal, even populist in its various generic and linguistic trappings. In this light, Lope's address to Madrid intellectual elites becomes even more ironic, as his material success can be seen to arise from the *peasant*'s attraction for aristocratic culture, an attraction emanating from Madrid itself. We can conclude that Lope seeks to convert the cultural capital gained through his success into a preeminent symbolic position, not within the academies of the Court, which he has summarily rejected, but within the Court itself. As Juan Carlos Rodríguez has argued, Lope does not see himself as an up-and-coming *letrado* in an emergent cultural field of practice, but rather as an artistic aristocrat with a court of his own: 'Lope thoroughly carries out the rules of the Master/servant dialectic; for this reason he admires and serves the *Señores*, until he drowns himself in them, but at the same time he despises the "grandees" of his own circle; he does not settle for being *primum inter pares*, rather, he always wants to be the first' (*El escritor* 50). Read through de Man, the historical relationship between Lope's art, already popular, and his theory, which comes after the fact, reflects its ideological nature and function, which is to naturalize and legitimize a de facto and contingent aesthetic institution, the *comedia nueva*. In dialectical terms, the (anti-) theoretical treatise works to show how Lope's theatre was *always-already* theoretically sound in its intuitive response to its historical context.[3]

Ritualization deploys an analogous sleight-of-hand, which leads to its being 'experienced as deriving from powers or realities beyond the community and its activities, such as god or tradition, thereby depicting and testifying to the ultimate organization of the cosmos' (Bell, *Ritual Theory* 207). Both practices (re)produce a resistance to rhetorical or historical analysis, as Karen Pinkus's characterization of Counter Reformation emblematics demonstrates: 'an ideal Tridentine emblem would be valued for its economy of expression and for its powers to exclude questionable attributes' (54). In the case of Juan de Borja, this resistance to theory is just about absolute.

Like Lope, Borja appears to have no practical need to justify his aesthetic enterprise, but for very different reasons. For starters, he was born into the uppermost echelons of Counter Reformation political and social castes. Third son of (San) Francisco de Borja (a cousin of Carlos V), married to the granddaughter of Ignatius of Loyola's older brother, and ambassador to the court of Rudolph II under Felipe II, Borja has no social or political need to situate himself in relation to emblematists of more pedestrian pedigrees.[4] As Fernando Bouza points out in *Communication, Knowledge, and Memory in Early Modern Spain*, Borja's obvious disdain for intellectualism situates him quite comfortably on the side of innate (caste) superiority in opposition to learned 'pedantry or affectation' (19). Maravall has argued, however, that in spite of its seemingly confident tenor, this rigid posture is itself a dramatic reaction to the crisis that shook the 'monarchical-seignioral pyramid' of Spanish society in the sixteenth and seventeenth centuries (*Culture* 28). Like Lope, Borja's consideration of previous and current theories of the emblem, or, in this case, the *empresa*, takes the form of a collective and sarcastic dismissal.

In the Prologue, Borja takes issue with all previous theories of the *empresa* in a nonchalant gesture that effectively cancels their legitimacy and continuing influence in a single stroke. Equally important, his anti-theoretical strategy subsumes theory under seemingly pragmatic considerations:

> Although the laws that some new Authors have published, concerning the making of *Empresas*, are as rigorous as they have wanted to make them; adding some, removing others according to their *taste*; it did not seem to me that they were worth considering, except with regard to whether they are reasonable, since neither the authority nor the antiquity of the Authors

was so great that to fail to follow them was of much importance; indeed, not even in their own Empresas have these same Legislators rigorously applied the laws that they themselves have written.

[Aunque las leyes, que han publicado algunos nuevos Authores, de la manera de hazer las Empresas, son tan rigurosas, como las han querido hazer; añadiendo unos, y quitando otros à su beneplacito; no por esto me pareció, que obligavan à la observancia de ellas, sino en quanto llevan razon, por no ser, ni la authoridad, ni la antiguedad de los Authores, tanta, que dexarlos de seguir, importe mucho; pues, ni aun los mismos Legisladores en las Empresas que han hecho, han guardado sus leyes con el rigor, que las han escrito.] (B2)

Borja is very conscious of the fact that his rendering of emblem theory deviates from and challenges previous models, which he accurately describes as inconsistent both in theory and practice. The 'Authores' to whom Borja refers would most likely include humanists such as Paolo Giovio, who emphasizes that the meaning and efficacy of the *empresa*, or hieroglyphic, depend on the surprising and difficult internal relationship between the *pictura* and *subscriptio*.[5] However, no actual names are cited, which makes the critique universal. Also of note is the ironic use of juridical language in Borja's acerbic critique of the unstable 'laws' of emblem 'legislators.'

One of the most important aspects of the *Empresas morales* is the tacit way in which Borja completely redefines his chosen emblematic vehicle, the *empresa*. García Mahíques and Pedro F. Campa have pointed out that most Spanish emblem books are in fact collections of *empresas* with a didactical-moral intention, which tells us much about the influence of Borja's work, not to mention the ideological climate in which emblem books were produced in Spain.[6] According to its humanist theorists, the *empresa* differs from the emblem in that it contains and expresses a future, personal goal, often associated in the Renaissance and early baroque with feats of martial or amorous prowess.[7] Pinkus writes: 'this theoretical corpus constructed a hierarchy of forms in which the most notable achievement was not the emblem … but the *impresa*, a form that, in turn, reproduces the humanist subject' (129).

Returning to the prologue, Borja begins by stating that these emblematists are new authors; in this way he endows his even newer enterprise with the gravity of antiquity while initiating a rhetorically fallacious thrust which elides any serious consideration of theory by redirecting his criticism towards the theorists themselves. With this gesture he is free to disregard emblem theory altogether through a disparagement of its practitioners, declaring that their authority rests entirely on their own shoulders, or on the manner in which they assemble the privileged thoughts of ancient and classical thinkers and artists. Let us recall that individual wit and ingenuity are the main criteria by which the performances of *empresas* are interpreted and judged, which means that Borja's critique is not really directed against poorly executed *empresas* at all, but encompasses instead the wider enterprise of individual symbolic expression. To strengthen his point he repeatedly dismisses the authorial claims of these 'legislators' by opposing his self-evident definition of reason to what he characterizes as the frivolous activities of the *empresa* theorists, more tied to fashion than reason: 'the laws ... are as rigorous as they have wanted to make them; adding some, removing others according to their *taste*.'[8] Through this attack against the anonymous authors, who are apparently 'too clever by half,' Borja invites his readers to join him in rejecting and ridiculing the selfish and undisciplined claims of an arrogant intellectual elite. This is an important moment in the work, and the emblem in general, because we see Borja's explicit recognition of the epistemological instability at the heart of the very artifice he seeks to deploy in the reinforcement and expansion of a socially conservative ideology. Even more interesting is the appearance of an incipient, moralistic, and anti-intellectual populism which can be read as an aesthetic and social bridge between Borja's new vision for the *empresa* and Lope's theater, whose triumph is still a couple of decades away.

After discrediting the humanist theorists – he never actually discusses their theory – Borja frames the *empresa* within the sphere of *costumbres*, more conventionally associated with the emblem, and in this way the whole problem of aesthetic devices is effectively framed by moral customs. In the words of García Mahíques, 'Juan de Borja formally composed in the Italian manner, adapting and inventing conceptual artifices according to the model provided by *empresas*, but eliminated from these their particular character – associated with the knight's intention or the praise of his virtues – and makes them applicable to the moral universe' (Introducción 45). In essence, Borja converts a heretofore individualistic enterprise into what Maravall would term a 'program of cultural guidance,' as preexisting predispositions for allegorical play are set in motion around a newly articulated reading practice (*Culture* 57). *Empresa* becomes emblem, the personal becomes collective, and individual wit gives way to collective ritual.

Borja's rhetorical efficiency is nothing less than confounding, as instead of articulating a new taxonomy and set of rules for his *empresas*, he settles the whole debate by judging whether or not his *empresas 'llevan razón.'* This seemingly transparent solution is yet another example of Borja's theoretical resistance, which in this case conceals an entire array of politically informed suppositions which will act as the unrecognized foundation for an emblematic hermeneutics tied to his personal and institutional concerns. Maravall cites a similar definition of reason in Saavedra Fajardo's definition of *razón de Estado*:

> [T]he most certain is that which natural reason dictates, which, due to its conservation and evolution, does not require study; study actually confounds it, and, confused by the variety of discourses that speculation brings, it does not know how to resolve it. We have learned more from animals than from men, more from the unlearned than the learned.

> [[L]a más segura es la que dicta la razón natural, la cual, por su conservación y aumentos, no es menester el estudio; antes con él se confunde, y dudosa con la variedad de los discursos que ofrece la especulación, no sabe resolverse. Más hemos aprendido a vivir de los animales que de los hombres, más de los rústicos que de los doctos.] ('La literatura' 167)

We have already seen this 'naturalistic,' anti-intellectualist ethos in Lope's 'Arte nuevo': in both Borja and Lope, disciplined study and the knowledge that comes with it are completely overridden by what can only be called a plea for common sense. *Llevar razón* thus evokes a *sensus communis* in defense of these new artistic projects, producing what Gumbrecht calls '"phenomenalization," that is, a habit of confusing effects of language with a closeness to, if not with a possession of, what are taken to be real-world phenomena' (*Powers* 34). The establishment of this 'firm' terrain, as we have seen, is accomplished by positing an asymmetrical, dialectical opposition with the fanciful and imaginative theorists of the *empresa*.

Meditative Confusion and the Ritualistic Resistance to the Material World

Upon reading Borja's emblems it quickly becomes apparent that his opposition to the humanist emblematic project is more serious than a mere quibbling over rules of engagement. Instead of participating in an ingenious semiotic joust with social implications, or penetrating the hieroglyphic sign in search of ideal and original knowledge, Borja's reader is guided towards a hermeneutical practice in which all signs only point to the inexorable impossibility of illumination and transformation of the worldly self and, by extension, society. The gaze turns inward to one's own deviance and castigation, warding off any possible encounter with knowledge in and of the world. In this context, *llevar razón* coincides with the individual's rejection of the idea that self-transformation and improvement are possible in the earthly arena of social interaction. According to García Mahíques, 'he falls back on cultural mechanisms to disseminate ideas such as it is not good to occupy high places, since being at great heights implied the danger of being brought down from there and taking a fatal fall; or that the wise man was the one who always knew how to find the middle way, this being the true path to virtue' ('La emblemática y el problema' 82).

The 'reasonable' relationship between the deceptiveness of earthly appearances and the security of obedience and self-abasement is readily identifiable with the wide dissemination of Ignatian meditative techniques, where ideas such as the superiority of reverence over reason, or the dangers of society – even of one's own family – to salvation, or the view of the self as perverse or monstrous, and the mortification of the senses and the body are recurring acts in a ritualistic drama of self-rejection and discipline.[9] If the image of the Other that inhabits Borja's prologue takes the form of the upwardly mobile, humanist intellectual, and the chaos that his social mobility would introduce into Borja's estatist worldview, the Other that emerges from reading the emblems arises from the corporeal baseness and historicity of the meditative subject himself. The tacit linking of the two reveals the ideological unconscious of the *Empresas morales*.

Julián Gállego informs us that Borja's father, Francisco de Borja, presented the manuscript of Ignatius's meditative treatise to Pope Paul III, who printed its first edition (88–9). But rather than follow the more obvious diachronic thread leading from Loyola to Juan de Borja, I would prefer to take the term *genealogy* much more literally and explore the relationship between the works of father and son. Due to their concrete imagery and overreaching erudition, I find the religious and moral works of Francisco de Borja to be even more revealing of the intimate relationship between early Jesuit thought and the *Empresas morales* than the *Spiritual Exercises*. In a striking departure from the sensual starkness of Ignatius's seven-step program, Borja the elder's writings are filled with vivid images that function simultaneously as rhetorical ornaments and moral *exempla*: serpents, bees, ants, and rosebushes appear alongside the more Ignatian brambles, spines, splinters, worms, and so forth. Francisco de Borja might easily have become the first emblematist of Spain, as at one time he wrote a series of meditations to be published with engravings (Campa, 'La genesis' 45). He concludes the introduction of his treatise 'Espejo de las obras del cristiano' by connecting the usefulness, or profit, of his work to the biblical concept of *talento*: 'And although each one may take the fruit according to the "talent" that God has given him, we will touch on this exercise here, so that, once the intention is understood, each may profit according to his good desires and diligence' [Y aunque cada uno podría sacar el fruto según el talento que el Señor le ha dado, se tocará aquí algo de este ejercicio, para que, entendida la intención, cada cual se aproveche según sus buenos deseos y diligencias] (69).

Eugenio Frutos has studied the concept of *talento* and its relation to the theological doctrine of the two *gracias* in Calderón's *autos sacramentales*. According to Frutos, God bestows the first *gracia* on all human subjects equally, while the second must be earned by man through his moral action in the world – *el obrar bien* – for which he may be rewarded with a seat at the table of the Eucharist, once he is dead. Constitutive of this doctrine is the following definition of reason: 'More than rational, reasonable is the man who does not allow himself to be pulled along by the sensual Appetites or their interior effects, but also not by the errant Will nor by the doubtful Understanding' (539). Note how Frutos's explanation underlines the movement away from the philosophically informed world of reason towards the more worldly and pragmatic notion of reasonableness, or common sense. Much like the emblematic conversion of texts and the world into a series of unconnected signs, Frutos demonstrates how the human subject becomes a fragmented collection of faculties whose internal conflict and recomposition track the movement of what Pinkus calls an 'auto-logico mastery' (6).

Nothing is more indicative of this fragmentation than the separation of the subject from the direct realization of his God-given talent, which opens a space for further disintegration and the disciplined reconstitution of the reading subject. Once transducted into this reading practice, the identification of the idea becomes less important than the imitation of a set of practices bent on instituting what Tony Bennet calls a 'cultural technology of self-control' (109). In the movement from the *empresa* to the dogmatic emblem of meditation, the symbolic capital sought by the maker of *empresas* in the world of the court is exchanged for the less material but no less socially and politically determined spiritual capital (*provecho*) of Ignatian meditation. Bell observes that by centering on the action of the individual, such ritualistic practices 'convey a biased, nuanced rendering of the ordering of power so as to facilitate the envisioning of personal empowerment through activity in the perceived system' (*Ritual Theory* 84). This is where personal redemption meets redemptive hegemony in the sense that the personal redemption of the reader is directly tied to the redemption of the symbolic order that frames and thus limits his 'individual' act of interpretation.

In the next paragraph of the treatise, Francisco de Borja's meditative process is unveiled: 'Three considerations must move you, devoted spirit, so that your works may be sound and, purified … beginning in the morning UPON GETTING DRESSED: the first consideration will be of confusion. The second of giving thanks. The third will be the plea' [Tres consideraciones te han de mover, ánima devota, para que tus obras sean de peso y, purificadas … tomando del principio de la mañana AL VESTIR: la primera consideración será de confusión. La segunda de hacimiento de gracias. La tercera será la petición] (69; caps in original). The meditative program begins with the first act of consciousness, which should be to cover one's body. As the practicant moves through the hours of the day, every mundane act becomes a performance, an event, a ritualistic opportunity to place oneself, not in contact with, but rather in relation to, the divine. The material body in time, that which 'clothes' the soul of man in his sinful condition, becomes the primary locus of ritual activity. Bodily organs become emblematic symbols, removed from their material context and functions in the world. In the words of Bakhtin, they are 'smoothed out' so that their regenerative properties are marked with the degenerative sign of spiritual death (*Rabelais* 29). Like nature itself, the body is separated from the mental locus of reasonable elections in the human subject.

The reigning attitude in these meditative performances is one of *confusión*, which will require a short explanation. The 1729 *Diccionario de*

Autoridades contains nine entries for *confusión*, whose connotations are worth noting.[10] The first entry refers to 'the disorder, perturbation, bewilderment and revolution of things' [desorden, perturbación, desconcierto y revolución de las cosas], from the Latin *perturbatio*. This might well form the basis for the baroque understanding of an upside-down or topsyturvy world. The second entry repeats the first but adds the idea of a perturbed soul arising from the 'confusion of the senses,' which brings us very close to the philosophy of *desengaño*. In the third entry, exemplified by a citation from Santa Teresa, we begin to recognize the kind of confusion that Borja is preaching in his treatise, which finds its clearest articulation in the fifth entry: 'It is taken at times for dejection, bashfulness, embarrassment and shame, born from knowledge of oneself, or from the excess with which one has been favored' [Se toma algunas veces por abatimiento, encogimiento, empacho y vergüenza, nacida del propio conocimiento de sí mismo, u del exceso con que uno se halla favorecida].[11]

Francisco de Borja's expression of confusion is as follows: 'When getting undressed at night. *Confusion*. Because you are undressed, sleeping and Christ dressed [with your sins] for you, having nowhere to recline his head' [Al desnudar a la noche. *La confusión*. Porque te desnudas, dormiendo Cristo por ti vestido, no teniendo do reclinar su cabeza] (72). The goal here is the interiorization of the passion of Christ and the concomitant self-abasement of the practicant. During his uncomfortable and innocent vigil, Christ is dressed with the sins of man, which should cause man no little *confusion* in his naked, simulated death (sleep). As the sign of man's fallen condition, the naked body becomes the focus of a ritualistic process that converts physical presence into nothingness through the punishing gaze of a moribund Christ. As the work progresses, seemingly every possible contingency in the life of the practicant is reallegorized according to a particular moment in the passion of Christ, from riding horse to being deceived by one's friends. If we return to the first definition of *confusión*, it becomes apparent that this meditative program depends on a perpetual 'revolución de las cosas,' which allows all of (human) nature and life itself to be converted into signs, deterritorialized from what we might term their socio-historical and political contexts of meaning. Current theories of reception have little to add to this overwhelming program of guidance; nevertheless, Gumbrecht designates three aesthetic operations in his anthropological model of reception: thematization, interpretation, and motivation (*Making Sense* 45). Thematization describes the process of selection, which centres here on the human body and the senses; interpretation corresponds to the frame of *desengaño*, according to which these themes are situated; while motivation corresponds to the orientation towards a future action, or inaction, as the case may be.

In the section titled 'The second part Proceeds with how we will be confused by what we see on the earth' [Prosigue la segunda parte cómo nos confundiremos en lo que vemos en la tierra], man is compared to inanimate objects and forces in the natural world: 'Oh, how reasonable and right it is that man should be confused by his inobedience, when only he fails to keep his nature!' [¡Oh, con cuánta razón se puede confundir el hombre por su inobediencia, pues él solo deja de guardar su naturaleza!] (84). Water, fire, air, and earth are praised for the way in which they reflect the pain and loss of Christ's passion, while man, in his alienated self-involvement, is distanced ever more forcefully from nature and its creator. In Calderón's *La vida es sueño*, this sentiment is repeated almost verbatim by Segismundo, who laments his relative lack of freedom when compared to the birds of the air and the fishes of the sea (1.102–72). Man in this scheme is cut off, exiled from the natural world, which, due to its sinless – and undivided – existence, is closer to God. One curious effect of this development is that there is literally no sign of the first or natural grace with which all human beings are supposedly blessed at birth; rather, the emphasis is placed entirely on the sinful and entropic nature of human existence.

This isolation and paradoxically narcissistic self-obsession prevents the practicant from taking action in the world of human society, converting him instead into a silent emblem of piety. Most importantly, the temptation to critique the shortcomings or excesses of one's equals or superiors is curtly rejected and redirected into the all-encompassing process of punitive introspection and self-loathing: 'When dealing with the great power of the grandees, regard your own nothingness and what little you can accomplish, although at times you decide to act' [Cuando tratan de la gran potencia de los grandes, mira tu nada y lo poco que puedes, aunque algunas veces lo determinas de hacer] (91). The personal meets the political in a strikingly transparent way when we recall that the Borjas in fact embody the power and privilege of these 'grandees,' which takes us directly to Bell's concept of redemptive hegemony: 'ritualization does not simply act, unseeingly, to bring the social body, the community, and the largest image of reality into some reassuring configuration of coherent community. More fundamentally, it also appropriates this coherence in terms of the interests of persons or groups' (*Ritual Theory* 114). What is redeemed here are the monarchical-seigniorial segments of Spanish society, where families like the Borjas wield an enormous amount of power and influence, much of which they employ in the legitimation and defense of this same power and privilege. 'Ask your spirit what it is or what it has and how it is joined with the body and from this you will become confused, not knowing who you are nor how you come to be nor how you cease to exist. Since in your own house you know so little, what will you do in another's? Such that in what you fail to see you may remain confused' [Pregunta a tu ánima qué cosa es o qué cosa tiene y cómo está unida con el cuerpo y desto te confundirás, no sabiendo quién eres ni cómo eres ni cómo dejas de ser. Pues si en tu casa sabes tan poco ¿que harás en las ajenas? De manera que en lo que dejas de ver puedes quedar confundido] (99–100). Seduced into ignorance of 'one's own house,' the only way back to self-knowledge in this scheme is via the path laid down by Borja, which establishes the impossibility and/or sinfulness of social transformation. It is worth noting that the narrative voice of this 'reasonable' enterprise is situated outside of history – and humanity – embodying a timeless and unquestionable authority. It is here where R. de la Flor locates the contiguity between Ignatian meditation and Catholic mysticism: 'The mystic, in reality, is the one who submits him- or herself with unusual mildness to the torment of impositions, until s/he finds him- or herself on occasion at the point of abandoning the carnal and historical sheath in which s/he is inscribed' (*Barroco* 29).

Returning to the *Empresas morales*, the emblematic translation of Francisco de Borja's transcendental historicism becomes evident in an *empresa* titled 'Spes inanis,' which Borja the younger translates as 'Esperança vana' (figure 1). The motif is a typical emblematic image of a hand and arm leaning on a broken cane. Its message mimics the program of *The Spiritual Treatise* by urging the reader to place his hope and salvation in God and not in earthly vanities. At the end of the commentary we find a warning for those who persist in placing their hopes and desires in more worldly endeavors: 'Because whoever does so, rather than being sustained, will instead be injured, as truly happens to those who place their hope in Egypt, failing to place it in the true God of Israel, who will save them' [Porque èl que assi hiziere, en lugar de sustentarle, le herirà, y lastimarà, como verdaderamente acontece à los

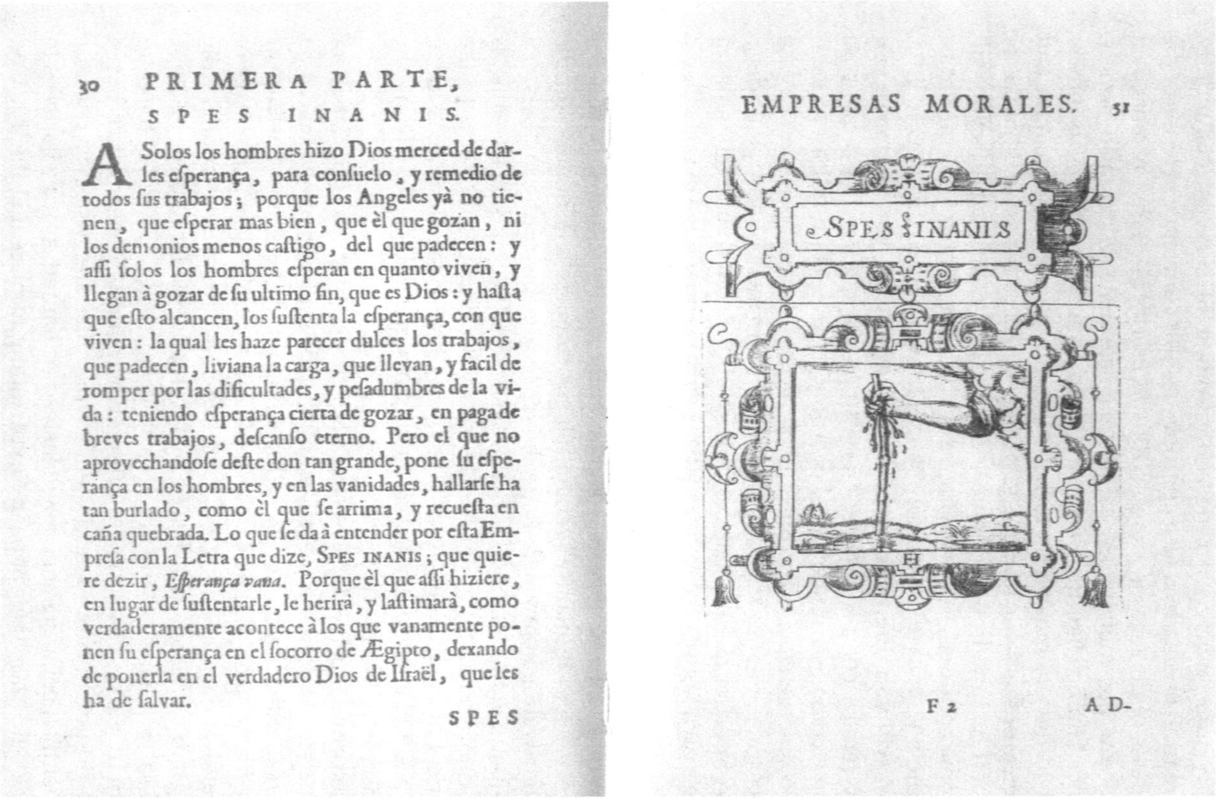

30 PRIMERA PARTE,

SPES INANIS.

A Solos los hombres hizo Dios merced de darles eſperança, para conſuelo, y remedio de todos ſus trabajos; porque los Angeles yà no tienen, que eſperar mas bien, que èl que gozan, ni los demonios menos caſtigo, del que padecen: y aſſi ſolos los hombres eſperan en quanto viven, y llegan à gozar de ſu ultimo fin, que es Dios: y haſta que eſto alcancen, los ſuſtenta la eſperança, con que viven: la qual les haze parecer dulces los trabajos, que padecen, liviana la carga, que llevan, y facil de romper por las dificultades, y peſadumbres de la vida: teniendo eſperança cierta de gozar, en paga de breves trabajos, deſcanſo eterno. Pero el que no aprovechandoſe deſte don tan grande, pone ſu eſperança en los hombres, y en las vanidades, hallarſe ha tan burlado, como èl que ſe arrima, y recueſta en caña quebrada. Lo que ſe da à entender por eſta Empreſa con la Letra que dize, SPES INANIS; que quiere dezir, *Eſperança vana*. Porque èl que aſſi hiziere, en lugar de ſuſtentarle, le herirà, y laſtimarà, como verdaderamente acontece à los que vanamente ponen ſu eſperança en el ſocorro de Ægipto, dexando de ponerla en el verdadero Dios de Iſraël, que les ha de ſalvar.

SPES

EMPRESAS MORALES. 31

SPES INANIS

F 2 AD-

Figure 1 'Spes inanis,' in Juan de Borja, *Empresas morales*, part 1 (1680), 30–1[12]

que vanamente ponen su esperança en el socorro de Ægipto, dexando de ponerla en el verdadero Dios de Israël, que les ha de salvar] (30). If we look to Francisco de Borja's *Instrucción para el buen gobierno* for clarification, we find that the God of Israel is approached through the sacrament of confession: 'And no one will be saved if he is not of the Israelites, not according to the Jewish people, but rather spiritually speaking, if they are not of those who see God; since if in order to see him it is necessary to confess to him, it is a great thing to reign in Judah' [Y nadie se salvará si no es de los israelitas, no según el pueblo judáico, sino espiritualmente hablando, si no fueren de los que ven a Dios; pues si para verle es menester confesarle, gran cosa es reinar en Judá] (189). This passage follows a portrait of the ideal exemplum of good self-governance, King David. David is a model ruler not because of his martial exploits but rather because he yokes his desire to rule under the duty that a faithful subject owes to his lord, even if his master is the excessive and violent Saul. The control over one's earthly desires is equated here with the death of Saul, which, in a decidedly Freudian turn, means that one becomes one's own excessive master, thus making Saul's material presence unnecessary. The implication is that by turning away from Egypt through self-mastery and the purification of confession, one is freed from slavery to one's own desires. Another way to say this is that David moves from being Saul's vassal to a modern subject of ideology: authority becomes internalized in the relation between the subject and the world.

The most important motif in this passage is 'blindness.' Although I will analyse the dialectic of blindness and insight in more depth in my study of *El gran mercado del mundo* (chapter 3), it is worth pointing out that the meditative act requires one to turn a blind eye to the material world – including the alluring aspect of the visual image – and activate a spiritual sense of sight directed towards immaterial as opposed to material or social truths. The 'inability' of the Jew to see the godliness of Christ places him in an antagonistic relation with his own biblical role; thus, to question these spiritual truths is tantamount to being a blind and heretical materialist, in short, the Other. In both texts, the God of Israel is disengaged from the Jewish people and placed at the centre of a Christian allegory of exodus from the earthly world of sin. If we take the allegory one step further, the Counter Reformation persecution of Jews (and converts) would seem to suggest that the Jew is now the antithesis of Israel, or the figure of Egypt herself. Such radical

78 PRIMERA PARTE,

HODIE VIVE.

EL diferir, y dilatar, poner en execucion, lo que ſe ha de hazer, es la coſa mas dañoſa, que puede haver, y de donde no ſuceden ſino grandes daños; y aunque eſto ſea aſſi verdad en las coſas de la paz, y de la guerra, pero en ninguna es de mayor daño, el dilatarla, que en emendar la vida, por ſer eſto la coſa de mayor importancia, que tenemos, y como tal en ninguna nos ponen nueſtros enemigos mas eſtorvos, ni mayores dificultades. Porque aunque muchos entienden el mal camino, que llevan, y mueſtran deſſear retirarſe dèl, ſon muy pocos los que lo executan, y ponen por obra; y aſſi à los mas acontece, que primero, que comiencen la vida, en que querrian acabar, ſe les acaba la vida, que viven; lo que ſe da à entender en eſta Empreſa del carro de dos exes, con la Letra que dize en el primero, CRAS. *Que es mañana*, y en el ſegundo, HODIE. Que es, *Oy*. Y la Letra de la Empreſa que dize, HODIE VIVE. Que quiere dezir, *Vive oy*. Porque aſſi como es impoſſible, que el que eſtuviere ſobre el poſtrer exe, alcance al que eſtà en el primero, porque ſiempre va delante; aſſi ſe deve vivir bien, oy, ſin dexarlo para mañana, pues nunca el dia de oy alcançarà al de mañana.

HODIE

EMPRESAS MORALES. 79

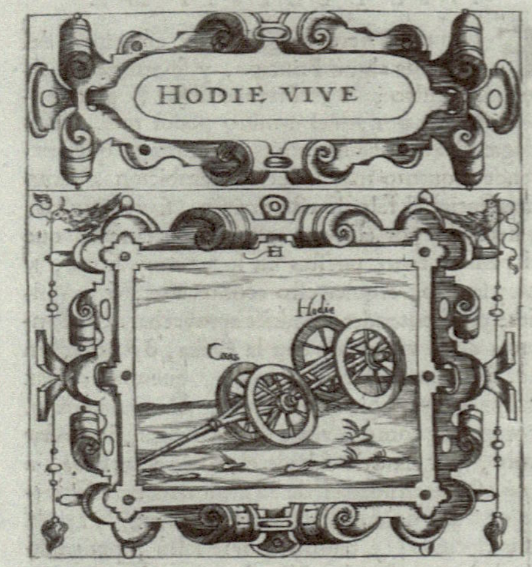

M 2 IPSE

Figure 2 'Hodie vive,' in Juan de Borja, *Empresas morales*, part 1 (1680), 78–9

reorganizations of ideas and symbols are one of the effects of emblematic allegorization, as all nature and history are read through the eyes of Counter Reformation ideology. In Benjamin's words, 'Any person, any object, any relationship can mean absolutely anything else. With this possibility a destructive, but just verdict is passed on the profane world: it is characterized as a world in which the detail is of no great importance' (*Origins* 175). This dynamic relationship with history and texts has serious implications for emblem studies, since the search for classical and medieval sources and correspondences is one of its most established means for constructing the 'correct meaning' of an emblem. If the emblem is constantly recontextualizing images and verbal motifs, committing what Russell calls the 'willful' subversion of sources, then many emblem studies are overlooking one of the most effective practices of the emblem: its ritual practice of textual and historical revisionism (*Emblematic Structures* 168).

In this regard, one of more instructive aspects of Borja's emblematic program is the (mis)use he makes of a series of motifs related, in one way or another, to the Horatian ethic of carpe diem. The emblem entitled 'Hodie vive' features the image of a horse-drawn cart whose front axle is labeled *Cras*, 'que es mañana,' and the second one *Hodie* (figure 2).

The main idea is that the back axle (today) will never reach the front axle (tomorrow), so one ought to worry only about today. So far there is nothing that would stifle Garcilaso's exhortation to 'gather the sweet fruit of your joyful springtime' [coged de vuestra alegre primavera].[13] Borja's commentary, however, establishes a different take: 'To defer and delay to put into execution what must be done is the most harmful thing that can occur and from whence only great harm can come; and although this is manifestly true in matters of peace, and of war, nowhere is it more harmful to defer it than in correcting one's life, since this is the matter of most importance' [El diferir, y dilatar, poner en execucion, lo que se ha de hacer, es la cosa mas dañosa, que puede haver, y de donde no suceden sino grandes daños; y aunque esto sea assi verdad en las cosas de la paz, y de la guerra, pero en ninguna es de mayor daño, el dilatarla, que en enmendar la vida, por ser esto la cosa de mayor importancia] (78–9). Borja converts the Horatian cry for freedom and sensual exploration – knowledge of the world – into its exact opposite: a turning inward and acknowledgment not so much of the existence of death but of its necessity. In this sense, emblematics fits very well the Deleuzian definition of ideology as a 'semiotic

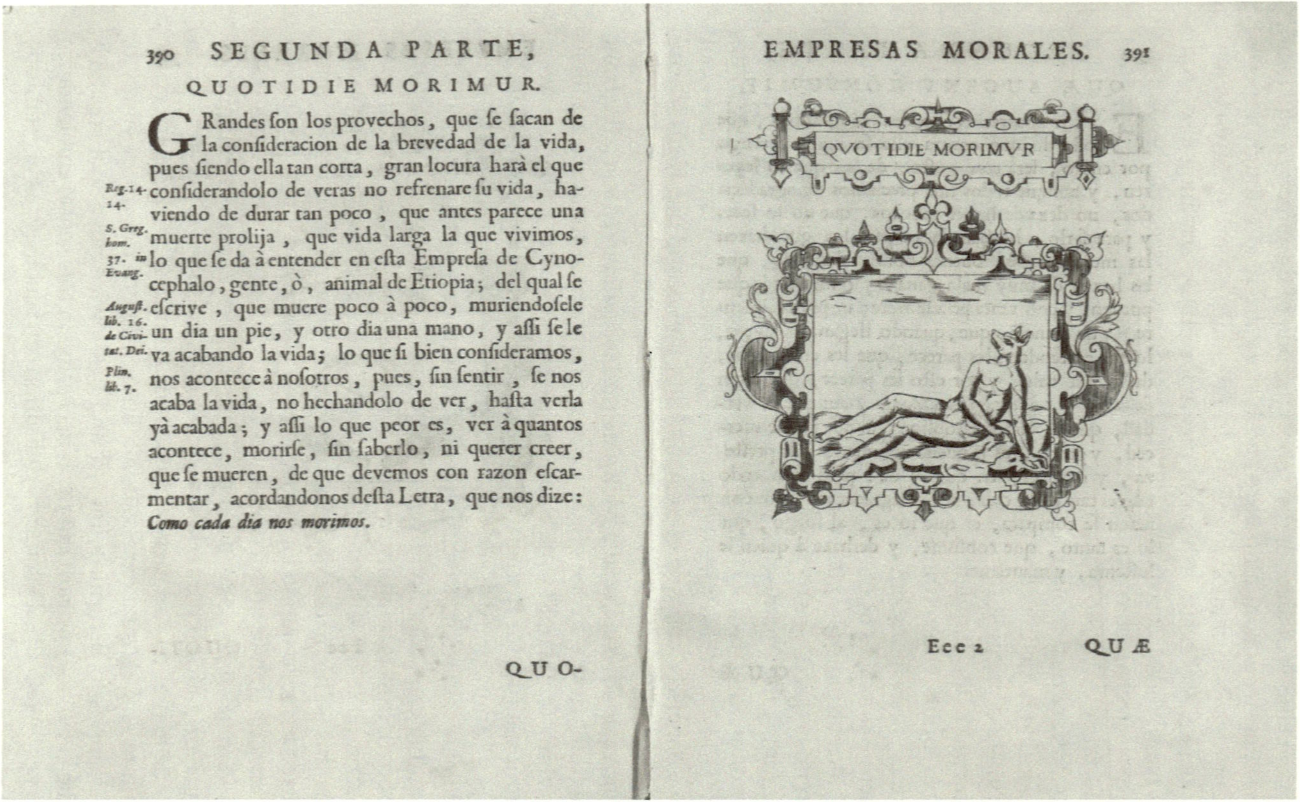

390 SEGUNDA PARTE,

QUOTIDIE MORIMUR.

GRandes ſon los provechos, que ſe ſacan de la conſideracion de la brevedad de la vida, pues ſiendo ella tan corta, gran locura harà el que conſiderandolo de veras no refrenare ſu vida, haviendo de durar tan poco, que antes parece una muerte prolija, que vida larga la que vivimos, lo que ſe da à entender en eſta Empreſa de Cynocephalo, gente, ò, animal de Etiopia; del qual ſe eſcrive, que muere poco à poco, muriendoſele un dia un pie, y otro dia una mano, y aſſi ſe le va acabando la vida; lo que ſi bien conſideramos, nos acontece à noſotros, pues, ſin ſentir, ſe nos acaba la vida, no hechandolo de ver, haſta verla yà acabada; y aſſi lo que peor es, ver à quantos acontece, morirſe, ſin ſaberlo, ni querer creer, que ſe mueren, de que devemos con razon eſcarmentar, acordandonos deſta Letra, que nos dize: *Como cada dia nos morimos.*

Reg. 14. 14.
S. Greg. hom. 37. in Evang.
August. lib. 16. de Civitat. Dei.
Plin. lib. 7.

QUO-

EMPRESAS MORALES. 391

QVOTIDIE MORIMVR

Eee 2 QUÆ

Figure 3 ‘Quotidie morimur,’ in Juan de Borja, *Empresas morales*, part 2 (1680), 390–1

machine,' as Borja proceeds to perform the same transmogrifying ritual on a series of *empresas* with similar results (Deleuze and Guatarri 136).

In the emblem entitled 'Quotidie morimur' (figure 3), 'we die a little each day,' he explains: 'It is given to understand in this Device of the Cynocephalus, a people, or animal, of Ethiopia; of which it is written that he dies little by little, one day a foot, another a hand, and so his life leaves him ... and the worst part is to see how many people this happens to, dying without realizing it, nor wanting to believe they are dying' [se da à entender en esta Empresa de Cynocephalo, gente, ò, animal de Etiopia; del qual se escrive, que muere poco à poco, muriendosele un dia un pie, y otro dia una mano, y assi se le va acabando la vida ... y assi lo que peor es, ver à quantos acontece, morirse, sin saberlo, ni querer creer, que se mueren] (390–1). Again, instead of turning the reader's gaze toward a possible engagement with the material or social world, death, and in particular the piecemeal mortification of the body, is placed in the foreground as the object of contemplation. And so it continues: the image of a hand, the 'measure of one's life,' is accompanied by the inscription 'Vita Brevis' (38–9) (figure 4). The image of a snake devouring itself, which Ficino takes for an embodiment of time, falls under the inscription 'Omnia Vorat' (figure 5). Praz notes that this image occurs in other contexts under the *inscriptio* 'Amor aeternus' (106).

Conclusion

If we permit ourselves to nationalize a literary genre, as does García Mahíques, just what is the *hispanic empresa* that Juan de Borja configures in his *Empresas morales*? It should be clear that the Hispanic device is only related to the Italian device of Giovio, Ficino and company dialectically: more specifically, in the way that it systematically denigrates and abases an intellectualist, erudite humanist culture in which meanings are constantly in play and subjects are visible and mobile. By performing what Van Gennep has called 'the pivoting of the sacred,' Borja removes classical and biblical motifs from their historical and aesthetic contexts and transforms them into rituals of self-abasement according to the spiritual program of Ignatius of Loyola (cited in Bell, *Ritual Perspectives* 37). If we follow this line of thinking, García Mahíques's definition of the Spanish device ties both the emblem and early modern Hispanic culture to an exclusively Counter Reformation

38 PRIMERA PARTE,

VITA BREVIS.

POcas razones ſeràn meneſter para perſuadir que la Vida ſea breve, pues à todos nos lo parece, y aſſi ſi no ſon algunos, que por falta de animo, para paſſar los trabajos, deſſean que ſe les acabe; ò, otros mas perfectos, que por la eſperança cierta, que tienen de la Vida eterna, deſſean acabar eſta temporal: à todos los demàs les parece tan corta, que muchos dixeron, que no tenia de largo ſino un palmo, comparandola à tan pequeña medida, por ſu gran brevedad: que es lo que ſe dà à entender en eſta Empreſa de la mano abierta, midiendo un palmo, con la Letra que dize: VITA BREVIS. Que quiere dezir, ***La Vida es breve.*** Y es lo tanto, que ſi bien ſe conſidera, ſe verà que los mas mueren primero, que comiencen à vivir aquella, en que penſavan, y deſſeavan acabar: de los quales con razon ſe puede dezir, que ſe les acabò la Vida primero, que commençaſſen à vivir; que es coſa que con razon nos deve hazer vivir mas recatadamente.

VI-

EMPRESAS MORALES. 39

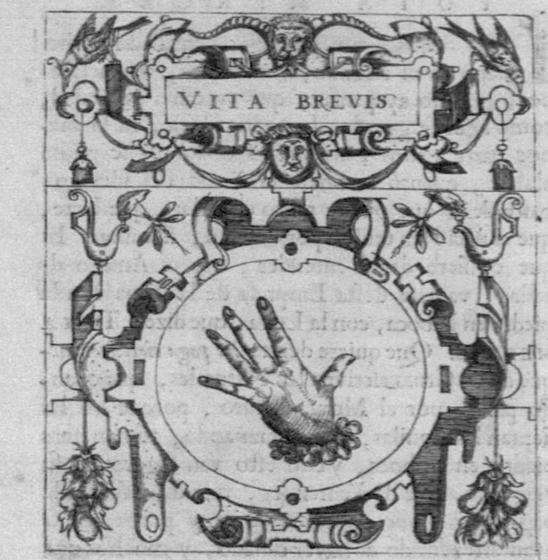

G 2 TUTA

Figure 4 'Vita brevis,' in Juan de Borja, *Empresas morales*, part 1 (1680), 38–9

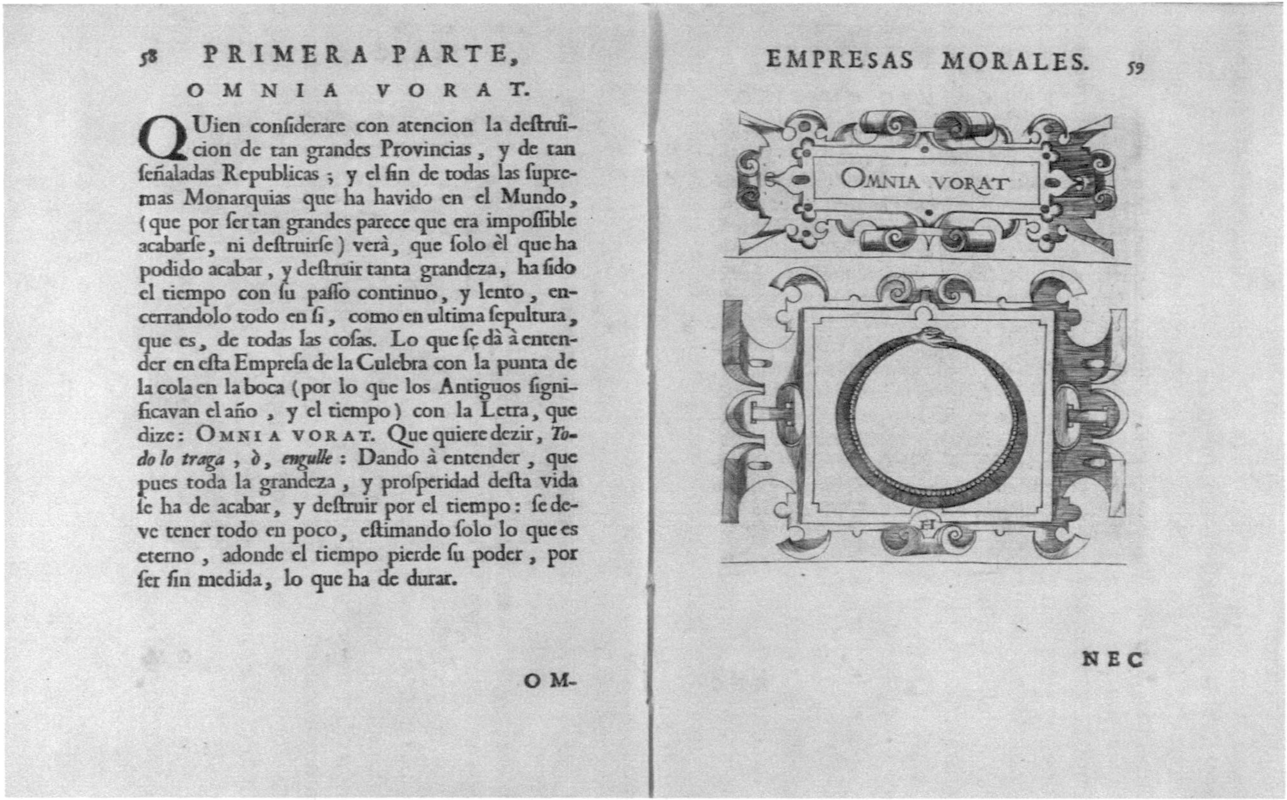

58 PRIMERA PARTE,

OMNIA VORAT.

QUien conſiderare con atencion la deſtruicion de tan grandes Provincias, y de tan ſeñaladas Republicas; y el fin de todas las ſupremas Monarquias que ha havido en el Mundo, (que por ſer tan grandes parece que era impoſſible acabarſe, ni deſtruirſe) verà, que ſolo èl que ha podido acabar, y deſtruir tanta grandeza, ha ſido el tiempo con ſu paſſo continuo, y lento, encerrandolo todo en ſi, como en ultima ſepultura, que es, de todas las coſas. Lo que ſe dà à entender en eſta Empreſa de la Culebra con la punta de la cola en la boca (por lo que los Antiguos ſignificavan el año, y el tiempo) con la Letra, que dize: OMNIA VORAT. Que quiere dezir, *Todo lo traga*, ò, *engulle*: Dando à entender, que pues toda la grandeza, y proſperidad deſta vida ſe ha de acabar, y deſtruir por el tiempo: ſe deve tener todo en poco, eſtimando ſolo lo que es eterno, adonde el tiempo pierde ſu poder, por ſer ſin medida, lo que ha de durar.

OM-

EMPRESAS MORALES. 59

OMNIA VORAT

NEC

Figure 5 ‘Omnia vorat,’ in Juan de Borja, *Empresas morales*, part 1 (1680), 58–9

frame of reference. Later chapters in this book will show that the historical evolution and deployment of emblems in Spain tests and often exceeds this definition in a number ways. By recontextualizing Lope's *Arte nuevo* in light of Borja's anti-intellectualist appeal to common sense, my goal was to shed light on the rhetorical manipulation that makes the social and moral dominance of the upper echelons of Spanish society appear natural and right. According to this view, Lope's theatre and dramatic theory do not so much represent a new populist, i.e., democratic, vindication of the common man as put into play a well-established discursive practice for separating that which is natural from that which is learned, that which is morally superior from that which is inferior, according to what J.C. Rodríguez calls the traditional, organicist view of the estatist world (*Theory* 54–5). The ritualistic nature of Borja's and Lope's artistic enterprises allows, or even demands, that the theoretical notions and definitions of both artists remain vague, empty, or lacking altogether.

According to Bell, '[ritualization] is a process of "free play" in which the drawing of distinctions endlessly defers signification, meaning, and reference from the present signifier to a potentially infinite number of signifiers. Not only is "meaning" never arrived at; it is never present in any sense at all' (*Ritual Theory* 105). Bell's point becomes readily apparent when we consider Borja's theoretical keystone, *llevar razón*. Borja makes no attempt to define reason in a positive or concrete sense, since the entire enterprise consists of 'reasonable' *empresas*; moreover, the meditative process becomes reasonable in the same tacit fashion that the *empresa* is converted into an emblem. Theoretical reticence, thus, is not an indication of the solidity of the philosophical and theological edifice on which Borja's enterprise rests but rather marks a situational strategy he employs in order to preempt any criticism or contestation. As such, the emblem is more than the communication of ideas; it is the communication of a reading practice that converts the encounter between the subject and the world into a ritual of allegoresis.[14] The *hispanic empresa* treats human and textual bodies in identical fashion, uprooting selected members and passages so that they can be set in motion around early modern social, cultural, and ideological centres of gravity.

2 Anamorphosis and Theoretical Depth of Meaning: Juan de Horozco's *Emblemas morales*

History, poetry and painting symbolize between each other and are so alike in appearance, that when you write history, you paint, and when you paint, you compose.

[La historia, la poesía y la pintura simbolizan entre sí y se parecen tanto, que cuando escribes historia, pintas, y cuando pintas, compones.]

Miguel de Cervantes, *Los trabajos de Persiles y Sigismunda*

The force of spells of evil ones and enchanters, which do exist, makes us see one thing for another and remain fixed from here on, as there is no one who changes their first nature for another.

[La fuerza de los hechizos de los maléficos y encantadores, que los hay, nos hace ver una cosa por otra y quede desde aquí asentado, que no hay gente alguna que mude en otra su primera naturaleza.]

Miguel de Cervantes, *Los trabajos de Persiles y Sigismunda*

Questions of Methodology

In 'Influencias e interferencias en los orígenes de la Emblemática española,' Santiago Sebastián states that 'Emblematics is a fundamental science for the reading and comprehension of artistic works, and for this reason it is of great interest to historians of Art' (445). By calling emblematics 'fundamental' to the wider and more institutionally secure field of Art History, Sebastián manages to blur the formerly clear line dividing two fields of analysis. His research convincingly proves his point, as his emblematic readings of paintings, especially those of

Diego Velázquez, provide startling insights while challenging established readings. In creating a bridge between Iconology, Philology, and Art History, Sebastián is not only responding to the tendency of the latter, or any other 'autonomous' discipline, to define and protect its borders but also furthering an influential school of emblematics which advocates the division of emblem studies itself into more discrete areas of inquiry in the interest of a 'total understanding' of the phenomenon.

In *Método iconográfico*, Jesús María González de Zárate marks off the terrain he deems appropriate for the scientific discipline of Iconography, one of any number of subdivisions that might be carved out of emblematics. In his estimation, Iconography should confine itself to the description and diachronic and synchronic cataloguing of the forms that the visual images take, a project that would ostensibly complete the field of formalistic research (113). *Iconographers*, however, should not confuse their practice with that of *iconologists*, who should limit their own analyses to the semantic properties of the image with the goal of arriving at the 'ultimate significance of the *imagines*' (113). In sum, Iconography is descriptive while Iconology is interpretive, although both are necessary, according to the author, in order to move past the current field of Art History towards a 'Historia total' of the image (115). García Mahíques proposes a similar division between the semantic study of meaning and the semiotic study of form ('La emblemática y el problema' 62). In a type of postmodern Scholasticism, the fields of Art History and Emblematics are divided and subdivided so that each discrete entity can be rationalized according to its own 'self-evident' properties and then reincorporated into a total understanding of the visual symbol. The ultimate goal of such projects is to correctly 'control the context' so that the interpretation of the meaning of the emblem may be 'fixed': 'we should be clear that the point of view of the iconographer/iconologist, like the Art historian, consists of focusing his interest especially on *the meaning* the work assumes in its *moment of creation*' ('La emblemática' 62; my emphasis).

García Mahíques offers four affirmations subtending his approach, the first two of which are particularly relevant to earlier discussions in this book: '(I) that the meaning of a work, in its moment of genesis, is based on a fundamental denotation; (II) that the spectator may construct different meanings from those originally denoted starting from concrete connotations, which then become denotations' ('La emblemática y el problema' 63). There are several points to be made here, the first of which concerns the problematic nature of the 'moment of creation.' As we have seen with Alciato, the moment of creation of an emblem book, as with any text, is multiple, contingent, and dependent on a number of material factors that make it impossible to isolate such a moment. This does not mean that the critic should ignore the problem of authorial intent, but it does mean that its definition should always remain open, multiple, and subject to those contingencies and materialities that come between the author and his text, between the author and his reader, and, finally, between the author and his own intention. As Gumbrecht suggests, 'Within the framework of a descriptive history of reception I would like to recommend using the meaning intended by the author as a background against which other meanings can be understood and compared' (*Making Sense* 17). There are several advantages to this position, not the least of which is the explicit resistance to the phenomenalization of authorial intent, which would seem to be the goal of Mahíques's approach.

The second problem is the elision of the question of reception, or, more accurately stated, the conflation of the moment of creation with the moment of reception, which converts the historian into the ideal reader of a singular, ideal meaning. In my view, literary history and criticism should consider the multiple ways in which criticism selects and edits the very texts on which the discipline depends. As the classicist Sean Gurd argues, 'Textual criticism is the *substance* of ancient literature, not a tool used to recover it' (45). Gurd's vision for a 'radical philology' is based on the idea that the 'specificity of ancient [or Golden Age] literature is not based on any geographical, chronological, or linguistic delimitation, but rather on a particular relationship with the modernity that possesses, produces, and invokes antiquity [or the baroque] endlessly in its own process of self-delimitation' (34). Rather than maintaining and essentializing the historical distance between the critic and the text, Gurd suggests that this frontier, or space, always be in view in order to question and analyse the ways in which critics and theorists edit, or even create, the past.

Finally, the idea that the meaning of the work is based on a 'basic denotation' denies the possibility that a single work may purposefully contain more than one meaning, and that these meanings may be placed, either by the author or the reader, in problematic juxtapositions. More fundamental in the case of the emblem is the fact that all emblematic images, due to their indivisibility and opacity, inherit multiple denotations, and that the meaning of the emblem is not established in a creative moment, but rather by moving back and forth between the commentary, which attempts to fix the reader's gaze on one or several of these meanings, and the image, which ultimately escapes complete identification. In the words of Egginton, 'Rather than attributing meaning to an original intention, for example, we conceive of meaning as being the shuttling between positions of intention and reception or being nothing other than the very force of attribution itself' (*Philosopher's Desire* 64). The force of attribution at work in the emblem would be seen by Egginton as a primary source of repression exercised on the infinite circulation of possible meanings that characterizes the signifier. This critical posture repositions the act of making emblems toward an ideological as opposed to strictly iconological study; or, in Mitchell's words, 'make[s] the notion of ideology itself the subject of an iconological analysis' (*Iconology* 159).

Both García Mahíques and González de Zárate seemingly want to clear out a space in which the visual symbol can be studied in its 'objective' meaning and form. Standing in the way of such an attempt to arrive at the empirical stability of hieroglyphic meaning and form, however, are precisely those material forces that affect their realization in time, such as artistic form, social convention, individual style, technological limitations, or editorial choice, all of which immediately lead to questions of social practice and context. Such methodological 'contamination' is in fact what places the emblem at a particularly rich crossroads of aesthetic and social inquiries. Returning to Mitchell: '[I]f we were to understand the text-image relation as a social and historical one, characterized by all the complexities and conflicts that plague the relations of individuals, groups, nations, classes, genders, and cultures, our study might be freed from this craving for unity, analogy, harmony, and universality, and might, in the process, be in a better position to move toward some sort of coherence' (*Iconology* 157). According to this logic, any study of the visual sign or hieroglyphic would have to confront what Gurd terms a 'multiple plurality' of textual dispositions before considering the question of meaning. Russell characterizes the emblematic image as completely 'detachable,' which suggests that, much as occurs with alphabetic language after the invention of the printing press, the meaning of the emblematic image arises from its grammatical and rhetorical relationship to the other components of the emblem, including its theoretical corpus, not to mention its wider cultural contexts and functions, be they devotional, literary, celebratory, theatrical, propagandistic, commercial, architectural, and so on and so forth (*Emblematic Structures* 28). Similarly, R. de la Flor locates the source of the emblem's popularity, longevity, and ideological mutability in the insistent polyvalence of the visual sign, 'infinitely open towards connotation' (*Emblemas* 12). Like Egginton, he equates the delimitation of connotation with the ideological deployment of the emblem, which suggests that all attempts to control the context of philological interpretation are subject to homologous symptoms of institutional and ideological embeddedness. The following study of Juan de Horozco y Covarrubias's *Emblemas morales* will show how classical antiquity in early modern Spain is an exemplary case of how the definition and deployment of a remote literary and cultural corpus says as much or more about those who study it as it does about the object of study itself.

History Framed: Anamorphosis and Other Tricks of the Perspectival Trade

Gumbrecht defines five basic philological practices: 'identifying fragments, editing texts, writing commentaries, historicizing, and teaching' (*Powers* 4). The multiple tasks of the emblematist are very similar if not identical to this list, which is what makes the emblem a useful stage on which to view philological performances. To exemplify how this works, I would like to return for a moment to the *Empresas morales*. Borja's philological practice and rhetorical subtlety come to the fore in an *empresa* whose inscription reads 'Satiabor cum apparverit,' or 'I will be satisfied when it appears' (figure 6). This legend is placed above an image in which a 'hieroglyphic' sign, the Egyptian letter TAV, is sculpted on the face of a perspectivally rendered pyramid. The subscription reads as follows:

> That which our Lord Christ won for us with his Cross, as the Egyptians signified in their Hieroglyphic Letters with the Cross, as seen on the Obelisks, which they made with the letter: TAV. Which signifies the Cross, for which they understood the life that was to come, as very serious Authors declare it, and thus it is reasonable that we work, and await the respite from this life, which is to come, which he won for us through so many trials.
>
> [La qual nos ganó Christo nuestro Señor con su Cruz, como lo significavan los Egipcios en sus Letras Hieroglyphicas por la Cruz, como se vee en los Obeliscos, que hizieron con Letra: TAV. Que significa la Cruz, por

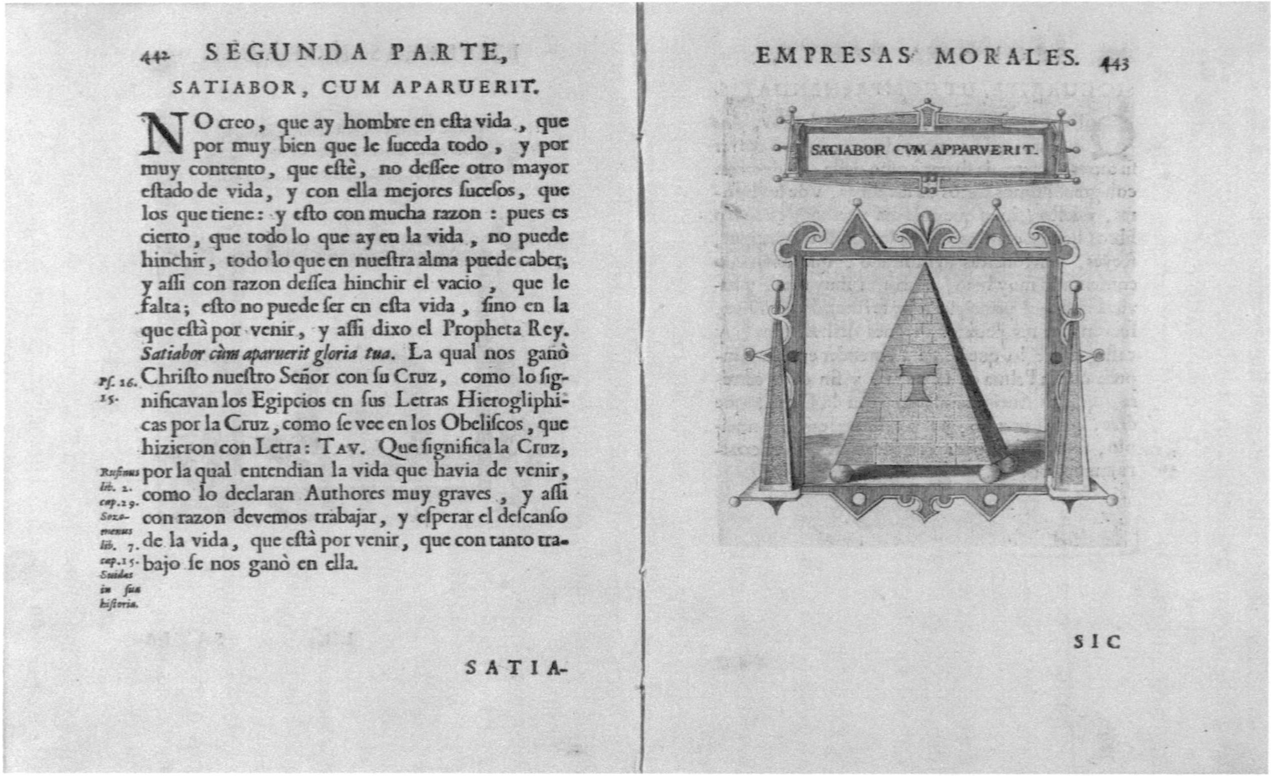

442 SEGUNDA PARTE,

SATIABOR, CUM APARUERIT.

NO creo, que ay hombre en esta vida, que por muy bien que le suceda todo, y por muy contento, que estè, no dessee otro mayor estado de vida, y con ella mejores sucesos, que los que tiene: y esto con mucha razon: pues es cierto, que todo lo que ay en la vida, no puede hinchir, todo lo que en nuestra alma puede caber; y assi con razon dessea hinchir el vacio, que le falta; esto no puede ser en esta vida, sino en la que està por venir, y assi dixo el Propheta Rey. *Satiabor cùm aparuerit gloria tua.* La qual nos ganò
Ps. 16. 15. Christo nuestro Señor con su Cruz, como lo significavan los Egipcios en sus Letras Hierogliphicas por la Cruz, como se vee en los Obeliscos, que hizieron con Letra: TAV. Que significa la Cruz,
Rufinus lib. 2. cap. 29. Sozomenus lib. 7. cap. 15. Suidas in sua historia. por la qual entendian la vida que havia de venir, como lo declaran Authores muy graves, y assi con razon devemos trabajar, y esperar el descanso de la vida, que està por venir, que con tanto trabajo se nos ganò en ella.

SATIA-

EMPRESAS MORALES. 443

SATIABOR CVM APPARVERIT.

SIC

Figure 6 'Satiabor cum apparverit,' in Juan de Borja, *Empresas morales*, part 2 (1680), 442–3

> la cual entendian la vida que havia de venir, como lo declaran Authores muy graves, y assi con razon devemos trabajar, y esperar el descanso de la vida, que està por venir, que con tanto trabajo se nos ganò en ella.] (442–3)

According to Gumbrecht's philological vocabulary, the fragment selected by Borja is the image *tau*, which the author will illuminate by writing a commentary that abstractly cites 'serious Authors' in its attempt to teach the reader about the history of the hieroglyphic. There are several aspects of this emblem which reveal the power of the philologist in his attempt to guide the reader to a/the correct interpretation of the central textual problem: the meaning of *tau*. First, the reader is placed in a 'weak' position through the use of the passive verb form of *satiabor*. According to this grammatical relationship, the sign and its meaning will self-consciously appear to the patient reader as if they were protagonists in the denouement of an epic story, which in fact they are. Next, Borja creatively misconstrues the Egyptian alphabet by reading the letter *tau* as a pre figuration of the Christian cross.[1] Jan Assmann's differentiation of the *semantic* and *material* sides of the linguistic sign is germane here, as Borja strategically confuses alphabetic and ideogrammatical images, appropriating 'hieroglyphic' symbols and their ideal knowledge in the name of Spanish Catholicism by playing on the iconic similarities between *tau* and the Christian cross. More importantly, by confusing a letter and a symbol, he grafts, or projects, the allegorical operation he has just performed onto the sign itself. To paraphrase Edward Said, the scientific practice of the philologist brings about the objectification, essentialization, and metaphysical fixing of the object of study (*Orientalism* 97). Another way to say this is that Borja 'puts the image in a state of vacancy with respect to itself … by saying what it meant to say but that it will never say, by giving its implicit spoken discourse and by revealing its secret' (Marin 207). By objectifying *tau*, Borja can exert absolute power over the meaning that its mysterious visual presence seems to promise.

As in the case of 'Spes Inanis' (chapter 1), the knowledge and signs of Egypt only become legible and profitable when placed within the symbolic order of Counter Reformation values or *costumbres*, wherein the aura that emanates from their resistant iconicity and Otherness is linked to a concrete semiotic and political project through what Jesús Maestro calls 'transducción': 'The problem of transduction … is generated and resolved, as a formal and functional means that (empirically) permits the (intersubjective) normalization of (ontological) difference' (45).[2] The ontological differences that Borja so elegantly normalizes, or transducts, include the aforementioned difference between alphabetic and hieroglyphic signs, which stands in as a metaphor for the differentiated relationship between modern and primitive, Christian and pagan, Spanish and Other. Wlad Godzich suggests that conceptual marriages such as the one between *tau* and the crucifix '[are] meant to allow thought not only to embrace all of the real but to annihilate it in its very alterity, that is, to appropriate the real to thought as a form of organized knowledge' (*The Culture of Literacy* 23).[3] The semiotic analysis of Borja's emblematic practice demonstrates that the emblematist is free to redefine symbols according to his strategic practice as long as their meaning is contained within a linguistic and cultural universalism consonant with Counter Reformation doctrine. Seen another way, we can say that universalizing linguistic regimes place all of history in a relativistic relationship to their own historical and cultural unconscious, overwriting any resistant historical or cultural specificity with the universalizing thrust of imperialist allegories. The dialectical turn from *other* to the *same* occurs when the vacant image *tau* becomes what it 'always already' was – a prefiguration of the crucifix – by absorbing and erasing the active transduction of the emblematist. Neither Iconography nor Iconology, alone or together, is sufficient to tell us either what the emblem means or how Borja 'makes' it mean. Any attempt to retrieve the original, which is to say, Egyptian meaning of *tau* would only open Borja's method and meaning to further scrutiny and, ultimately, doubt, and not corroboration. To follow how Borja makes a distant object, in Hiedeggerian terms, 'ready to hand,' or to analyse how the mysterious hieroglyphic becomes part of the way we 'experience the world and its objects as always already interpreted,' it is useful to approach the object of analysis from another place (Gumbrecht, *Powers* 19).

Bell calls the creation of a sacred symbol out of a pagan sign 'framing,' which helps move us toward the world of Renaissance perspective, one of the predominant themes of Horozco's theoretical treatise (*Ritual Theory* 89–93). Just as Sebastián brings emblematics into the world of painting, we can now consider emblematics according to the central technical and (eventually) philosophical development of early modern painting. In his definition of the emblem, Horozco makes clear that the composition and interpretation of emblems are subject to the same representational rules that drive perspectival painting. For

Konrad Hoffmann, it is precisely this relationship between single-point perspective and the emblem that characterizes the emblem as a modern representational phenomenon: 'The pictorial interpretation of surrounding reality that is constitutive of and underlies emblematics is not a more or less accidental expansion of the medieval repertoire of representation by individual motifs. Here it has more to do with the central art-historical event which led to the formation of a spatial imagery that was both distanced perspectively and related to the observing subject' (1). Echoing Russell, Hoffman concludes that the dynamic and interactive nature of perspectival space is more important to the emblem than the residual effects of the fourfold structure of medieval allegory. By positioning objects or scenes either closer to or farther away from the viewing-reading subject – *visos* and *lejos* in Spanish perspectival language – the eye may be guided through the various geometrical planes toward a single meaning. Ideally, the viewer follows the narrative sequence established by the spatial discourse through which the artist has organized the representation (Andrews 91). Abstract and empty space thus becomes the hermeneutic condition by which the individual is interpellated into the reconstruction of the spatially organized ideas of the visual narrative.[4] In this new rationalized system of perspective, images function like an independent and self-contained language (*letras*), as they are positioned in naturalistic spatial and temporal *grammars* through which they rearrange motifs and ideas even as they disguise the historically grounded act of their production. We have already seen Borja translate a sign (the cross) into a letter (*tau*) and back into a hieroglyphic sign by closing the distance between ancient Egypt and imperial Spain. Such perspectival procedures and 'tricks' of Renaissance and baroque art are part of what Martin Jay refers to as the baroque 'madness of vision,' otherwise known as *anamorphosis* (114–33).[5]

The most famous example of pictorial anamorphosis is *The Ambassadors* by Hans Holbein, a painting which offers different images and meanings when seen from different spatial coordinates. When one stands directly in front of the painting, regarding the tableau from what is called the *vanishing point*, there appears to be an elongated smudge or stain in the foreground of a heroic portrait of the diplomats Jean de Dinteville and Georges de Selve. The two aristocrats stand on either side of a table that displays the technological and artistic instruments representing the intellectual power of man in the world. As one moves off to the side, however, the stain resolves itself into a skull, or symbol of death, which both visually and rhetorically reduces the heroic portrait to a blurred and imperfect, i.e., fallen, status. Thus, the meaning of the painting changes as the viewer changes position. More importantly, these perspectives tell us that the imagined eye of the spectator is incorporated into the visual grammar of the painting: 'if you stand here you will see this; if you stand there you will see that.'

Most analyses of Renaissance perspectivalism place anamorphic tricks on the opposite end of an aesthetic and moral continuum from the more naturalistic paintings of the Renaissance masters. From one point of view, we encounter the coincidence of scientific modes of thought and modernity, a relation which privileges the distanced, 'objective' Cartesian point of view; an oblique gaze, however, unveils the playful and witty games of deception and disillusion made possible by the mathematical grids deployed by mannerist and baroque artists. Jurgis Baltrusaitis sees both paradigms as representative of perspectival art: 'It is a science which fixes the exact dimensions and positions of objects in space, but it is also an art of illusions which recreates them' (4). According to Panofsky, the constitutive element of such representations, or illusions, is the creation of an abstract and 'empty' space in which objects can be arranged in any number of ways (63). As a result of this new freedom, Renaissance perspective disrupts the metaphysical unity of matter and form that characterized medieval aesthetic and theological conceptions of the world. In the words of David R. Castillo, 'Faced with unstable and changing images, the spectator is invited to distance him or herself from fixed interpretations and to reflect on the uncertainty and artificial or constructed nature of meaning' (*(A)wry Views* 1–2). Bakhtin notes a similar occurrence in language due to the rise in status and visibility of vernacular literatures. In both cases the 'high can be brought low' and the 'low made high,' resulting in a panoply of potentially liberating or chaotic possibilities (*Rabelais* 363). As Borja's *empresas* demonstrate, however, this new freedom of movement for objects and signs can be guided to more conservative ends.

When Borja anamorphically frames a mysterious Egyptian 'hieroglyphic' in order to reconstitute it under another guise, it becomes clear that framing devices are not limited to emblems, but can be applied to all manner of historical objects and events in the interest of producing distinct semantic, ideological, even behavioral effects on the reader or spectator. As indicated in the first epigraph for this chapter, the translation of represented objects from one medium to another is a frequent subject of commentary in the Renaissance and the baroque. Horozco's emblem book establishes this aesthetic homology early on when he states: 'The emblem is a painting that signifies a warning under some or many figures' [Emblema es pintura que significa aviso debajo alguna o muchas figuras] (f10). His opening treatise is a wide-ranging affair that touches on many different discursive forms – poetry, theater, theology, law, etc. – all in the interest of situating his enterprise in the most authoritative light possible. After Borja's elegant dismissal of theory, Horozco's long treatise begs the question as to why he felt so compelled to construct what is, in effect, a universal history of art, poetry, and visual signs as a prelude to his emblems. The work itself provides a satisfactory answer, but, as in the previous chapter, I would like to frame my discussion of Horozco within another text, which both helps to explain the social and historical context in which the *Emblemas morales* was written and demonstrates the importance of rhetorical decisions in the creation of anamorphic effects.

In an astute reading of what many would consider a decidedly unliterary text, Jack Weiner suggests that, unlike the deference shown by Borja to the spiritual works of his father, the sons of Sebastián de Horozco 'manifest great hostility towards their father whose maternal ancestors come from Jewish blood' (*En busca* 135). Due to the inability of Horozco and his brother Sebastián de Covarrubias y Horozco to produce authoritative depositions concerning their ethnic *limpieza*, a requirement for being named to official positions, 'the two brothers receive one rejection after another in their search for social acceptance and equality' (*En busca* 135). In the case of Horozco, his failure to gain entrance into the Colegio Mayor de San Salvador is followed by an equally frustrating experience with the Holy Inquisition. He is finally named bishop towards the end of his life, first at Agrigento (1594–1606) and then in Guádix (1606–10). Both dioceses were in Andalusia, where the laws and legal processes pertaining to blood purity were apparently less rigorously enforced (Weiner, *En busca* 136). Even so, as part of the juridical-ecclesiastical interview process, Horozco was subjected to an inquiry into his genealogical background, and it is this testimony to which we now turn.

Weiner records the 26 questions asked of each witness, the first twelve of which are directly related to the candidate's 'qualifications.' It appears that item three had been the stumbling block for the brothers and their guarantors: 'if they know if the abovementioned is born and procreated from a legitimate marriage and by honorable and catholic parentage' [si saben quel susodicho es nacido y procreado de ligítimo matrimonio y de padres honrados y cathólicos] (Weiner, *En busca* 139). According to Weiner, Horozco's success in this particular process is due to two editorial decisions: first, the priority and prominence given to the Covarrubias bloodline by the witnesses interviewed; and second, the establishment of the purity of the Horozcos, whose homeland is stated as being the Old Christian stronghold of 'la montaña.' By placing the Covarrubias nobility in the foreground, supported by the vague allusion to the Old Christian status of the Horozcos, two genealogical *costados* are established, which are apparently sufficient to occlude the Jewish heritage of Juan's paternal grandmother, María de Soto, at least in Andalusia. A figural reading of the geographical origins of the Horozco clan, *la montaña*, turns the description into a 'naturalistic' portrait of the honorable cleric, who is portrayed standing on the firm and naturalized ground of his ancestral nobility.

In strikingly real and effective ways, Horozco's editing of his own genealogical text reveals an 'editor-subject [who] constitutes itself in these multiple acts of choosing' (Gumbrecht, *Powers* 28–9). To ensure his social and economic survival, Horozco has no choice but to risk gaining or losing his identity through an unpredictable trial of his blood. In emblematic terms, the deposition acts as an *empresa* through which Horozco rewrites the meaning (soul) of his genealogical text, as he and his ancestors become transducted into that which they always-already were – provided, of course, that the verdict declares him and his family pure – an honorable and ethnically clean Israelite family. We will see a similar spell cast by Horozco's philological ingenuity in his new history of emblematic art.

Emblem as the Aesthetic Culmination of Literary and Artistic Mimesis

Horozco's *Emblemas morales* (1603) is divided into a Prologue and three books, which can be further subdivided in the following manner: a theoretical description and philological study of the history of the emblematic modes of representation, including detailed definitions and examples of *empresas*, insignias, symbols, hieroglyphics, and of course emblems; a second book that combines a Prologue and a collection of emblems; and a third book of emblems, many of which echo efforts from earlier in the collection. I will limit my comments here to

Horozco's Prologue and first book, which attempt nothing less than a complete revision of the history of artistic mimesis.

The Prologue begins with a generic study of poetry: the roots of poetry, Horozco states, are found in the songs that spurred ancient soldiers to battle. The most ancient and thus 'natural' function of poetry is not lyrical, but hortatory, as poetic mimesis originated and was performed in warfare. The treatise continues with a catalogue of discourses that at one time or another had been expressed in verse in order to facilitate the memorization of cultural, religious, and legal codes: Law, Philosophy, Theology, Mathematics, in short, all instances in which poetry had been used as a socially and morally decorous, mnemonic and mimetic strategy. Having established poetry as a historical as opposed to artistic space, Horozco now begins to populate this *mise en memoire* with unspecified deeds performed by heroic individuals in great battles, fashioning yet another natural link between the glorious history of a 'nación' and the use of poetry in the construction and maintenance of this historical space. In this way the Spanish nation becomes a reflection of the mimetic ability of poetry to create an ideologically informed locus, which literate subjects may then rhetorically and imaginatively discover and inhabit through the recitation of heroic verses. In the words of Godzich, 'The introduction of print technology ensured that the ideological commitment of humanism to linguistic universalism received the support of literacy, itself a requirement of the caste expansion of the state' ('Language' 357). The model for all similar intitiatives in early modern Spain is of course the Prologue to Antonio de Nebrija's *Gramática de la lengua castellana*, in which the influential humanist-philologist situates the Spanish language at the culmination of a linguistic and cultural genealogy stretching from the ancient Hebrews to imperial Rome.

Moving from the establishment of a military regime to a juridical one, Horozco then explains how poetry facilitated the memorization of laws in ancient Crete, ancient Spain, and in the Bible. In this way he is able to assemble a single, self-reflexive, and continuous representation of history by connecting ancient cultures to a mythical, prehistoric Spain and, finally, to the Holy Scripture of the Israelites through a strategy of juridical metonymy. Mitchell explains: 'A modern nation is not a natural fact: its origin, history, and destiny are the stuff of myth, made and not given' (*Pictures* 273). Just as the true meaning of the Egyptian hieroglyphic *tau* was obscurely covered until the time of Felipe II's Catholic Empire, only then ready to reveal its true meaning to its chosen reader/people, the natural function of poetry and emblematic representation – the realization of the Hispanic Empire – can be found lurking behind the masks of all nations and creeds:

> And to conclude it will suffice to say that the authority and esteem of orderly poetry will be clearly comprehended by showing the seriousness of the saints, both Greek and Latin, who performed similar exercises of virtue and ingenuity, imitating the sacred tomes, where five entire books are written in verse, as it is known in the original, and as the learned Saints observe.
>
> [Y para concluyr en esto bastara dezir q la autoridad y precio de la concertada poesia, se entendera claramente poniendo delante la grauedad de los santos assi Griegos como Latinos, que se ocuparon en semejantes exercicios de virtud y de ingenio, imitando los sagrados volumines, donde se hallan cinco libros enteros escritos en versos, como se conoce en su original, y lo advierten los Doctores santos.] (8)

Horozco's narrative plots a course through vast and largely depopulated historical landscapes, and this emptied space becomes the ontological and epistemological condition for his historical practice, in which the allegorical techniques of anamorphosis can convert a letter into a symbol, or a pagan into a saint.

The Prologue ends with a proclamation that the goal of the book is the expansion of the already universal realm of the Spanish language: 'the book will also profit from our tongue being so widespread in the world, because it is already becoming as universal as Latin, and to some it even appears more so, or it will be very soon' [y para los de otras partes se vee q tambien aprouechara el libro por estar nuestra lengua tan estendida en el mundo, que ya viene a ser tan general como la Latina, y aun algunos les parece que lo es mas, o lo sera muy presto] (8). In similar fashion, the colonization of ancient and classical history in the Prologue prepares the ground for Horozco's forthcoming theoretical and historical study of the emblem. Classicism functions here along the same lines as Said's reading of nineteenth-century Orientalism: first, Horozco's philological practice reveals an ancient world that is more 'valuable as a sign of … [Hispanic] power over [Antiquity] than it is a veridic discourse about [it]'; next, 'authority … means for "us" to deny autonomy to "it" … since we know it and it exists … *as* we know it'; finally, Horozco establishes 'scholarly study [as] a branch of national policy' (*Orientalism* 6, 26, 32). This approach to the study of the ancient world makes all historical knowledge absolutely relative to the epistemological necessity established by imperial subjects. Horozco's book, in fact, signals the end of political history, just as the emblem signals the end(s) of poetic and iconic history, or philology.

Chapter 1 is entitled 'En que se declara que cosa son Emblemas, Empresas, Insignias, Diuisas, Symbolos, Pegmas, y Hieroglyphicos,' yet the first topic refers to none of the above, but rather to painting:

> As all things that represent the Divine virtue that shines forth in them bring us to the consideration of the Author of the universe, and in this manner please the soul; thus painting these same things according to their likeness also guides and amuses us, in such a manner that sometimes what is natural does not provide as much satisfaction as a close imitation. And in part we will say that painting has a great eminence: which is that it arranges things in such a way that one could say they endure.
>
> [Como las cosas todas representando en si la virtud Diuina q en ellas resplandece, nos lleuan a la consideracion del Autor del vniuerso, y en esto recrean el alma; assi la pintura de las mismas cosas en la razon de semejança, tambien nos lleua y recrea, de manera, que algunas vezes lo que es natural no da tanto contento, como lo que se vee con propiedad imitado. Y en parte diremos, que la pintura tiene gran excelencia; y es que pone las cosas de suerte que se puede decir permanecen.] (9)

It is significant that he begins with the properties of painting, just as it is significant that the Prologue is dedicated to a discussion of poetry. Both are situated at the forefront of Platonic and Aristotelian theories of mimesis, and any privileging of the emblem as an art form capable of offering models of reality worthy of imitation will have to pass through these canonical concepts of aesthetic philosophy. The chapter opens with the Neoplatonic view that the ability of the artist to create images, or appearances, imitates the all-encompassing creative powers of the 'Author' of the universe. This privileging of the divine powers of mimesis is a clear reference to Thomas Aquinas, who advocated the use of surprising images for teaching divine truths (Russell, *Emblematic Structures* 46).

The key to Horozco's project, as E.H. Gombrich has demonstrated, will be the containment of Neoplatonic idealism, crystallized in the hieroglyphic image, within Aristotelian theories of poetic mimesis, grounded in language (190). The emblematist employs aspects of both notions, placing a painterly emblematic discourse of semblance within an ideologically informed poetic frame, which seeks to privilege his scholarly practice by equating the emblem's manifold potential with a God's-eye view of reality. Christian Bouzy identifies the divine nature of Horozco's universalist point of view as one that represents 'God as a dramatic archetype' ('Dios' 151). This aesthetic genealogy deploys the presence-based, Neoplatonic privileging of the image as the cipher for an immobile centre of universal Ideas, all the while channeling the image's interpretation through institutionally bracketed expressions of poetic language, thus guiding its infinite connotative potential toward the metonymical expansion of the Spanish Empire. Another name for this is *self-reflexivity*, as Spanish identity recognizes its origins in antiquity just as the true meaning of antiquity is reflected in the Spanish will to empire.

As he continues his comparative treatise on art, literature, and science, Horozco moves from the semblances produced by painting, admirable for their representation of memorable stories, to the Egyptian hieroglyphics, which, in his view, are the only 'letters' that teach truths:

> [O]f all the letters, only those [hieroglyphics] that teach truths and the path to virtue should be called letters; they were called sacred, in imitation of which we have introduced those that in the present book we call Emblems, many of which may also be called, as we will see, *empresas*, and these are the ones that pertain to one's individual intention. But reduced to the common good through advice that may be of profit to everyone, they cease to be *empresas*, and are Emblems.

> [de todas las letras solas aquellas [hieroglyphicos] que enseñan las verdades, y el camino de la virtud, se deuen dezir letras, les dieron nombre de sagradas, a imitacion de las quales se han introduzido las q en el presente libro llamamos Emblemas, pudiendo muchas dellas llamarse, como luego veremos, empresas, y son aquellas q tienen respecto al intento particular de alguno. Mas reduzidas al bien comun en algun auiso q puede aprouechar a todos, dexan de ser empresas y son Emblemas.] (10)

Like Borja, Horozco takes liberties with what he calls a hieroglyphic. Bouzy notes that Horozco explicitly compares the hieroglyphics of the Aztecs to those of the Egyptians. He comes to no firm conclusions concerning the ontological status or meaning of the American ideograms, which would be theologically problematic, but the comparison is enough to enlarge his linguistic universe as well as establish the subservient role of colonial iconography to Spanish language and history: 'This convergence between Egyptian and Aztec *hieroglyphics* could pass for an attempt to reconstruct the unity of the world, which was lost following the delusional enterprise of the Tower of Babel' (Bouzy, 'La poètique' 90).

As in the case of poetry, the etymological and historical survey of emblematic images (*empresas*, insignias, symbols, etc.) spans centuries of historical and literary knowledge. Chapters 2 through 14 read much like the first edition of Cesare Ripa's *Iconologia*, in that there are iconographical descriptions and iconological applications of a virtual encyclopedia of symbols, without a single visual image to aid the imagination of the reader. One important difference is that, in Horozco's survey, all historical and mythological references to the emblematic mode are incorporated into a narrative of Spanish dominance. Following Bell's notion of redemptive hegemony, all subjects who participate in the emblematic project redeem their own innate and previously unrecognized *casticismo* at the same time as Spanish history, all history for that matter, is redeemed.

Conclusion: Unequal Modes of Reception

In the chapters that lay out the rules for the construction of emblems, Horozco discusses the types of *empresas* appropriate for public festivals and celebrations. His most pressing concern is 'clarity of purpose and meaning,' which he also takes up in a subsequent chapter. In both chapters it is evident that the material artifice of emblematic language, like the surface of a painting, should not bring attention to itself but should act instead as a transparent window through which the spectators may gaze on the constructed meaning. All spectators are not equal, however, for what he is actually proposing are two distinct modes of cultural reception and production. Maravall reminds us that Counter Reformation Spain is a crisis-filled society in which caste lines that were at one time written in blood are now being rewritten with money and culture, changing, in other words, to class lines.[6] As we have seen in the case of Juan de Borja, the creation of a literary sphere and its accompanying literary instrumentality is one of the most notable and effective responses of Spanish elites to the social, economic, and ethnic fragmentation of early modernity: according to Godzich and Spadaccini, 'The political, and seeming cultural, fragmentation could not provide the assurance of any common readership ... such a readership could only be constructed, that is, formulated, as a project for the future' (43). The emblem is at the heart of this futurist project, which can be observed when Horozco adds yet another factor to this social drama by conceptualizing a mode of cultural capital that would divide society along symbolic lines. Literate subjects, or *letrados*, have the opportunity to participate in the material processes that produce culture and, subsequently, are able to cultivate their own symbolic capital – prestige – from their surplus of cultural capital. Illiterate subjects, on the other hand, who are lured into the artifice by spectacular public festivals and celebrations where emblematic and hieroglyphic constructions are much more clearly and simply constructed, merely consume and reproduce the emotional feelings aroused by the collective experience of the multimedia spectacle – at least in theory.[7]

Let us recall that, according to Weiner, Horozco had been excluded time and again from a sphere of social elites constituted and defended by doctrines of blood and caste. In these stifling conditions, the *converso* attempts to redraw social hierarchies by assembling a cultural hierarchy in which his scholarly practice functions like a passport, redeeming both his own intellectual labors and the history of the social and political body he is attempting to penetrate. He is not necessarily challenging the political status quo; indeed, his treatise places questions of religious and national destiny in the foreground. He is, however, creating a space in which his social practice could bring him and his country honour. The moral imperatives of the community are not just respected and maintained; the emblem works to expand the range of institutional power and increase the voluntary participation of Spanish subjects. He is articulating, in Bell's words, 'a dynamic of social empowerment,' one that leads in two directions at the same time (*Ritual Theory* 181).

To properly arm this emergent subject of representation, Horozco composes new rules for emblematic assemblage to accompany and redirect the more traditional guidelines regulating its rhetorical composition. Where Borja offers a single rule of common sense, Horozco composes a ten-rule program, the first five of which are taken from Giovio's aforementioned treatise, to which he adds five of his own.[8] 'The sixth rule that I am adding, and which must be the first, is that the aim and intention be good' [[L]a sexta regla que yo añado, y ha de ser la primera es, que el proposito y el intento sea bueno] (50). By rhetorically situating the sixth rule as the first, traditional rules concerning the difficulty and proportion of the triplex form are subordinated to a new imperative, which, almost identical to Borja, privileges the dogmatic concept of the proposal at hand. Also like Borja, the criterion used to judge these emblems is an abstract notion which can only be understood by taking into consideration all that has preceded this chapter of the book: 'good' thus describes any emblem which unilaterally contributes to Spanish universalism.

With the seventh rule, the manner in which the emblematic mode will attempt to guide the imagination of readers becomes more explicit: 'The seventh rule is, in addition to the purpose being good, that when it is chosen, it should be in such a manner that neither in the figure nor in the letter may it be distorted, and of this there are many *empresas* with remarkable failings' [La septima regla es, que de mas de ser bueno el proposito, lo que para el se escogiere se procure que sea de manera, que ni en la figura, ni en la letra se pueda torcer, y desto ay hartas empresas con falta notable] (51). When dealing with discursive modes based on visual symbols in early modern Europe, we should keep in mind that there were individuals and groups that 'erroneously' attributed magical or, at the very least, mystical qualities to certain symbols, including many that eventually became standard emblematic signs. Hans Belting reminds us that Horozco's project is not unique but rather intimately connected to a more general effort to rationalize the meaning and use of religious images and icons: 'As an obligatory part of the church inventory, images were given a fixed place and a precisely defined function. By elevating every image to the same rank, … the doctrine of images sought to dispel the magical fascination that certain images exerted as physical objects. The philosophical explanation denied the image's miraculous power and defined the image with a pictorial type that could be duplicated at will' (183). William Christian's and Sarah T. Nalle's work on the efforts of religious authorities to perform a similar standardization of religious beliefs in early modern Castile is also helpful for contextualizing Horozco's *Emblemas morales* in the Hispanic context. As in the case of *tau*, signs must be emptied of any 'foreign' content before their potential signification can be linked to the interests of specific social and ideological fields. The emblem exemplifies this push for symbolic hegemony, as the naturalistic representation of the images together with the philological method of exegesis naturalizes their new meaning and function: it acts, in other words, as a 'vanishing mediator.' Knowledge, along with the artistic competence attained through practice and repetition, is naturalized, while the intellectual tools required to take full advantage of the rhetorical game become the patrimony and cultural capital of the members of an emergent sphere of cultural elites. What we are witnessing is the emergence of a new protagonist onto the stage of history, one who harnesses philological practice to the engine of empire.

PART TWO

Applied Emblematics

3 Lope de Vega's Emblematic *Indios*: The Discovery of America, or the End(s) of History

Globalization begins at home.

Homi Bhabha, *The Location of Culture*

It is almost a truism of emblem studies that theatre is the most emblematic cultural practice of early modernity. This can be read two ways, of course, which is my intent: on the one hand, theatre is at the centre of the emergence of a formidable culture industry, one which becomes increasingly sensitive to the tastes and desires of urban consumers. In this sense, theatre is emblematic of the emergent phenomenon of mass visual culture. In a more properly literary frame, the formal and thematic homologies between the construction and reception of emblems and the way in which theatre involves the spectator in the staged imitation of actions reveal that the 'emblematic mode of representation' is an omnipresent source of literary themes and dramatic staging techniques in the plays themselves. According to John T. Cull, the theatrical use of emblems includes: 'the invention of original word emblems, the emblematic argument in dialogue, the epigrammatic maxim, the emblematic character, the emblematic backcloth, the inclusion of actual emblems in the dramatic action, the use of emblematic stage properties, the use of chorus to provide emblematic commentary, and the extended emblematic portrayal conveyed by such dramatic forms as the dumb-show, the masque, pageants and processions' ('Emblematics' 115).[1] I would add that the combination of easily recognizable figures and symbols, formulaic plots that employ strategies of misdirection and discovery to create suspense, curiously framed and therefore compelling objects – such as letters, daggers, devices, etc. – and witty and portentous dialogue 'are enough to make us suspect that there is an intimate kinship between baroque theatre and the emblem' (Maravall, 'La literatura' 149).

The goal of this chapter is to deploy the emblem as a critical and theoretical frame for the analysis of the staged encounters and misencounters between the Old and New Worlds in Lope de Vega's historical-religious honour play *El nuevo mundo descubierto por Cristóbal Colón*.[2] I am particularly interested in the way Lope stages the ritualistic-emblematic fragmentation and reconstitution of the central religious symbol of the Counter Reformation: the cross. Through a detailed analysis of this process, I hope to demonstrate that both the *indios'* initial surprise, caused by the sudden appearance of the cross on their beach, and their eventual acceptance, or recognition, of the presence of Christ in the image of the crucifixion reveal how baroque ideology is extended in time and space in order to construct and then fold a 'tamed' image of New World Otherness into the symbolic economy of Counter Reformation imperialism.

The key figure in this play is the *indio*, and I will retain Lope's terminology throughout this analysis because I do not want the reader to confuse this aesthetic invention with an actual historical entity more properly, or anthropologically, termed the indigene or Amerindian. In spite of the play's ostensible aesthetic and historical relationship to colonial America, what we find in *El nuevo mundo* is a series of theatrical figures who, in Said's words, become 'fixed in a visionary cosmology without much regard for anything except their "function" and the patterns they realize on the stage where they appear' (*Orientalism* 70). It is these patterns and their relationship to history and historiography which most interest my analysis, in particular the way in which Lope stages the 're-creation of past experience and its empty protensions' through a series of discursive performances by the *indios* (Gumbrecht, *Making Sense* 71). What is meant by this is that the play takes the spectator 'back in time' in order to experience the past as a space with multiple possibilities. These possibilities are performed on stage by the *indios*, whose various encounters with the cross configure an increasingly complex tableau of 'readings' in which the *indios* attempt to make sense of the cross and, by extension, the Spaniards. These readings are situated in parallel relationship to an allegorical scene in which the Spaniards erect and dedicate the cross to the success of their enterprise. The *indios'* interpretation of the strange, emblematic icon is thus framed within a Christian ritual of discovery, giving the play's spectators the impression that, in Gumbrecht's words, they 'understand the conditions under which various meanings of a given text [object] are generated by readers whose receptive dispositions have different historical and social mediation' (*Making Sense* 15). Adding to the impression that we are witnessing a unique moment in history is the anthropological role played by the Spaniards themselves, who observe these primitive rituals from the safety of their ships. Since the central semiotic event, or performance, in the play is a progressive effort to come to terms with the historical and cultural meaning of the placement of the cross on the shores of *La Deseada*, emblematics plays a constitutive role in the play.

There are several moments in the play in which the characters, both European and 'American,' strike more or less consciously allegorical and ritualistic postures in the attempt to construct a metaphysical framework for anchoring the meaning of this mythological moment of the first contact. Not only does Lope invent a theatrical figure he calls *el indio*, he also gives this image of the Other a constitutive role in the realization, or making present, of the messianic vision of the Counter Reformation monarchy.[3] As with the ontological and historical distance I have attempted to situate between Lope's dramatic *indio* and the historical, documentable Amerindians, we should not confuse the staged agency of the *indio* in his voluntary embrace of Spanish vassalage with the violent historical process of conquest and domination; or rather, we should see the highly framed representation of the *indio*'s voluntary assimilation as one of the most effect tropes in the representation of conquest and domination as a peaceful and progressive historical process.

Lope's play exemplifies colonial discourse in the sense that his anthropological and ethnographic figures are embedded in a cultural presupposition that places the *indio* in an asymmetrical cultural, political, and historical relation with the European. This relationship, embodied in emblematic images, produces a sequence of privileged symbolic moments in which the *indios* act as a cipher for the Europeans' desire to both consume the material riches of the New World and legitimize that same desire by framing the supposed cultural inferiority of the inhabitants. In the first instance, the symbolic differences produced by the contrasting interpretations of the image of the cross are best understood within the dialectic of iconoclasm and iconophilia. According to Mitchell, 'totems, fetishes, and idols ... are ... productions of colonial discourse, and are often identified as the "bad objects" of empire, the things that produce ambivalence and need to be neutralized, merely tolerated, or destroyed' (*What Do Pictures Want?* 146). Thus, the *indios'* initial reactions to the cross, which appear to treat the object as an idol or fetish, will be corrected and then fixed according to allegorical meanings consistent with Counter Reformation theology. This intellectual deficiency of the primitive subject of colonial power is most readily recognized in the image of the cannibal. The deconstruction of this image of Otherness, which also appears in Lope's play, will bring us to the second movement, summarized by Jerry Phillips: 'Colonial discourse was heavily invested in the spectacle of savage cannibalism because, as Marx pointed out, "civility", as a cultural ethics of negotiating stark human differences, was obliged "to go naked" in the colonies – revealing itself as a "morality" of plunder and murder' (196). In other words, we can reverse the original mirror image by seeing the *indios'* eventual consumption of the sacramental body of Christ as an oblique gaze upon the Europeans' simultaneous absorption and erasure of American Otherness.

I have found it necessary to begin with this interpretive frame, as the play stages the complicity of the colonized subject in his own subjugation by deploying what Mary Louise Pratt calls an 'ethnographic discourse.' In *El nuevo mundo*, 'ethnographic texts are a means by which Europeans represent to themselves their (usually subjugated) others' (*Imperial Eyes* 7). In this case, the American Other projects an un-self-consciously allegorical worldview, one which intuits and thereby recognizes the universal destiny of the Spanish empire. Much like Bell's discovery of the ideological unconscious of modern anthropological narratives concerning primitive myth structures and content, Pratt underlines the unacknowledged blind spot of empiricist narratives of Otherness. My claim is that the so-called realistic representation of New World Otherness on the stage of Counter Reformation Spain is better understood as the channeling of hegemonic imperialistic discourses through a domesticated image of Otherness, or the emblematization of the Amerindian Other.

As we have seen in the previous two chapters, Horozco and Borja exemplify the emblematist's peculiar obsession with ambiguous signs, which is manifested in the numerous and contentious attempts to (re)unite the fragmented symbolic body of what Edmundo O'Gorman has called the 'Ecumene,' or Christian world view, inherited from the Middle Ages (21). What Russell describes as the ambiguous and polyvalent meaning of emblematic signs (167) places the emblem in close proximity to Bell's characterization of ritual discourse: 'some type of ambiguity or blindness in ritualization is linked to its distinctive efficacy' (*Ritual Theory* 109). Nothing could be more ambiguous and thus more open to ritualistic and emblematic play than the discovery of the New World. As O'Gorman states, 'The events … only receive their full meaning … if they are projected and framed within the image of the world that constitutes their own historical circumstance' (21). In this reading, I will borrow O'Gorman's historiographical approach and analyse the image of the world that Lope invents and then projects onto his audience within the baroque world of the image. Toward this end I will use the emblem as an analytical tool akin to Maravall's definition of a historical structure, which 'reflects the mentality of an epoch and at the same time wields influence over that mentality … not as a passive means of expression, but rather as an active principle which imposes an organized ensemble of distinctions and values on thought' (*Teoría del saber histórico* 191). As we have seen in the first two chapters, the emblem embodies a modern mentality that seeks to erect epistemological guarantees on the remains of a medieval, allegorical worldview that is in decline.

Image of the World; World of the Image

Turning the tables on Maravall, one could characterize his by now canonical if highly contested reading of *baroque guided culture* as 'emblematic.' The first chapter of his monumental study *The Culture of the Baroque* describes how the baroque mentality is conditioned by a perceived loss of social, economic, and political stability and cohesion; and the subsequent emergence of a historical consciousness acutely attuned to crises, both imaginary and real. It is in the context of this perceived social instability and fragmentation that the monarchy and the Church are embraced by the elite, not as an absolute presence in the medieval or iconic sense of the word, but as an *empresa*, in the medievalizing emblematic sense. The Church and the emergent Absolutist State become dominant figures in the representation and propagation of a largely unfulfilled desire for hegemony – a device – constituted through the rearrangement of politico-religious estates and symbols. Like the emblem, absolutist ideology simultaneously looks to the past, as an age of lost plenitude, and to the future, where, ostensibly, the desire for wholeness – and absolute meaning – will be fulfilled. As R. de la Flor argues, the fragmented world of the baroque teeters precariously on the edge of history, simultaneously invoking and reacting to a series of 'national' crises. Joaquín de Entrambasaguas and Robert M. Shannon make much of the fact that *El nuevo mundo* appears in one of the weakest moments of the economic, political, and social decline of the Hapsburg regime.[4] The monarchy's recent declaration of bankruptcy (1596), a series of 'humiliating' treaties with the heretical powers of Europe, and the futile efforts to protect the colonies from privateers financed by France, Holland, and England converge at the time the work was probably written (1596–1606) and point to the mentality studied by Maravall.[5] Lope's very baroque answer to this state of affairs is the construction and invocation of a national *empresa* of universal proportions.

The most well known study of emblems in Lope de Vega's theatre is Warren T. McCready's oft-cited '*Empresas* in Lope de Vega's Works.' Of particular interest for *El nuevo mundo* is McCready's catalogue of Lope's repeated usage of the Carolingian device *Plus Ultra*. Starting with the early and numerous allusions to the columns of Hercules, which invoke the double *empresa* of Carlos V – *non plus ultra* and *plus ultra* – and continuing with the insistent parallels between the Colón brothers and another pair of brothers divinely charged with the pilgrimage of the Israelites to their promised land – Moses and Aaron – Lope composes a messianic enterprise that spans almost a thousand years of Iberian history in yet another emblematic transduction of Hebrew history. From King Rodrigo's seduction of la Cava (alluded to by the Moorish king Mahomet in the first act) to the death of another sensually enslaved Rodrigo (Terrazas), the work is millenarian in both temporal structure and religious theme.[6] Given the decidedly spiritual connotations of the Hapsburg device, it is not surprising that the columns of Hercules appear so often in the work. As Sandra Sider observes, '"Plus Ultra" certainly involved a striving toward moral excellence and eventually referred to political expansion into the New World. It had its origin, as we know, in the religious fervor of the early sixteenth century, and I would argue that the incredible popularity and power of this device were based on this compelling religious symbolism. "Plus Ultra" reached toward Africa, America, and the East; it also reached toward the stars' (261). This emblematic fantasia culminates in the dénouement of the play with the appearance of a newly invented *empresa* framing Colón's discovery within Spain's universal destiny. Having been knighted 'Duke of Veraguas,' Colón carries a banner with his new coat-of-arms as he parades before the Catholic monarchs, who ask him to read the blazon. He proudly accedes to their command: 'For Castile and Leon, Colón found a New World' [Por Castilla y León, / Nuevo Mundo halló Colón] (2960–1). Due to the rhyme scheme, his very name seems to form a neologism composed of the united kingdoms of Castile and León. The meaning seems clear, yet Lope's invocation of a collective destiny begs clarification, especially since the device refers to the past and not to the future, a significant breach of the *empresa*'s conventional performative functions.

As I have indicated earlier, the *empresa* is the most noble and ingenious of the various emblematic modes. While the aim of the emblem is the moral education of the reader or spectator, an *empresa* entails the public representation of an individual, aristocratic subject. Its history is somewhat different in Spain, however, as from a fairly early date the Spanish term *empresa* was tied to the reconquest of *Al Andalus*. In the words of Campa, 'The first imprese in Spain are associated with the founding of military orders during the Reconquest from the Moors … During this period the real enterprise (empresa/impresa) is the Reconquest' ('The Space' 58). From time immemorial, then, the Spanish *empresa* had been associated with what came to be regarded as a collective, historical-religious-ethnic project. One might even suggest that the etymological history of the term in medieval and early modern Iberia influences Borja's redefinition in his Prologue. On the other hand, since the Reconquest was not declared over until 1492, for a long period of time this *empresa* was not the symbolic expression of an established reality but rather the expression of a longed for if unrealized goal. My point is that in their projection towards the future, both the *empresa* and the emblem function as '*modus operandi* [and] *modus vivendi* of history: [they] reveal … how from the bosom of a determined image of the world, narrow and particularistic, archaic, a historical entity surges which, as it proceeds constituting itself into being, operates like a dissolvent of the old structure and how, at the same time, it is the catalyst that provokes a new conception of the world' (O'Gorman 15).

For an illustration of this movement, we can refer back to Borja's *empresa* entitled *Satiabor cum apparverit*, or 'I will be satisfied when it appears,' where the Egyptian letter *tau* is emptied of any historical meaning related to the place where it was ostensibly produced. At the same time, the significance of the 'religious' symbol becomes absolute when it is fully incorporated into the Catholic allegory. This ideological extension, and not the elucidation of the linguistic history of the

Egyptians, is the product of the emblematic practice of the author.[7] In this way, the ancient Egyptians are made to carry, unconsciously, the future enterprise of the Spanish Empire in their 'pregnant' signs. The Catholic cross faces a similar destiny, at least semiotically, becoming a multiple possibility, infinitely scattered across a historical and textual landscape and thus open to infinite recontextualizations.

The mediation and channeling of the movement from signifying chaos to 'motivated' meaning is the emblem's primary role in Lope's play, as the symbolic expansion of the Spanish empire is universalized through the repeated play of allegorical images and discourses. Most of this semiotic work occurs in Act 2 of the play, when the Spaniards arrive on the shores of the island *Deseada*. Mimicking Borja's *empresa* of the letter *tau*, both the reader's passivity – 'I will be satisfied' – and the unprecedented appearance of the cross come into play when Colón plants the symbol on the beach in his first act of imperial possession. Given the liminal location of the geographical and symbolic beachhead, Homi Bhabha's concept of the boundary helps explain how the placement of the cross effects a negation of the Otherness of *La Deseada* as well as how Lope both triggers and overcomes the strangeness of the *indios*: 'The negating activity is, indeed, the intervention of the "beyond" that establishes a boundary: a bridge, where "presencing" begins because it captures something of the estranging sense of the relocation of the home and the world – the unhomeliness – that is the condition of extra-territorial and cross-cultural initiations' (13). By positing America as 'Other,' it becomes clear that it can only be understood and thus appropriated through its difference to the 'same.' The containment and conversion of this difference is the fundamental theme of the allegorical plot. We should note that the arrival on the shores of the New World occurs exactly three days after Colón's impatient and rebellious mariners give up their admiral's *empresa* for dead, thus situating the discovery within messianic time. In spite of the sailors' desperation and rage, God's providential instrument is not thrown overboard, and, more importantly, what follows the resurrection of Colón's *empresa* is a series of emblematic commentaries on the meaning of his initial, imperialistic gesture.

The hero himself begins the emblematization of the cross by proclaiming that 'this will be the lamp that will give new light to the world' [éste el farol ha de ser / que dé al mundo nueva luz] (vv. 1571). Father Buyl continues, sanctifying the 'Blessed sands and shores that merit such a plant' [Dichosa arena y orillas / que tal planta merecéis]

(vv. 1576–8). Colón responds with: 'Illustrious bed on which the God-Man died ... You are the beautiful banner' [cama ilustre, donde Dios – / – Hombre murió echado en ella / Vos sois la bandera bella] (vv. 1580–2). And Buyl replies, 'Mast of the beautiful ship of the Church, glorious ladder that Jacob saw, what sail could be more blessed than a bed sheet, a shroud, what pilot more great?' [Árbol de la nave hermosa de la Iglesia / escala la que Jacob vio gloriosa, / ¿qué vela más venturosa que una sábana, mortaja? / ¿qué piloto le aventaja?] (vv. 1589–91). This series of apostrophes achieves several objectives, the most important of which is the animation of both the newly discovered *ínsula* and the symbol of Spanish domination over it. This rhetorical gesture creates a dialogical link between the passive land and the active symbolic activity of the conquerors, thus the penetration of the beachhead by the cross becomes a meaningful encounter between two animate beings rather than a violent imposition of symbolic and military superiority. Later, when the *indios* approach the cross, they become organically linked to the land and then to the cross in the same way.

In this preliminary scene, the allegorical fragmentation of the cross results in its metamorphosis into a lantern (of faith), a miraculous plant, a (death) bed, a banner of faith, a ship's mast, a flagpole, and Jacob's ladder. Even more interesting is the deterritorialization of the shroud and body of Christ into sail and navigator. The allegorical excursus is extended by the other explorers, and the cross fuses with the staff of Moses, while the crown of thorns becomes a laurel of victory; finally, the cross merges with David's harp, whose strings are held in place with three pegs/nails. The baroque concert ends with a return to the motif of the sheet that adorns the semi-nude body of the dead Christ, a common motif in many Renaissance representations of Christ's death and resurrection.[8] According to this emblematic parade, the discovery of the New World signals the redemption of Colón, the redemption of Queen Isabel's faith in his enterprise, Spain's redemptive role in universal history, as well as a number of 'resurrections': once again, the resurrection of the seemingly moribund Colón; the resurrection of the Universal Church; and, not least, the resurrection of the *indios* from their spiritually morbid and moribund beliefs. Finally, Terrazas – later Rodrigo – prays: 'Holy shirt, stained with the innocent blood of Joseph, for whom Jacob and Maria tenderly wept, be our banner and guide amongst this barbarous people' [Camisa santa, teñida / de aquella sangre inocente / de Josef, que tiernamente / lloró

Jacob y María, / sed nuestra bandera y guía / entre esta bárbara gente] (vv. 1632–7). Here the motif of brotherly enmity is introduced in a Hebrew context, as the Other is once again equated with the heretical Egyptians: the false blood on Joseph's colorful coat is transformed into the real, sacramental blood on the shroud of Christ, who, like and unlike Joseph, is raised from the dead in a barbarous land. What also becomes apparent is the conversion of the discovery into a text, first by focusing on the fabric of Christ's-Joseph's shroud-coat, and second by framing the discovery within the textual world of the book. The discovery thus becomes a literary as opposed to an exclusively historical event. Finally, it is noteworthy that the most malevolent character in the play provides the most theologically explicit commentary on the discovery. As Brotherton explains, 'in this unconventional context, this New World, Lope chooses the same character to explain the doctrine of the Holy Trinity, the Fall of Lucifer, and the concept of Transubstantiation to the ignorant natives, and he does so with admirable clarity' (43). In his sophisticated and explicatory role, Terrazas is closely analogous to satanic characters in the *auto sacramental*, a structural characteristic that will be developed in the next chapter.

Just as Borja colonizes the Egyptian letters with a latent religious meaning, Lope frames the cross inside the most recognizable moments and symbols of the Old Testament, colonizing the history of the Jews through allegoresis. What I want to highlight in this static and ecstatic moment in the play is the way in which the movement from speaker to speaker resembles a small book of emblems. In each *empresa* we are delightfully surprised and then satisfied by the allegorical interpretation of yet another marvelous facet of the crucifix, leading towards a progressive expansion of temporal and spatial depth through the accumulation of thread after biblical thread into the tapestry of the discovery. The number of motifs effortlessly subjected to emblematic allegoresis in this play seems potentially infinite: the cross is transformed into a lantern, the shroud into a sail or flag, the nails on the cross into the keys of a harp, Christ into a sailor, and, finally, wood into a tree (of life).

Given the sandy locale, the tree image invokes another common emblematic topic, that of the palm tree. Pedro A. Galera Andreu explains: 'The consideration of the palm tree as *arbor victoriae* is strongly rooted in ancient sources in that their palms were chosen as rewards for the victors in contests or jousts' (63). Thus, the ultimate victory of the Spaniards over the *indios* is prefigured in the first act of discovery. Parallel to this scene, in the last act of the play, Colón's cross is made to spring from heretofore unseen roots after the *indios* pull it out of the sand. This wordplay centering on the wooden cross actually begins in Act 1, when Colón tells the Catholic Kings that he learned of the existence of the New World while he was nursing an old sick sailor, who lived (and died) on the island of – where else – *Madera* (vv. 65–136).

Although we appreciate the poet's quick wit and *inventio*, the dramatic emblems and their inventors should not surprise us, since the Spaniards are exemplary Christians. More to the point, the emblematic tableau ties the practice of Christianity to the creation of emblems, i.e., allegorical readings of the transcendental significance of personal experiences and contingencies, exemplifying Bell's concept of ritual mastery: 'Ritual mastery is the ability – not equally shared, desired, or recognized – to (1) take and remake schemes from the shared culture that can strategically nuance, privilege, or transform, (2) deploy them in the formulation of a privileged ritual experience, which in turn (3) impresses them in a new form upon agents [spectators] able to deploy them in a variety of circumstances beyond the circumference of the rite itself' (*Ritual Theory* 116). Fundamental to Bell's definition is the way in which the ritual act extends itself beyond the 'circumference of the rite' and reaches into the 'real' of historical events. It bears mentioning that the *indios* witness this entire scene along with the spectators in the *corral*. This scopic structure corresponds to what Thomas E. Case terms a 'minidrama,' in that we witness both the original moment of discovery and the witnessing of this same moment by the native inhabitants of *La Deseada*. Later on, this structure will be reversed, with the Europeans gazing on the verbal performance of the *indios*.[9] In the meanwhile, what we learn – both *indios* (unknowingly) and spectators (knowingly) – is that although the fragmentation of the cross is infinite, its interpretations all lead toward a single, absolute, and universal meaning: the idea that Colón and, more importantly, Spain are the chosen participants in what Entrambasaguas calls an 'epic and providential drama' (IX).

Emblems and *Indios*

The first signs of the unexpected arrival of the fleet, the gunshots celebrating the discovery of *La Deseada*, interrupt a war, or duel of honour, between two quasi-epic warriors, Dulcanquellín and Tapirazú: Dulcanquellín has abducted the wife of Tapirazú. Lope frames our interpretation of this barbaric spectacle of honour by alluding to the invasion of the 'Muslim horde' and the potentially tragic parallel with the conflict between the infamous King Rodrigo and Don Julián over the former's abduction and seduction of la Cava, the latter's daughter. José Cartagena Calderón also finds parallels between the *indio* warriors and an earlier scene in the play that takes place in Granada, just before its conquest by the Catholic monarchs: 'Lope will interlace, connect and create contiguity between the … demasculinization of the moor and the representation of the natives of the New World, who will look similar to Tarfe, the Boabdil king, Zelindo, Abindarráez and other muslim heroes consumed and defeated by emotional instability, surrender to passion for a woman, lechery, lasciviousness, or sexual abandon' (129). Lost in this emblematization of an American scene of conquest between rival *indios* is the potential parallelism between the Muslim horde and the Spanish *conquistadores*, as the dramatic emphasis is placed on the implicit identification of the lovesick Dulcanquellín with the unfortunate and lustful Visigoth king Rodrigo. Although this analogy may not be developed by the spectator, it is an interesting example of how difficult it is to control allegorical connotations once the wordplay is set in motion. Bhabha observes that this identification of the other effectively cancels his otherness (88), as from this point on the *indio* becomes a mobile figure in a Spanish drama of (re)conquest as opposed to a sign of that which lies beyond the European mentality. Just as significant is the way in which the appearance of the cross immediately pacifies the *indios*, who have only recently become violent due to the illegitimate and lustful act of their commander, yet another structural parallel with honour plays like *Peribañez y el Comendador de Ocaña*.[10] In this case, however, rather than have the king play the role of deus ex machina, it is the cross itself that pacifies the barbarian mob, underlining what R. de la Flor calls the 'active nature' of the emblematic image (*Emblemas* 118). The subsequent staging of emblems arises from the *indios'* attempts to understand the mysterious images, symbols, and words of the alien race and their marvelous ships.

In the eyes of the barbarians, the fleet is perceived as a wonder – monstrous and/or divine – whose cosmological significance becomes the object of their hermeneutic vacillations. This dramatic structure, which combines the appearance of mysterious images (*picturae*) with mottos shouted in an unknown language (*inscriptiones*), both of which are subjected to the equivocal commentary of the *indios* (*subscriptiones*), illustrates the classic triplex form of the emblem. The *gracioso-indio* Auté initiates the savages' speculation with the following 'translation': 'They said "God," "land," and "Virgin," which must be their houses, unless God and the Virgin are called their father and mother, and the land is some friend who travels estranged from his fatherland' [Dios, tierra y Virgen decían, / que deben ser sus casas, / si no es que Dios y la Virgen / su padre y madre se llaman / y la tierra algún amigo / que anda ausente de su patria] (vv. 1509–14). *Dios, tierra,* and *Virgen* function here as transcultural and translinguistic signifiers in that the natives pronounce these words in Spanish and then are portrayed 'translating' them into their native tongue. They become, in other words, universal mediators of difference – in Spanish of course – and thus demonstrate once more how the movement between distinct orders of signs, i.e., alphabetic and hieroglyphic, is much more fluid than is generally recognized. The struggle of the *indios* to come to terms, metaphorically, with the marvelous arrival of the Spaniards corresponds to early modern linguistic views on the savages. Gombrich explains: '[Vico] developed his theory of the mentality of primitive man who becomes a poet by force of circumstance, creating images and symbols not out of superior wisdom, but as tools to come to terms with a world he does not understand' (184). Previously, Auté had identified the ships as 'houses,' so his subsequent confusion of the Spaniards' spiritual parents with the ships or (symbolic) edifices of the mysterious visitors works perfectly within the theological symbology of the play, while also highlighting the penetration of the simplistic intuition of the *indios* by elemental theological notions supposedly emanating from the cross. If we add the architectural nuances of the word *nave*, as well as the symbolic association of the Church with the womb of the Virgin, or the house of God, the implications of the naïve *gracioso*'s musings can be seen to lead towards the same absolute goal as the previous emblematic scene.

The chief Dulcanquellín continues the speculation and even appears to contradict the *gracioso* when he calls the ships 'fish that roar, which, walking through these islands to gorge themselves on human flesh, have eaten these men' [peces que braman, / que andando por esas islas / a hartarse de carne humana / se han comido esos hombres] (vv. 1515–18). The provocative possibilities of this suggestion of anthropophagy by a barbarian who, later on, prepares a welcoming feast for the visitors by ordering the culinary preparation of a few of his servants deserve a study of their own, for Dulcanquellín's words identify cannibalism as a universal marker for the Other, even among savages. Let us not forget that the goal of the Spaniards is the absorption of American Otherness into their own political body. Nevertheless, what interests me here is how Dulcanquellín 'naïvely' alludes to the biblical monster that swallowed Jonah, a story mentioned earlier by the friar Buyl. Caroline Bynum informs us that the story of Jonah and the whale had been a popular figure of Christ's death and resurrection from the very inception of the Christian Church (186–200). The fact that these ravenous 'fish' have disgorged their human cargo on the shore is yet another indication that the arrival of the Spaniards is a resurrection of sorts, if the spectators have not already been yoked to the messianic plotline. In both scenes centering on the cross, the emblematic exclamations of Christians and *indios* – the former conscious of the metaphysical significance of the discovery, the latter unknowingly and unconsciously allusive – deploy tropes of resurrection, redemption, and triumph in these ritualized moments of allegorical and quasi-allegorical reception. One way to understand the surprising intuition of the *indios* is to concede, heuristically, that Catholic religious allegories are indeed innate, akin to Neoplatonic Ideas, and that the natives are starting to remember their 'true selves.' We can connect this Neo-platonic reading to Eugenio Frutos's explanation of the two *gracias*: in this case, the quasi-poetic conceits of the *indios* may be taken as an indication of the first, or sufficient, *gracia*, which will be redeemed when the savages take consciousness of their sinful nature and repent, thus achieving efficacious or efficient grace through their voluntary submission to God's – and Spain's – will. In either case, any substantive Otherness, anything that might place the *indio* outside of the European and, specifically, Catholic ecumene and thus threaten its universality, is elided.

In the attempt to find a figure from 'his own cultural history' with which to identify the strangers, Tapirazú alludes to a story, or myth, about giants 'as tall as a tree who came to these mountains' [de la altura de un pino / [que] vinieron a estas montañas] (vv. 1533–4). The dishonoured *indio* recalls that in this pre-historic period – in which 'men joined with men … one day the heavens opened up in various places and a youth descended with a white shirt who made war on them, throwing many flames at them' [juntaban hombres con hombres … un día se abrió el cielo en partes varias / y bajó dél un mancebo / con una camisa blanca / que hizo con ellos guerra / tirándoles muchas llamas] (1535–46). Entrambasaguas argues that Lope takes this legend from one of the chronicles of the Araucanians of Chile.[11] If we look to the Old Testament, however, whose overriding presence in the play has already been established, sexual abominations and the rain of fire are among the most recognizable motifs of the biblical story of Sodom and Gomorrah. Furthermore, the image of the white shirt echoes the Christological emblems, such as the shroud, the sail, and the 'camisa santa,' mentioned earlier by the Spaniards. Rather than opt for one or the other of these interpretations, I think it is more useful to consider that Lope is working syncretically – allegorically – much as does Juan de Borja when he projects the form of the cross onto the accidental matter of the African letter *tau*, and, in so doing, creates a historically and spiritually pregnant image. Following Borja's model, the arrival of the Spaniards would open the way to the *indios*' spiritual redemption and rebirth to historical self-awareness at the same time as the ontological dichotomy of the European and its self-fashioned Other is, in O'Gorman's words, 'cancelled' in a staged act of mutual recognition. The 'Araucanian' anecdote functions as a hieroglyphic, or letter, that only achieves its true meaning when framed within a teleology that transcends the sign's primordial moment of articulation in time and space.[12] Like *tau*, the *indio*, along with the entirety of his cultural archive, is impregnated – Brotherton would say contaminated – with the universal history of Spain.

In discussing the emblems rendered by the *indios*, I have attempted to highlight the apparent innocence, or lack of allegorical self-awareness, characterizing their initial interpretations of the trans-Atlantic encounter. What such naïveté demonstrates is that even though the *indios* are intuitively correct in their interpretation of religious symbols, they are unable to fully possess the theological meaning, which exceeds their innate capacity for (ir)rational thought, according to St Thomas and his humanist translator Francisco de Vitoria (M. Castillo 'El secreto'). Brotherton states that 'while they share the *lengua* (Spanish) of the spectators, their *lenguaje* is a very specifically constructed theatrical and, more significantly, ideological sub-set of that *lengua*' (37); Case is even more explicit on this point: the *indio* 'is an incomplete human being' (19). The distinction is vital because if, on the one hand, this universal emblematic mentality establishes the essential similarity of the *indios* to the Europeans, on the other, the metaphysical shortcomings of the former act as a distinguishing characteristic that we can equate with their American, or barbaric, Otherness.

Moisés Castillo convincingly connects this ontological lack of the *indio* to the debates between Ginés de Sepúlveda and Bartolomé de las Casas concerning the humanity or inhumanity of the Amerindian populations. According to Castillo's juridical-philosophical reading, the central issue is 'the functioning of the understanding for Thomas Aquinas which constitutes the keystone – the participation of divine understanding in human understanding' (79).[13] This explains the difference between the formal perfection of the Christians' emblems and the nagging excess, or lack, obstructing the real meaning of the *indios*': 'Without the light of active understanding we are blind, we do not understand the *form* of things, their *perfection*, that for which they serve' (M. Castillo, 'Lope de Vega' 79). The evolution of the *indios* from blindness to sight, from imperfection to perfection, from first to second *gracia*, as evidenced by their increasing emblematic sophistication and perfection, is both mediated and witnessed by the European actors and spectators within the drama and in the *corrales*. Colón's retinue watches the *indios*' performance from the ships; the spectators watch both the *indios* and the sailors who watch the natives. The effect could be described as that of an emblematic *mise-en-abîme*, but Russell explains how this multiplication of frames can also function to close off interpretive possibilities: 'rather than empowering the individual, the anamorphic controls the individual perspective by framing or constructing the composition in certain ways that call for specific perspectives on the tableau' (*Emblematic Structures* 241). Thus, rather than a confusing multiplication of interpretive frames, we experience an increasingly focused telescoping effect. In this structure, the raw material of the *indios*' proto-theological conceits is channeled through the reception by the Spaniards and handed to the spectator fully formed.

The apotheosis of this impregnation of an almost empty, proto-European mentality into the naked body of the American *indio* occurs in Act 3. A miraculous cross appears, sprouting from the hole from which the first cross had been violently removed by the offended *indios* during their aborted massacre of the greedy and lecherous Spaniards. What is interesting here is that the *indios*' rebellion is caused by a European character, the aforementioned Rodrigo Terrazas, who 'seduces' the previously kidnapped wife of Tapirazú, Tacuana.[14] With this crime, Rodrigo replaces the *indio* as the antagonist of the imperialistic enterprise. The initial ontological transplant occurs, however, in Act 2 when the Christians return to their ships, permitting the *indios* to approach the new adornment on their shores. For Entrambasaguas, this scene is one of the greatest achievements of the play: 'the impression produced by the arrival of the Spaniards is astonishing' (VII). I agree with Entrambasaguas, but not because Lope represents the indigenous Amerindian in a natural or historically accurate way; to the contrary, what we witness here is the invention of what M. Castillo has called 'a new ontological entity' ('El secreto' 397): to wit, a quasi-emblematist *indio* who, in his Adam-like innocence, is able to 'unconsciously' intuit and communicate the most profound mysteries of the Christian faith thanks to the sufficient grace Christ endows him with at birth. Thus, the plot of the play concerns the *indios'* struggle to attain efficient, or efficacious, grace through their embrace of Christian doctrine.

We begin with the comments of the three protagonists of the quickly forgotten conflict concerning Tapirazú's marital honour. Tacuana, the hostage, exclaims 'What light!' [¡Qué lustre!]; Dulcanquellín, her abductor, finishes off the quatrain, 'looking at it is blinding' [El mirarla ciega] (vv. 1749). The offended Tapirazú points out that 'it has three irons nailed into it' [Tres hierros tiene clavados]; and Dulcanquellín speculates that 'This tree, with these irons, they erected on this sand … in order to bring their houses to land from the sea and to tie those ropes to these irons' [Esta, con aquestos hierros, / en esta arena fijaron … para meter a la tierra / las casas desde la mar, / y en estos hierros atar / aquellas cuerdas] (vv. 1752–62). Sensing the implications of this literal (and metaphorical) beachhead of imperial conquest, Tapirazú asks Dulcanquellín why he hesitates to order the removal of this 'pier' from his beach. When the natives lay their hands on the cross, however, Tapirazú suffers inexplicable (mystical?) pangs of regret: 'By my life, it has occurred to me that we have deceived ourselves, and that by removing it we err!' [¡Por mi vida que he pensado / que nos hemos engañado, / y en quitarla yerro hacemos!] (1767–9). The word-play with the homonyms *hierro* and *yerro* connects the avoided error of the *indios* to the crucifixion of Christ, which is an omen that they will be saved. Tacuana validates Tapirazú's intuition, declaring, 'It must be some sacred thing' [Que debe de ser / alguna cosa sagrada] (vv. 1770–1). The emblematic repartee resumes with yet another pregnant image: that of a watchtower that the bearded strangers could use 'to raise themselves up … and look from there at their houses, shores and beach' [para subirse sobre ella … y mirar desde ella sus casas, ribera y playa] (vv. 1774–6).

Let us pause for a moment to summarize what we have just seen and consider how it is related to the previous emblematic scene because, although we are indeed presented with a series of emblems, the position and characterization of their enunciation and reception have changed significantly. First, we must recognize that if the emblems created by the Spaniards are marvelous, we should not be surprised that the European characters know the theological rudiments of Christianity; rather, what amazes us is the anamorphic sequence of images and the *inventio* of the poet who fills them with meaning. The metamorphosis of David's harp into Christ's cross and vice versa is fluid because the figure is completely subject to the commentary of the emblem. In Aristotelian terms, the image is only an accidental body, or instance, of a transcendental form, or soul. In the case of the *indios*, however, the semi-allegorical emblems maintain an unyielding materiality, or duality, due to the speakers' ontological incompleteness, which is symptomatic of their lack of transcendental (self) awareness. There is a minimal but unresolvable vacillation between the 'real time' enunciation of their words and their ultimate meaning and intent. When Dulcanquellín comments on how the nails on the cross are used to moor the ships, or how the strangers climb up the cross to look at their houses and shores, our perception of his 'primitive,' natural understanding remains, at least in part, literal. The way Lope positions the spectator underlines Dulcanquellín's 'empty' or 'unfinished' mind, as the *indio* seems to imagine real ropes physically extended between the ships in the bay and the cross on the beach; or bearded men physically perched on the cross while they look at their unmetaphorical houses. In short, Lope provokes us to laughter with the denotative nature of the *indios'* exclamations. At the same time, and unlike the parallel scene with the Spaniards, here it is the spectator who is invited to invest the metaphor *in potentia* with allegorical meaning in order to fill in and complete the apparently incomplete – imperfect – devices of the *indio*.

Equally important is the perception that the *indios* have a natural intuition of Catholic truths;[15] or, conversely, that Christian truths are in fact universal, both contained and communicable in the very materiality of their symbols. M. Castillo explains that since Dulcanquellín's forefathers had previously been visited by an apostle of Christ, only to be turned away from the true faith by Ongol – a.k.a., Idolatry – what we are actually seeing is a reconquest of America, as opposed to the discovery and recognition of something new: 'In this sense, "discover" actually means returning America to her being (ontology) as well as to "un-cover" America's being (epistemology); so that in this fashion it may be known, re-conquering her meaning, that which had been concealed by Idolatry' (75). America functions like a hieroglyphic whose true meaning, after centuries of pagan and heretical obfuscation, is rediscovered by the penetration of Christian insight. It is impossible for the *indios'* understanding to be more correct, since they have never before seen such things; in fact, the true meaning of their own words is hidden from them. What is more, if the *indios'* understanding lacks enlightenment, the emotions and fear they feel before the cross supersede the necessity to come to an absolute understanding of the sign. As Gombrich states, 'this effect of the image on our passions and emotions would have been accepted as a proof of its true correspondence to the heavenly idea, a natural outcome of its magical efficacy' (195).

This scene is doubly effective because it reintroduces the technique of 'the play within the play,' or, more precisely, an 'appearance' within another 'appearance.' The miraculous appearance of the cross is framed by the marvelous appearance of land to the Spaniards, who observe the *indios'* insular reactions with much interest.[16] Far from introducing ambiguity into the meaning of the staged encounter, this play with point of view effectively frames the actions and words of the *indios* by recontextualizing them according to an outside and 'objective' – Pratt would say 'ethnographic' – point of view. The embrionic emblems of the *indios* are brought to term by the historical spectator with the help of the on-stage spectators, who have just provided the correct commentary on the meaning of the cross. Allen Carey-Webb explains: 'the *indio* needs the Spaniard (as the peasant needs the aristocrat) to bring about "rational" exchange' (433). All the same, the fact that the *indios* are not fully aware of their necessary role in the providential history of the Hapsburgs suggests that they might wander off the true path at any moment. The agent of this detour arrives on the shores of *La Deseada* embodying the messianic undercurrent that has connected the Visigoth king Rodrigo to Dulcanquellín, and his name is *Rodrigo* Terrazas; similarly, la Cava, *La Deseada*, and Tacuana form an emblem of paradise lost and potentially redeemed.

At the end of the previous scene, Tapirazú's servant/*gracioso* arrives in a state of panic and gives an admirable description of a two-headed man/beast – a man on horseback – which leads to another attempt to remove the cross from the sand.[17] This time the Christians fire their shotguns from the ships, which results in the timid obedience of the *indios* and momentarily contradicts the representation of the colonization as peaceful and voluntary.[18] This suggestion of violence is quickly overridden, however, by the apology of Palca, who concludes that 'these guests are not warlike but peaceful' [estos huéspedes no son / de guerra sino de paz] (vv. 1890–1). How much more effective these words are coming from the mouth of a native! Her declaration is followed by another litany of potentially Christological emblems motivated by the mysterious appearance of the deafening explosions. In this case, the allegorical allusions are easier to identify: Tacuana exclaims, 'Holy mast, beautiful mast, unknown God in you' [Palo santo, palo hermoso, / Dios en ti no conocido] (vv. 1846–7).[19] Dulcanquellín proceeds to compare the revival of the cross to that of the phoenix (vv. 1855–62).[20] Tecué follows with 'Barren tree, may you be fruitful' [Árbol seco, así te veas / con fruto],[21] while Tacuana concludes: 'Thus from these holes flow spirits ... that heal any wound' [Ansí de estos agujeros / mane un licor ... que sane cualquiera herida] (vv. 1874–9). This last image resonates with the Italian legend of the icon of Lucca: '[The Lucca image] came into the possession of a Jew who pierced the icon of the crucified Christ with a lance in order to avoid suspicion of being a clandestine Christian. When the image began to bleed from the wound, the Jewish community was converted to Christianity and repented of its hostility toward images, which God seemed to reveal to be a sin by this heavenly miracle' (Belting 305). In both cases, the displacement of the mysteries of Catholic faith into the mind of the Other makes the sacramental rite totally palpable, concrete, and incarnate. The first declaration of Tacuana also underlines the reason for the natives' imperfection: like the Jews, they lack Christian insight.

It is apparent that Lope is more concerned with staging the presence of Catholic mysteries than with the accurate representation of the Amerindian Other. Far from relativizing the legitimacy of the conquest and colonization, as many critics of this play have argued,[22] Lope impregnates the New World with a utopian ideology through the creation of an unconsciously emblematic *indio*. Thus, rather than constituting a rare case in which the American reality is made to cross the threshold of European consciousness, what we see in these scenes corresponds to Pratt's previously cited definition of ethnography, which means that the *comedia* functions as a tool of colonization. As O'Gorman concludes, not only does the recognition of a New World not subvert the tripartite European *ecumene* inherited from the Middle Ages, the product of this 'ontological process' is yet another concept, or ideological activity, more useful for safeguarding and mollifying a crisis-driven mentality than for opening a space for the measured consideration of Otherness.

Conclusion

By way of conclusion, I would like to comment on the *empresa* with which Lope ends his play. As I mentioned earlier, one curious aspect of the motto is that it looks to the past rather than the future. The same can be said of Borja's oft-cited *empresa* of the letter *tau*. In both cases, an imperfect and spiritually empty history reaches fruition and perfection – termination – in the allegorical enterprise of Counter Reformation Spain. What the *indio* is missing, or that which exceeds his capacity to know himself ('that which is in him more than himself'), is his destiny as a future subject of Spain. As Žižek points out in *Organs without Bodies*, the product of this dialectical process is the cancellation of difference along with the contradictions this difference discovers within ideology itself: 'The Hegelian dialectical process/progress is … the very model of a pseudo-development in which nothing effectively New ever emerges … All that happens is just the passage from In-itself to For-itself, that is, in the course of the dialectical process, things just actualize their potentials, explicitly posit their implicit content, become what (in themselves) they always already are' (14). What the *indio* is lacking in fact corresponds to the metaphysical surplus of the European: the ability to recognize his own innate identity as a future subject of empire. When he finally does recognize Christ in the miraculous appearance of the cross, the dramatic act of emblematic understanding is completed, and the history of the New World as Other ends. According to Lezra, 'Events are what was silently predicted in the system to which they come. In this reading they are what returns to, not what arrives at, their own' (40). In a rigorously emblematic movement, the enigmatic image of the *indio* rediscovers its 'true' meaning in the historicizing allegoresis of the emblematist.

Before closing, I would like to review a few aspects of the play in order to shed some light on the baroque meaning of its dénouement. It is significant that Lope maintains the danger represented by the material and sexual interests of the Spaniards, a danger that follows the movements of the aforementioned Rodrigo Terrazas. The figure of Terrazas is closely connected to that of Idolatry, which is introduced in Colón's prophetic dream in the first act, and appears again in Dulcanquellín's own prophetic dream in Act 3, thus linking conqueror to conquered in the allegorical world of prophecy and predestination. If the *indios* – with the notable exception of Tacuana, the very willing, illegitimate lover of Rodrigo – represent an unknown form of the providential future of Spain, Terrazas represents the hidden face, the mask of the historical chaos embodied by the figure of King Rodrigo a thousand years before when he fell in love with La Cava. It is so hidden, in fact, that we don't learn Terrazas's 'Christian' name until the third act. At that moment, when his thirst for gold – awakened by Tacuana's Atahualpan promises of infinite riches – is married to his perverse desire for the exotic Other, Colón's *empresa* teeters on the edge of history. These selfish and lustful acts of yet another self-obsessed Rodrigo threaten the establishment of the kingdom of Christ on Earth, which in turn endangers the return to the Promised Land and the realization of the redemptive prophecy of God's people. Thus, Rodrigo represents the quasi-eternal catalyst of movement in time and history, the contingent, the accidental. He also corresponds to what Žižek calls the 'unthought' of Counter Reformation ideology: its need and, yes, desire for a transcendental threat, an Other to establish the necessity of its utopian drive towards completion. His violent death at the hands of the *indios* and the expulsion of everything he represents serve to close the final chapter of the universal history of Spain as well as the New World. At this point, the gold, the *indios*, and all of the New World's natural possessions can be brought to the centre of the empire to be given their true meaning and redeem their spiritual interest.[23] In this encounter between incomplete forms of Otherness and Christianity's most perfect beings, the movement of the drama comes to a point of complete rest, and we can appreciate the broad resonance of the play's closing words: 'here, senate, *the history of the New World is ended*' [aquí, senado, *se acaba / la historia* del Nuevo Mundo] (vv. 2973–4; my emphasis).

Octavio Paz has characterized the baroque world of New Spain as a hermetic world, a universe whose historical aim is to avoid the contingencies and changes introduced by time and by contact with the Other. The metaphor used by the Mexican poet to materialize the peculiar apocalyptic mentality of the Jesuits of New Spain is 'the world as a hieroglyphic' (163). Other theorists of the baroque have offered different allegories for the mentality, or historical structure, of the baroque, but I think that Paz's image includes the other concepts, many of which work as emblems. There is the *fold*, which Gilles

Deleuze uses to explain the way in which artistic, scientific, literary, and political discourses are extended in time and space in order to appropriate foreign objects and fold them into a constant movement of curves, veils, façades, shadows, and light (*Fold* 3). Benjamin focuses on the image of a 'death's head' as the symbol for a still life, disconnected and decontextualized, whose future destiny is servile in the powerful hands of the allegorist (*Origins* 166). More recently, Omar Calabrese (*Neo Baroque*) makes use of *fractal* and *episodic* edges and fragments to describe the repetitive phantasmagoria that hides the void that motivates and disturbs the symbolic movement of what R. de la Flor terms 'low' modernity (R. de la Flor, *Emblemas* 73). In all of these cases, the figures and motifs of fragmentation and freezing, absence and presence, movement and stasis bring us back to that moment, so accurately described by Pinkus, in which the humanist writer feels the loss of his power. Here, the image becomes a symbolic bastion, enlisted in and witness to an intensive attempt to detain a growing heteroglossia which signals the fall of the univalent universe. In *El descubrimiento del nuevo mundo por Cristóbal Colón*, an entire world is converted into a flag, a blazon, a hieroglyphic, in the attempt to alleviate the melancholy baroque mentality of its obsession with historical crises, and discovers that what this mentality most desires is the end of history.

4 From Hieroglyphic Presence to Representational Sign: The *Auto Sacramental* and the Ritual Colonization of Modernity

As they enter in a mixture of joy and fear, the curtain [peplos] before the icon suddenly is buoyed up as if a breath of wind [pneuma] moved it. Those who have not seen it cannot believe that the event takes place. All who have witnessed it see a miracle [paradoxon] in it, manifestly a visitation of the Holy Spirit [pneuma].

Michael Psellus, *The Miracle of the Curtain at Blachernae*, 1075 AD[1]

Will we be pardoned for showing the tapestry from the back?

[¿Se nos perdonará que mostremos el tapiz por su revés?]

Marcel Bataillon, 'Ensayo de explicación del "auto sacramental"'

Ritual Practice, or the *Modus Operandi* of the Dramatic Mass

If theatre is the most emblematic literary and cultural practice of the Spanish Golden Age, in the case of the *auto sacramental* the spectator confronts nothing less than a public performance of the emblematic modes of representation. In the words of Aurora Egido: '[T]he Calderonian *auto* operated like emblems. The title proposed the *inscriptio* that the staging visualized in the painting or *pictura* and that the *subscriptio* or poetic text extensively glossed, although in this case dramatizing it' (*La fábrica* 70). Egido's meta-emblematic characterization is a useful point of entry into what in practice is more akin to a Borgesian *mise-en-abîme* of more discrete and volatile emblematic structures and moments. As we have seen in Lope de Vega, emblematics is perfectly suited to both the fragmentation and making present of the divine body of Christ in the main dramatic performance of the Corpus Christi festival. In the world of theatricality, fragmentation could even be said to be constitutive of presence in the sense that the fragmentation of the spiritual body incites one's desire to recompose it, just as the empty tomb incites the desire for a bodily presence to fill it.

When speaking of the *auto sacramental*, critics are generally referring to Pedro Calderón de la Barca, who is credited with bringing this hybrid and idiosyncratic genre to its formal and thematic point of 'perfection.' Calderón's ingenious fusion of abstract ideas and allegorical tropes in the ritualistic structure of the *auto sacramental* has held as much power over critics as its performances ostensibly had over its spectators. As in the case of Alciato, it is easy to miss the forest of institutional, economic, social, political, and technological interests and players that went into the staging of the *autos* when concentrating on Calderón's solitary quill. In this discussion, however, I would like to bring the predominant dramatist of the Spanish baroque back into the crisis-filled world of early modern Spain. Following Gumbrecht's lead once again, I will consider the author from the central heuristic presupposition of New Philology: that is, the assumption of a 'weak editor-subject and a weak author-subject' (*Powers* 38). My goal is not to question Calderón's control over the aesthetic schemes and theological doctrine at the heart of the *auto* but rather to explore some of the gaps and contradictions in the tools at the artist's disposal: fissures, in other words, that open onto the consideration of other possible readerly dispositions than the one privileged in the plays and in most critical assessments.

To demonstrate how laborious this process proves in Calderón, his texts as well as the critical canon, I cite a recent study by Ignacio Arellano and J. Enrique Duarte. They define the main objectives of the *auto* in the following way: 'to provoke the emotive wonderment of the spectator – inducing an adhesion *without fissures* to the dogmatic exaltation – and to pedagogically fix the imparted doctrine' (72; my emphasis). This apparent lack of fissures between the ritual creation of divine truth and its reception by what can only be called a participatory practicant reminds us of Borja's, Horozco's, Lope's, as well as Mahíques's attempts to conflate the moment of creation with that of reception. Even those studies that question the efficacy of Calderón's plays in the heterogeneous social matrix of early modern Spain rarely pursue the possibility of a critical reception of its doctrine. Arellano's and Duarte's *El auto sacramental*, for example, which offers as complete a synthesis of the institutional history of the spectacle as one is likely to find, effects a noticeable divorce of the text of the *auto* from its communicative materialities. The goal of this chapter is to open up some space between the reception of 'profound truths' of sacramental theatre and their creation by considering both the institutional history of the *auto sacramental* and the multiple structural and rhetorical sleights-of-hand at work in the theatricized liturgy, or liturgical theatre, of Calderón's *El gran mercado del mundo.*

At issue is how the semiotic operation of the emblem makes an idea present: in Baena's words, '*Presence* is the operation that makes present [that which is present – that which is – is, in the end, the fruit of a previous operation of deferment ... which leaves (which *only* leaves?) traces]' (*Discordancias* 2n1). Baena's translation of Jacques Derrida's concept of *différance* to the discipline of Philology opens a fissure for critical analysis by introducing the element of time, *diferimiento*, into a phenomenon whose explicit goal is the collapse – or absolute expansion – of temporal and spatial limits into the experience of divine presence. The other key concept in this consideration of emblematic creation and reception is that of theatricality. For if the *diferimiento* of the semantic fulfillment of rhetorical gamesmanship opens a temporal space where criticism may inspect the choices made in discursive operations as well as the choices not made, theatricality opens a contingent space between the mask of the allegorical figure and the body of the historical, professional actor, whose goal is to usher the collective audience towards an authentic religious experience.

The *auto sacramental* is in many respects a theatrical transposition, or transduction, of the Catholic mass, in which the Eucharist – the hypostatic marriage of flesh and spirit – is the fundamental trope, dramatic climax, and liturgical *razón de ser* of the dramatic plot. Nevertheless, the ritual nature of Calderón's theatre has been left largely untreated by critics in favor of the dissection and celebration of his aesthetic ingenuity and control or, on the other hand, the orthodoxy of his dramatization of neo-Scholastic dialectics. As earlier noted by Gumbrecht, in both approaches the critic tends to act much like a museum curator, guiding the reader towards an appreciation of Calderón's theological sophistication – a curious conceit, by the way – or his wondrous yet controlled flights of artistic genius. Most attempts to marry the two philological approaches tend to pull back from the deconstruction of the meaning effects of the plays in order to frame the *auto* as the culmination of the varied festive and ritual activities of the

Corpus Christi celebration. What seems to be at stake is the making present of the genius of an author whose own goal is the staging of an experience of religious presence.

In my view, critical resistance to analysing the ritualistic nature of these modern dramas can be traced to at least three ideological presuppositions of modernity in general, and *auto* criticism in particular: first, modern prejudices against the allegedly primitive and/or magical nature of ritual activities; second, the desire of a secularized school of philology to find modernity in religious phenomena as opposed to the other way around; and finally, the inability, or refusal, of the critic to get beyond what Pierre Bourdieu calls 'the realism of the structure' (*Outline* 72). Much as we have seen with Borja's invocation and subsequent construction of a *sensus communis,* 'liturgical performances ... establish conventional understandings, rules and norms in accordance with which everyday behaviour is supposed to proceed' (Rappaport 195). Even as they seek to refute Menéndez Pelayo's infamous dismissal of Calderón's *autos* as 'una aberración,' many critics tacitly and perhaps unconsciously either bracket off the ritualistic nature of this early modern enterprise or take the liturgical form for granted, overlooking its historical and ideological embeddedness.

Henry Sullivan and Carroll B. Johnson's socio-economic readings of *El gran mercado del mundo* (1993) and *El gran teatro del mundo* (1997), and the work of Jean Flecniakowska on the reactionary political activism embedded in the plays stand out amongst recent efforts to bring discussions of the *auto sacramental* into the critical mainstream.[2] Nevertheless, Viviana Díaz Balsera points out that 'The vision of the Calderonian *auto* as theological art has in this century impeded our openly approaching this body of texts from the point of view of its contradictions, its paradoxes, the inevitability of its participation in the shattering of the human condition it represents' (4). I would like to take up Díaz Balsera's critique by privileging and analysing Calderón's unequal deployment of distinct emblematic modes of representation and reception in the ritualistic and theatrical performance of divine presence. Rather than link Calderón's discursive gamesmanship to the theological meaning of the play, my goal is to treat these multiple, meaning-producing strategies as 'heuristic constructs' with 'the expectation of producing a plurality of different positions' (Gumbrecht, *Powers* 36). By plurality I do not mean to suggest that I will be looking for subversive messages in Calderón's text; rather, I am more interested in the structural and theological fissures which simultaneously call for and resist the aesthetic and semantic closure of the play. Fundamental to this approach is Iser's observation that 'so long as the critic's mind is fixed on the hidden meaning, he is incapable … of seeing anything' (6). In illuminating the multiple ways in which oppositional or antagonistic *dispositions* are performed and then erased, one comes to understand that the articulation and containment of structural and ideological conflicts are not residual effects but rather constitutive mechanisms in the staging of divine presence.

Due to its allegorical nature, the *auto* is where the central historical role of the emblematic mode of representation becomes most apparent, as the search for a semiotic and theological stopgap for the incessant movement of modernity – social, political, economic, theological, linguistic, etc. – meets the central mystery of the Catholic faith. Unlike the studies of critics such as A.A. Parker, Donald Dietz and, more recently, Antonio Regalado and Vincent Martin, my method does not begin with the assumption that Calderón's dramatic theory and practice constitute a finished and closed artifice, the penetration of which leads to an encounter with a pre-existing, consistent, and integral pearl of cosmological or theological wisdom. Rather, my critical practice examines what Bourdieu calls the *modus operandi,* as opposed to the *opus operatum,* of Calderón's *auto.*

My claim is that the plot, or *argumento,* of *El gran mercado del mundo* constructs a contest of reception in which the character who interprets the confusing appearances, or merchandise, of the great marketplace of the world more 'emblematically' ultimately wins the day. What is at stake is not just a way of reading or interpreting the meaning of material objects but a normative way of desiring meaning, which pits two semiotic regimes against each other: 1) a discourse of immanence, or earthly love of material existence, i.e., the marketplace; and 2) a discourse of deferral in which the relation between the subject and his reality is mediated by a third, imagined, authoritative gaze. This construction of legitimate and illegitimate frames for seeing and acting in the world is driven by the political need for identifying an ideological Other in the interest of a program of social control. In the end, the theatrical representation – as opposed to liturgical celebration – of eucharistic presence is structurally dependent on this internal threat posed by a diabolical, semiotic regime of fragmentation.

The State of *Auto* Criticism

The popular reception of the *auto sacramental* has been noted, and questioned, by virtually all of its critics, with tones ranging from mystification to applause, depending on the objectives and perspectives of the critic. For José María Díez Borque, as for Bruce Wardropper and Marcel Bataillon, the performance and reception of the one-act dramas are inseparable from the festive atmosphere and varied public spectacles of the Corpus Christi in which the *auto sacramental* plays but one part. Díez Borque writes: 'The *auto sacramental* is the crossroads of liturgy and theater, ceremony and scenic action, the supernatural and earthly contingency by means of the limited human means of allegory, and other scenic elements, in order to penetrate the transcendental' ('El auto' 49). By recognizing the ambivalent structure and problematic nature of liturgical 'performances,' Díez Borque begins to answer the challenge of Bataillon, who states that criticism should be directed towards 'a complete politics of spectacles ... maintaining a fair balance between the popular thirst for diversions and the austere demands of the reforming spirit' ('Ensayo' 479). This appreciation for the complex and contradictory nature of early modern religious and festive culture carries serious methodological and philosophical implications for the aesthetic as well as the theological models of *auto* criticism, although two recent monographs would seem to contradict such a statement.

I am referring to Viviana Díaz Balsera's partial deconstruction of the internal contradictions in Calderón's dramatic and theological practice, *Calderón y las quimeras de la culpa*, and Vincent Martin's rescue and vigorous defense of Calderón's marriage of baroque aesthetics and neo-Scholastic theology, *El concepto de 'representación' en los autos sacramentales de Calderón*. Although both works seek to plumb the depths of Calderón's dramatization of aesthetic contradiction and religious paradox, neither can be said to provide a rigorous analysis of the sociopolitical role or communicative materialities of the *auto sacramental* in the crisis-plagued reality of the Spanish baroque. Díaz Balsera's 1999 study stops short of her stated intention to resituate Calderón's discursive contradictions within a more critical discussion: 'in considering the ambivalence and opacity of the *auto,* I do not seek to accomplish a deconstruction of it, if by deconstruction we mean a radical play of signifiers that incessantly defers a transcendental signified' (8). Due to her decision not to follow this critical path to its logical ends,

Díaz Balsera's pointed questions concerning Calderón's ambivalent use of poetic imagery are easily answered by Martin's study, published in 2002.

Martin's book hearkens back to more traditional studies of Golden Age religious theatre, exemplified by critics such as Parker and, more recently, Ignacio Arellano and Enrique Duarte, and Antonio Regalado. As R. de la Flor writes in his Prologue, Martin's analysis 'approaches the nature of its object as if it were a long course on symbolic metaphysics realized by visual parables through which the things of the world (its fable and its *history*) were organized and interpreted according to an invisible plane which constitutes the "script" of the true *Author*, in relation to which Calderón is merely a subrogated author' (13). Read side by side, Martin's reconstitution of baroque aesthetic contradictions in the laboratory of neo-Scholastic dialectics brings Díaz Balsera's attempt to do the opposite back to where the latter starts, where a judicious use of 'postmodern' theory might have resulted in a more productive mining of the foundations of *auto* criticism.

The traditional bi-membration of the 'profound' conceptual material (content) and the exuberant and multi-sensorial spectacle of the *auto* itself (aesthetic form) – soul and body in emblematic terms – has tended to foreclose analysis of the *auto*, as if the separation of philosophical and theological concepts from aesthetic tropes were a truism. As I hope to have demonstrated in my discussions of Borja and Horozco y Covarrubias, the author himself produces this fragmentation of the integral, performative act into separate theoretical and practical fields when he defines the *auto sacramental* as 'sermons placed in verse' [sermones puestos en verso], or when he rationalizes its aesthetic and theological aspects into the much discussed *argumento* and *asunto*. From a more practice-oriented approach, Calderón's isolation of his dramatic art from his religious orthodoxy – and his valorization of the former – can be read in two ways: on the one hand, the separation of the aesthetic medium from theological doctrine makes the latter appear independent of its modes of dissemination and thus substantial; on the other hand, when Calderón shines a light on his artistic genius he is furthering a personal *empresa* directed at gaining social and political legitimacy.[3] The playwright repeatedly stages the triumph of – redeems – his cultural and social legitimacy, even as he redeems Counter Reformation claims to hegemony, through the ritual dramatization of a competition between legitimate and illegitimate paths to knowledge of the self and of the world.

When he foregrounds the theatrical nature of his allegorical antagonists – Lutherans, Jews, and Moors, whose outward performance of Catholicism belies their essential deviance – he displays the inherent ambivalence of Counter Reformation culture towards theatricality. Stated otherwise, he stages the true faith in dialectical opposition to what are seen as blasphemous farces of religious belief. This strategy opens up a space in which to question Calderón's views on religious faith, especially if we are going to insist on his absolute artistic control. How can an artist who obviously understands the difficulty of distinguishing the public performance of sincere faith from that of mere consent – indeed, the success of this plays depends on it – remain unaffected by the inherent instability, deception, and vacuity of a theatrical world? Or, more to the point, how can the worldly spectator recognize the difference between sincere and insincere belief, especially in a spectacle whose presence effects depend on the professionalism, i.e., calculated detachment, of its actors? If we are going to celebrate Calderón's absolute artistic control, we should then also appreciate how the dramatic staging of an authentic religious experience requires a calculated manipulation of distinct religious points of view. Yet another contradiction, perhaps the most intractable from the point of view of material culture, arises from the fact that a complex confluence of increasingly professionalized religious, economic, bureaucratic, technological, and artistic institutions was charged with the task of orchestrating and communicating this same authentic religious experience. Once we begin to account for the complex material and institutional context of Calderón's practice, we are in a better position to pursue a fruitful deconstruction of the ideological forms and socio-political functions of the *auto sacramental.*

Liturgy 'Discovers' the Market

Gumbrecht and Egginton both describe how early modernity witnesses a shift from the predominance of medieval liturgical or courtly rituals towards the more contingent and open paradigm of theatrical representation. In the first case, the transcendental guarantees of earthly institutions of power are made present through the dramatization of archetypal events; in the second, the irrecoverable distance between universal truths and their contingent historical performance becomes a constitutive element in the spectacle of Christ's or the king's body.[4] The emblem proves useful for understanding and analysing this transition from presence to representation due to its simultaneous resistance to and dependence on the fragmented symbolic world of antiquity. Looking back to the Middle Ages, the emblem partakes of the mystical status of the hieroglyphic, or religious icon, which 'ensures "presence" of the idea in a way that a text alone could not do'; looking toward modernity, 'the emblem is in many respects an increasingly fragmented, secularized and decadent form of late medieval allegory' (Russell, *Emblematic Structures* 29, 40). The historical tension embodied in the form and function of the emblem is particularly important for understanding the *auto sacramental*, where one of the dramatic goals is the ritualistic making present of the indivisible body of Christ through a spectacle that leads the spectator to an experience of eucharistic transubstantiation in one form or another. As Russell's observations concerning the iconic degradation of the emblem demonstrate, transubstantiation becomes very problematic in early modernity, complicated even more by the Catholic Church's systematic attempts to divest religious icons of their 'magical' properties in the push for institutional control over religious images. According to the policy forged at the Council of Trent, 'due honour and reverence is owed to them, not because some divinity or power is believed to lie in them ... but because the honour showed to them is referred to the original which they represent' (Belting 554). This doctrine represents a sophisticated and contradictory expression of iconoclasm, which will function as the main axis of conflict in *El gran mercado del mundo*; just as important, the difference between the materiality of the religious image and its institutional meaning places the performance of religious belief in a theatrical space, making the religious experience of divine presence a matter of perspective.

The doctrine is directed at two different spaces: in geopolitical terms, its goal is to combat the hard line established by Protestant iconoclasm, which equates any use of religious imagery with idolatry; closer to home, it coincides with the attempt to repress the power of popular religious fervor by evacuating divine presence from religious imagery *tout court* and removing it towards the institutions that will henceforth determine their meaning and ontological status.[5] As Mitchell observes, the distinction is typical of the political element at the heart of iconoclasm: 'the first law of iconoclasm is that the idolater is always someone else ... The second law is that the iconoclast believes that idolaters believe their images to be holy, alive, and powerful. We might call this the law of "secondary belief," or beliefs about the beliefs of other people. Iconoclasm is not just a belief structure but a structure of *beliefs about other people's beliefs*' (*What Do Pictures Want?* 20). According to Mitchell's theorems, the Catholic interpretation of Protestant iconoclasm reveals that the law forbidding all religious imagery belies a great fear of the power of these images, which is itself a sublimated or unconscious form of idolatry. When placed alongside these modern reforms, the doctrine of transubstantiation – the ritual recitation of words and gestures, performed by and under the authority of a priestly emblematist, which guides the communicant to the perception and ingestion of the real presence and body of Christ – becomes the lone exception to an otherwise universal rule. It takes on a special status, which places it in dialectical relation to the merely evocative or mnemonic – theatrical – functions of other religious images, symbols, and gestures. Put another way, two ways of perceiving otherwise accidental objects become interdependent in a symbolic and theatrical shell game.

The appearance and eventual hegemony of the homogeneous theatrical space of the *comedia nueva*, as well as the ineradicable space between the modern professional actor and his or her theatrical role, place the *auto* in a highly contentious and mediated space, one in which the open space of the *corrales* – or public plaza – and the professional status of the actors work against the ritualistic alchemy of medieval rituals of presence. Egginton writes, 'the Middle Ages experienced space in a fundamentally different way: as full, impressionable and substantial, whose dimensions existed relative to observers and, more specifically, participants, as opposed to being empty and independent of them' (*How the World* 37). He also reminds us that the 'actors' in medieval spectacles are not itinerant professionals but ecclesiastical and public officials or, in the case of aristocratic society, monarchs and nobles whose dramatic roles are not entirely separable from their social and political status. Both Panofsky and Egginton underline how the nature of dramatic (as opposed to theatrical) space in the Middle Ages contributes to the making present of mysteries of the faith, as the goal of such dramatizations is not novelty or *admiratio*, in the modern sense, but rather the perfect imitation of a permanent and transcendent model.[6] Contributing to the communication of this effect is the architectural space of the temple or palace, which is already filled with sacred presence. Egginton summarizes, 'the hyperbolic solidity of the space of medieval drama reflected the instability of the distinction between the reality being represented and the reality of the representation' (55).

In the world of theatricality, on the other hand, as in the case of pictorial space, the gaze of the individual viewer becomes constitutive of the meaning, or presence, of the event. Bolívar Echeverría writes: 'The Judeo-Christian dramatization of human existence, with its cyclical sequence of the states of sin, guilt, and redemption, began to require the content of individual experience in order to materialize itself as such' (*La modernidad* 201). In *El gran mercado del mundo*, the space in which divine presence is performed becomes a metaphor for the baroque struggle in and against modernity, as we witness the movement of eucharistic presence into the marketplace. For Mikhail Bakhtin, the marketplace is a 'leveling' space, where rich and poor, male and female, religious and secular subjects and symbolic practices are brought into close proximity, with the advantage going to unofficial culture: 'the center of all that is unofficial[,] it enjoyed a certain extraterritoriality in a world of official order and official ideology, it always remained "with the people"' (*Rabelais* 153–4). With respect to the Corpus Christi, Bakhtin likewise contends that 'the popular marketplace aspect of this feast was, to a certain extent, a satirical drama which parodied the Church ritual' (*Rabelais* 230). Bakhtin's religious understanding of the immortal carnivalesque body, immortal because its dismemberment and death produce a regeneration of a *material* rather than an exclusively *spiritual* corporality, helps underline the carnivalesque residue at work in the death and resurrection – and ingestion – of Christ's body: the material excesses of carnival provide a deformed reflection of the *Santa Cena*. In this light, what Paz identifies as Calderón's conversion of the traditional miracle stories into 'intellectual allegories' can be read as an attempt to rationally colonize a traditionally uncontained space. Or, perhaps what we are seeing is the dematerialization of a space formerly filled with 'popular presence.' An important aspect of this colonization is the professionalization and rationalization of virtually every process in the production of the spectacle.

Wardropper observes that in the movement from medieval miracle stories to modern theatrical allegories, 'the custom was established in Toledo [1561] to contract exclusively with professional companies' (*Introducción* 80). Arellano and Duarte make a point of the fact that the performances pass from the hands of the clergy, or impassioned members of professional associations, into those of professional directors and actors, and even further, that the ordained clergy were eventually prohibited from participating in the plays. There are many reasons for this rapid secularization of performance practices, including the persistent residue of a confusing array of religious and ecclesiastical authorities and institutions under a monarchy seeking to extend its political and ideological hegemony into previously uncolonized spaces.[7] The professionalization of monarchical and ecclesiastical bureaucracies accompanies and informs a similar rationalization of the production and performance of the *auto*: 'the authorities began to regard positively the representations staged by experienced actors, *because they gained in authenticity and rigor*, soon becoming an essential element of the sacramental celebration' (Arellano and Duarte 23; my emphasis). What is curious is that this transition from passionate and interested celebrants to professional imposters leads to performances that gain in authenticity and rigour. Bataillon is more succinct: '[H]ere the symbiosis of sacred and profane theater intervenes, as the commission and remuneration fall, in both cases, to the same authors (directors) and the same actors. Literally the *auto sacramental* had the same destiny as the *comedia* ... Such is the path that is forged the moment in which edifying theater passes into the hands of professionals instead of remaining in those of pious amateurs' ('Ensayo' 197–9). Even though the baroque rationalization of festive culture is still a ways off, Maravall's observation that the 'institutionalization of the fiesta reveals its linkages with the social system and with the means of integration on which the baroque monarchy was based' holds true (*Culture* 244). By staging a theatrical representation of the Eucharist in the marketplace of the world, Calderón reconfigures the imaginary coordinates of the public sphere, and in so doing constitutes an emblematic moment where ritual and myth sanctify and domesticate a space characterized, at least in the medieval and early modern religious and aristocratic imagination, by transgression, conflict, and chaos. In a sense, it effects a reversal of the Gospel story in which a youthful Jesus throws the moneychangers out of the temple; here, Calderón will throw the moneychangers out of the marketplace itself while framing the market as a religious space.

In order to reconstruct the public plaza, the first thing Calderón does is to empty his dramatic world of any stable meaning outside of his virtual, representational space. Neither the *mercado* nor the signs that parade onto the stage at the beginning of the *auto* possesses any stable meaning apart from the dialectically opposed devices of the various characters. This wiping-the-slate-clean prepares the way for our heightened observation of the histrionic movements of the protagonists, *Buen Genio* and *Mal Genio*, whose rivalry achieves what Roy Rappaport calls the ritual reduction of a 'continuous complex to the binary,' thus transforming a varied and heterogeneous festive milieu into a final procession of conservative moral values (185).

In the interim, the audience will witness a contest between two competing schemes for interpreting and moving through this ambivalent space: an iconophilic discourse of immanence (the marketplace), framed as an errant, narcissistic, vulgar, and willful search for the immediate fulfillment of 'blind' desire; and an iconoclastic discourse of transcendence, which does not so much project meaning onto the marketplace as absorb the world's seemingly inherent meaninglessness and deception into its own consciousness, resulting in the deferment of the judgment of the world and one's actions in it to a third, authoritative gaze embodied by the figures of *la Gracia* and *El padre de familias*. As this ritual movement from chaos to order, from crisis to apparent resolution, becomes evident, the actions of *Buen Genio* will be seen to correspond to what Bourdieu calls 'structural exercises' in the 'projection of mythico-religious oppositions,' as he moves through the marketplace interpreting emblematically the spiritual value of the merchandise (*Outline* 89–96). *Mal Genio*, for his part, is made the source of all transgressive desire and thus becomes the central protagonist in what Bell calls the ritual 'motivation of bias' (*Ritual Theory* 172). In the end, the presence of the ecclesiastical body is not made present in the medieval sense of the phenomenon, but rather negatively suggested through this play of asymmetrical, conflicting perspectives.

El gran mercado distributes different facets of its eucharistic *asunto* into distinct paradigmatic or allegorical *argumentos*: a chivalric contest and romantic triangle, the biblical parable of the three talents, and the archetypal rivalry between brothers. To summarize, the two sons of the *Padre de familias*, *Buen Genio* and *Mal Genio*, vie for the object of desire, *la Gracia*, who, as the *serrana más serafín*, will accompany the winner across the threshold of life – death – to the *Santa Cena*. In emblematic terms, each brother can be read as the dramatic representation of the two competing emblematic modes discussed in chapters 1 and 2 of this study: the *empresa* and the *emblem*. Let us recall that where the Italian humanist Paolo Giovio privileges a high degree of difficulty in order to separate the ingenious, individual subject from the vulgar, both Borja and Horozco stigmatize the wit and ingenuity of the *empresa* as it relates to the individuality from which the '*poesía vana*' of the court springs.

In order to illustrate the problems that Borja and Horozco (and Calderón) most likely perceive in the device, I will comment briefly on a homologous mode of emblematic representation, *la invención*. Closely related to the *empresa, invenciones* were a favorite pastime of courtly subjects who often participated in the competitive creation and public performance of these witty devices. Theatrical in nature, the *invención* combines a clever motto with a visual *divisa* or *cimera*, as María José Díez Garretas explains: 'devices and crests will come to have the same meaning and function: they will be the decorative figure for the costumes and helmets of courtly subjects, always accompanied by a motto or slogan borrowed from the primitive device' (38). Similar conventions are used in allegorical theater, as attested to by the *disposiciones de los carros*.[8] Brian Dutton's immense anthology of *cancionero* poetry contains the following *invención* by 'Vicens':

> Vicens brought for a crest a mound of stones with a cross [,] and the words said: If she who brought my life to an end [,] with pain possessed a stone, losing it [my love? my life? the stone?] would not pain me.
>
> [Vicens trujo por cim*er*a un monto de piedres con huna crus y dezia la l*et*re[9]
>
> Si quien dyo fin a mi vida
> con dolor pyedra posyera
> p*er*derla no me doliera.] (151)

In the combination of *cimera* and *letre*, we can see how the poet uproots and re-frames a messianic metaphor around a personal amorous enterprise. The imagined figure on the empty cross is the lover himself, who would not regret losing his life were his beloved to possess a 'stone,' which we can take to be a jewel or *prenda* of some sort accepted and worn by the beloved. I have attempted to retain the ambiguity concerning the grammatical referent in the pronoun 'perder*la*' with the inset questions in the translation, since much of the ingenuity of the play on words hinges on it. From the angle of the stone, we can see how the beloved's hypothetical token of affection metonymically refers to the rocks that anchor and support the crucifix. As the meaning of the sacred enigma is theatrically subverted by the poet's genius, the religious connotations of cross, rock, and sacrifice are redirected towards a secular metaphor and, coincidentally, illuminate the poetic wit and *inventio* of Vicens. Also apparent, however, is the artificer's susceptibility to accusations of heresy or blasphemy, as religious symbols are translated into a personal enterprise, one having nothing to do with the religious function of the conceptual soul. The symbols are made ambivalent, and their meaning is shown to be dependent on competing points of view, the more secular of which is privileged. In the end, hieroglyphic presence gives way to a theatrical representation of wit.

For Borja and Horozco, such aesthetic power must be anchored in social and religious institutions. The desired effect of allegorization is the assimilation of hieroglyphic symbols and their transcendental knowledge to the symbolic program of Spanish Catholicism. Contrary to how the courtly poet directs the gaze of the reader-spectator to an appreciation of his wit, as well as evoking a surprised (and guilty?) enjoyment of the carnivalesque use of religious imagery, the emblem reader's eye is dehistoricized and absorbed by an absent authorial guarantee which gazes on its own retroactively constructed narrative of Catholic destiny and, in so doing, seeks to assimilate the psychic investment of the individual reader into a collective project. This conflict between two symbolic strategies takes centre stage in *El gran mercado*, which is a story about how one simultaneously navigates the world of signs and converts oneself into an emblem of a worthy intention, reflected in the names of the protagonists *Buen Genio* and *Mal Genio*.

The play opens with a problematic – and emblematic – invocation of *Fama*:

> *FAME enters, singing from high up on the stage in an appearance that moves from one side to the other.*
>
> FAME: Hear ye, mortals, hear ye, and present yourselves to the call of Fame!

> [*Sale la* FAMA, *cantando por lo alto del tablado en una apariencia que pasa de un lado a otro*
>
> FAMA: ¡Oíd, mortales, oíd,
> y al pregón de la Fama
> todos acudid!] (vv. 41–9)

What comes next is an anamorphic parade of allegorical commentaries that follow and react to the mobile figure of *Fama*. The main characters *Buen Genio* and *Malicia*, *Mal Genio* and *Gracia*, *el Padre* and *Inocencia* provide contradictory descriptions of *Fama* according to their own inclinations, or *genios*, but there is no attempt to establish what the real meaning of *Fama* might be. This is interesting in terms of reception, as Calderón stages the translation of a spiritual knowledge 'embedded in *monothetic* structures into the *polythetic* structural process of [its] acquisition.' Gumbrecht continues, 'it is through this specific performance of sense constitution that we become aware of the plausibility of favoring the narrow concept' (Gumbrecht, *Making Sense* 37). By juxtaposing the performance of contradictory devices concerning *Fama*, the characters offer *inscriptiones* designed to alternately privilege or discard traditional and/or novel meanings of her *carro*. Witty descriptions of the burnt feathers of Icarus or the desolation and destruction of Phaeton are contrasted to the wonder inspired by the untainted plumage of a magnificent bird that competes with the sun in power and beauty. In this world of enigmatic visual and aural clues, truth is not given positively; rather, it is suggested or intuited through a ritualistic architecture of mundane and spiritual planes to which the gaze of *el Padre* becomes the interpretive key.

The momentary confusion caused by the entrance of *Fama* is partially resolved by the explanation of *el Padre* in answer to a challenge by *Mal Genio*, who does not understand the pessimistic attitude of the patriarch towards what seems to him to be a sublimely beautiful ideal:

> FATHER: Because I also heard in FAME's summons that the World sells all kinds of things, and that only he who employs his talent well or poorly will be happy; but it must be noted that she said that good and evil will not be known until the end.

> [PADRE: Porque también de la Fama
> en ese pregón oí
> que vende el Mundo de todo,
> y sólo será feliz
> quien su talento empleare
> bien o mal; se ha de advertir
> que dijo que el bien o el mal
> no se conoce hasta el fin.] (vv. 72–9)

As in Lope's *comedia de indios*, the metaphor of spiritual 'interest' is grafted onto the economic activity of a culture increasingly based on consumerism. This is perhaps the most subtle and effective marriage of the mundane and spiritual worlds in the festive stage of the *auto*, one which speaks eloquently of the movement of mass spectacles from the hands of believers into those of a significant number of institutions whose goals are more temporal than transcendent.

It is important to note that *el Padre* does not give the correct meaning of the visual figure; indeed, the meaning of *Fama* is immaterial or even counterproductive to Calderón's purpose. Following the tradition of the *empresa*, the mottos are strategically elusive, shifting our gaze towards the way in which each character approaches the figure: *Buen Genio* simply observes what *Fama* does, neither desiring nor abhorring what he sees, thus reflecting a veritable blank canvas; *Mal Genio* is awestruck, lost in ambivalent desire but obviously enraptured and moved; *Gracia* is, naturally, horrified. Once presented with the hierarchical oppositions through which the idea is suggested, the reader-spectator is led to contemplate what it might mean to employ one's *talento* well and complete the concept in his or her own mind. The most stable point of identification in the play, *Padre de familias*, is also ignorant of the final outcome of *Fama*'s enterprise and must wait, like the rest of the characters, and spectators, for it to be played out on the stage. The fact that the most God-like figure of the play has no foreknowledge of the denouement could present a theological difficulty for the playwright, one which becomes more marked as the plot begins to unfold.

It seems there is a problem concerning the legacy of his two sons, *Mal* and *Buen Genio*. Arellano and Duarte paraphrase Ana Suárez: 'Just like Basilio [*La vida es sueño*], the paterfamilias ... does not know who the oldest of his two sons is and thus ignores who should inherit the estate; he fears that, according to the horoscopes, one will deserve it and the other will not' (127–8). At the end of the play, it is *el Padre* who delivers the hand of *Gracia* to *Buen Genio* and condemns *Mal Genio* to the flames that explode on stage to signal divine retribution. This spectacular representation of a vengeful god overrides the fact that at the beginning of the drama he is apparently nescient of who was born first, to such a degree that he resorts to astrology – unsuccessfully, I might add – in an illegitimate search for knowledge. Submitting this theological predicament to the dialectical operations of allegory, or vice-versa, one could argue that the mundane representation of religious truths – 'which are incomprehensible and which cannot be formulated with direct language, since human language is incapable of expressing them' – requires the author to manipulate theological doctrine in a sophisticated way for the benefit of his unsophisticated audience (Martin 35). For although the *paterfamilias* belongs to a paternal typology that includes Abraham and Isaac, the power he represents at the end of the play, in which malevolent characters are cast into hell, connects him directly to the Godhead itself. We should not pass over too lightly the relationship between the ignorant character at the beginning and the all-powerful god at the end. It also bears mentioning that the genealogical doctrine concerning the passing of the legacy to the firstborn son is placed in abeyance by Calderón. It is not completely subverted, but the mystery of primogeniture is overwritten by an ethics that privileges behavioral over genealogical criteria.

The amorous rivalry, if such a rigged affair can be so named, begins when *Buen Genio* offers to trade his entire inheritance, which he has not yet received, for the hand of *Gracia*. His brother immediately declares his own competing interest, but the comments of *Buen Genio* make it apparent that their desires are not equal: 'He does not do it for love but to contradict me' [No lo hace por amar, / sino por contradecir] (vv. 164–5). Where *Buen Genio* approaches his desire for *Gracia* through the mediation of *el Padre*, *Mal Genio* gauges his desire by comparing it with his brother's. This is Calderón's way of providing an interpretive rubric for all subsequent actions and judgments by framing *Mal Genio* for the crime of contradictory desire. On the other hand, *Buen Genio*'s criticism of his brother obscures the fact that his own preemptive desire for unilateral possession of *Gracia* provides the initial spark for the fraternal conflict. To place the brothers on equal footing for the competition, each receives the same *talento* from *Gracia*, whether he has earned it or not, which signals that the spiritual capital neither issues from them nor belongs completely to them. This *caudal suficiente* is represented by a rose, which *Gracia* gives to each brother. Since the rose is a symbol of earthly beauty and love, it is also used as an emblem of the transient nature of earthly beauty and of life in general according to the doctrine of *desengaño*. As Frutos explains, the material existence of man is itself a sign of a debt incurred in Eden which man is incapable of redeeming himself; or, in the words of Juan de Horozco, 'your hands formed me and were nailed [to the cross] to reform me' [vuestras manos me formaron / y para reformarme se enclavaron] (cited in Bouzy, 'Dios' 154).

When they begin their journeys, movement through space takes on allegorical significance within the plot as well as the theological doctrine of the play. *Buen Genio* undertakes an arduous pilgrimage through the mountains, while his brother initiates a quixotic romp over the plains, *el camino llano*. The first stop for both is an inn, where Calderón introduces the figure of *Culpa*, who will translate the meaning of these movements through her role as a self-proclaimed afterthought. She appears in the guise of a woman scorned with designs on revenge, and her theatrical shape-changing becomes the main testing ground and threat for the brothers. At the same time, as we have seen in Lope's character Rodrigo Terrazas, both her amorous pursuits and her theological explanations are vital for understanding the allegorical significance of the plot. In one and the same character we have theatrical *and* theological sophistication, in every sense of the word.[10] By embodying both in a single damnable character, one also skilled in the sensual arts, *Culpa* reveals as well as manipulates the fallen nature of humankind, and serves later on as kindling when the flames of retribution are sufficiently fanned. As Maestro observes, 'the Calderonian Devil praises and affirms the power of God, rather than demystifying, censuring, or defaming him, as occurs in the Old Testament' (82). We learn from *Culpa*, for instance, that *Buen* and *Mal Genio* represent the two inclinations that struggle against each other in man's divided conscience; if either fails to serve *Gracia* with perfect works, he will never receive eternal grace. *Culpa*'s role is to make sure that they both fail by confusing them with her changing appearances: 'Culpa: Since guilt was born from a lie; mutated into various forms, clothed in various costumes, I will see if their decisions endanger their undertakings, so that they will never be well regarded by Grace' [pues nació / la culpa de la mentira; / en varias formas mudada / en varios trajes vestida, / veré si de sus empleos / las elecciones peligran, / de suerte que nunca puedan / ser de la Gracia bien vistas] (vv. 492–9). Her function is more complex than first appears, as the diabolical Other becomes a constitutive element not *on* but *of* the path to knowledge.

Similar to the plays analysed by Díaz Balsera, *Culpa* acts as a malevolent impresario in this play within the play and thus represents a competing point of view to that of *el Padre*. Her deceptive use of poetic imagery exemplifies Counter Reformation doctrine concerning the inherent ambivalence (and evil) of material signs, and the illegitimate or diabolical status of sensual poetry.[11] Díaz Balsera writes, 'The *auto* is ambiguous because by making the representation of the evil of sin delightful, it ironically repeats that which Guilt and Lucifer do when they tempt Man' (92). However, if there is no chance for man to escape his fallen status, which is universally the case in a disillusioned world, then we are not really seeing ambiguity but rather an ontological extension of a totalizing ideology that equates historical change with chaos. Moreover, what Díaz Balsera is observing is how the spectator is led to experience the same temptations and to imagine the same punishments that *Culpa* and *Mal Genio* perform in the play. Thus, rather than reading this nuance as a theological-aesthetic paradox or, in Martin's view, as an example of Thomist dialectics at work, I think it is useful to view the role of *Culpa* as simultaneously underlining the genius of the artist in the allegorical artifice of the play while distancing her illegitimate and dishonorable arts of persuasion from Calderón's ostensibly more legitimate deployment of theatrical wit.[12] By representing *Culpa*'s activity as chimerical, the edifice of Counter Reformation dogma becomes by comparison substantial, or present, and thus shielded from the comparative lack of being in a theatrical world. Part scorned lover, part *Celestina*, the role of *Culpa* is that of an illegitimate mediator between the brothers' desire and the immanent worlds of the inn and the market. Calderón, for his part, becomes the legitimate, if absent, mediator between the public and the ideals of the monarchical-seigniorial segments of Counter Reformation society. Here, the iconoclasm-iconophilia dialectic is revealed as a 'rhetoric of exclusion and domination, a caricature of the other as one who is involved in irrational, obscene behavior from which (fortunately) we are exempt' (Mitchell, *Iconology* 113).

Calderón completes his characterization of *Culpa* with an *empresa* of heresy reminiscent of Borja's emblem on *tau* as well as Vicens's *invención*: 'I will be the rock of scandal and ruin' [seré la piedra / del escándalo y la ruina] (vv. 1351–2). Where the stone that the *cancionero* poet gives to his beloved represents the foundation of his absolute love for her, *Culpa*'s rock is the foundation on which the crumbling edifice of immanent and transgressive desire is erected. Later in the play, she will disguise herself as a male servant of *Gula*, naming herself *Pedro*, yet another anamorphic illusion of sanctity. Other emblematic images, such as the serpent and the basilisk – both mortal enemies of man, one through its voice and the other through its gaze – help complete the emblematic portrayal of evil.

When everyone arrives at the marketplace, *Mundo* introduces the various vendors and their merchandise in pairs of opposing allegorical figures: *Soberbia* and *Humildad; Lascivia,* disguised as *Hermosura,* and *Desengaño; Gula,* disguised as blind *Apetito* – and accompanied by an image-hawking *Culpa* – precedes *Penitencia;* finally, *Herejía,* who is loaded down with books of diverse sciences, accompanies blind *Fe,* who 'sells' flesh and blood, or bread and wine. The antagonistic characters are so theatrical in nature that they are disguised as other antagonistic characters. Hillaire Kallendorf informs us that the costumes of these characters were often drawn from emblem books, thus augmenting the visual spectacle of the play: 'the *autos sacramentales* have shown us that in Baroque Spain, fashion was used as a readable figurative code by playwrights trying to demonstrate clearly that morality *was* a set of fixed, immutable absolutes' ('Dressed to the Sevens' 181). There is no need to go into the merchandise, equally emblematic, that each brother purchases and its theological significance, but I would like to look more closely at two of the figures and their relation to the plot.

Apetito and *Fe* are both blind, but their disjunctively framed maladies symbolize the perspective that each of the brothers projects onto the stage of the world. *Apetito* is a desire that can only see material objects in the here and now, in the historical time of the subject, and judge them for what we might call their mundane exchange value in the marketplace. With respect to the Eucharist then, *Apetito* perceives the bread and wine as food for the body; on the other hand, once the victuals are transformed into the body and blood of Christ, he can be seen as a cannibal who desecrates the mystical body of the Church. As Martin observes, this desire to read the world more literally appears whenever Calderón brings his heretical characters onto the stage, which works to privilege the play's allegorical gyrations while branding all material knowledge of the world as demonic (29). *Fe,* on the other hand, is blind to all but the extensive, or hypostatic, meaning of material reality on the plane of transcendence. Through this opposition, all material existence is converted into ashes and dust, with the exception of bread and wine, which become hypostatically – emblematically – transubstantiated into the extensive body and blood of Christ. These two blind characters demonstrate that the performance of a point of view, or *habitus,* is constitutive of one's relationship to sin or salvation. If you cannot see things one way, you are saved; if your blind gaze goes awry, you are Other, the enemy, the heretic.[13] Much more problematic is the relationship of their limited perspectives to the ontological status of the sacramental body.

When *Fe* and *Herejía* debate the merits of their merchandise, the dogma of the Counter Reformation meets the aesthetics of the emblematic mode of representation, and emblematic iconology becomes acutely constitutive of ideology. Ostensibly one need not have scientific knowledge to function in this mode, as Calderón deploys the anti-intellectual populism introduced by Borja and Lope, denigrating erudition and science by equating a lack of education with the very cultural competence required to understand the doctrine of the *auto*. This is an interesting position to hold when one is as knowledgeable and sophisticated as Calderón. It is yet another example of a reactionary 'resistance to theory' and the way in which said resistance naturalizes the difficult doctrine of transubstantiation while delegitimizing the learned 'sciences' of *Herejía*.

Herejía's scientific books are those of Calvin and Luther, many of which were written for mass consumption; and the debate that follows is nothing less than the crux of the theological, aesthetic, and ultimately political conflict between Protestants and Catholics, or at least as Counter Reformation Catholicism represents it:[14]

> HERESY: This book affirms that every body should occupy a place, and that this is not possible, whereby the body of God is in the white Bread, since it occupies no space therein.
>
> FAITH: The extensive body I concede; but the body that is there in its indivisible form I deny, and in this manner the body of Christ is in the Bread of the Sacrament with indivisible form, and it provides an example for me: the soul of man occupies the whole man without our being able to find where this place is; since it fits so perfectly, after death the quantity remains as it was before he died; therefore, without occupying a place, God can be in that shroud, and his being or not being makes living Bread or dead Bread.

> [HEREJÍA: Este
> afirma que todo cuerpo
> ocupar debe lugar,
> y que no es posible aquello
> de que esté el Cuerpo de Dios
> en el blanco Pan, supuesto
> que en él no ocupa lugar.
> FE: El cuerpo extenso, concedo;
> el Cuerpo que está con modo

indivisible, eso niego;
y así está el Cuerpo de Cristo
en el Pan del Sacramento,
con el modo indivisible,
y declárame un ejemplo:
el alma de un hombre, ocupa
todo un hombre, sin que demos
lugar dónde esté, pues queda
tan cabal, después de muerto,
la cantidad, como estaba
antes que muriese; luego,
sin ocupar lugar, puede
Dios estar en ese velo,
y estar o no estar le hace
ser Pan vivo o ser Pan muerto.] (vv. 1271–93)

Calderón goes to great lengths to explain how Christ's indivisible body inhabits the extensive body of the bread, ending with *Fe*'s analogy concerning the indivisible presence of the soul in the body of man.[15] But we should take note of how both proofs are constructed through a type of post-mortem that demonstrates how transubstantiation works through its opposite: the ex-substantiation of the indivisible soul from the extensive body, which becomes an emblem consonant with Benjamin's definition of allegory: a hieroglyphic that stands in for that which has gone (*Origins* 33). The human body, like the emblematic sign, acts as a material and disposable screen for the divine soul, which is indivisible from the transcendental plane of existence. Human bodies thus stand in (and very shakily, at that) for the absence of something else, much as in the case of the religious image. At the same time, and through the liturgical dramatization of the Eucharist, the bread becomes more substantial than the human body itself; or rather, the body is reduced to the level of any other sign. According to Bell, as well as the philosophy of *desengaño*, this incarnation effect actually depends on the limits of human representation, much as *Buen Genio*'s goodness can only be correctly perceived when placed against *Mal Genio*'s carnivalesque excesses.

In the last scene, the two brothers approach the elevated gaze of *el Padre*, who judges their approach as if he were interpreting the meaning of two emblems. In fact, what we as spectators see are two 'Hispanic' *empresas* that point towards the already manifest works of their inventors. Wearing (*por cimera*) the sackcloth of *Humildad*, the misery of penance, and carrying the mirror of *Desengaño* along with the bread of the Eucharist, *Buen Genio* furiously – and nobly – races toward the finish line on horseback. *Mal Genio*, on the other hand, arrogantly conducts a vulgar carnival on foot, singing and dancing while accompanied by *Hermosura* and *Apetito* and carrying the heretical books of science. As they approach with their retinues of followers – *Inocencia, Fe, and las Virtudes* with *Buen Genio; Gula* and *Culpa* with *Mal Genio –el Padre* simply waits: 'Neither to one nor to the other, until I see to whom I should give it' [Ni a uno ni a otro, hasta ver / a quién se la debo dar] (vv. 1508–9). When it is clear that *Mal Genio* takes full and deliberate ownership over his deceptively beautiful merchandise and the earth-bound philosophy it represents, *el Padre* damns his keeping-it-real son, permanently expelling him from the heavenly realm. There will be no redemption here. Likewise, when it is clear that *Buen Genio* has purchased goods that reflect his ability to read their value from *el Padre*'s point of view – an act of judgment which exactly mirrors the absolute obedience *el Padre* demands – *el Padre* embraces him, and the Holy Trinity is reunited.

I have made a point of underlining several moments and structures in the play that display the inherent contradictions of Counter Reformation theology. These would include the tangible lack of omnipotence of *el Padre*, the use of *Culpa* as a source of theological sophistication, and the conscious knowledge that theatricality is ontologically opposed to the doctrine of divine presence. Another way to frame this problem is to see these contradictions as a necessary product, or dividend, of the material process of staging, or representing, religious truths which should be self-evident. These contradictions are, in other words, the 'unthought' of sacramental theatre: 'its disavowed presuppositions and consequences' (Žižek, *Parallax* ix). And of course a literal reading of the play, in which *Apetito* sells flesh and blood, *el Padre* is ignorant of the birth order of his sons, or *Buen Genio* instigates the fraternal competition, is proscribed by the dialectical operations of the play, which annihilate the literally inclined *Mal Genio* at the end. (This is also what makes the literal view so very interesting.) Since the figural point of view is spiritual, and since it depends in turn on the untrustworthy materiality of signs, the truth of the text is placed out of reach of both spectators and critics. It is our desire for fullness of meaning which leads us to substantiate theological paradox and turn away from the bothersome chaos and loose threads.

Conclusion: The Motivation of Bias, Both Critical and Poetic

In volume two of his anti-totalitarian critique of metaphysical historicism *The Open Society and its Enemies*, Karl Popper contends that the impetus for (traditional) historicist revisions of the past arises from the terror that the ruling classes associate with historical change. Much as we have seen in *El nuevo mundo descubierto por Cristóbal Colón*, by looking for the 'inner meaning' of historical crises the reactionary subject can, in effect, look beyond the material aspects of social and political change – and violence – toward a future moment of redemption: 'Change, by revealing what is hidden in the undeveloped essence, can only make apparent the essence, the potentialities, the seeds, which from the beginning have inhered in the changing object. This doctrine leads to the historicist idea of an historical fate or an inescapable essential destiny' (7). To arrive at these conclusions, Popper traces the genealogy of historicism back to the Greek philosopher Heraclitus, whom he credits with discovering the idea of change. He then considers how Plato takes this idea and comes to the conclusion that 'all social change is corruption or decay or degeneration' (19). By placing Plato's rationale within a socio-political, as opposed to a philosophical frame of reference, Popper finds that the de facto social and political arrangement, whatever that might be, would necessarily be the closest to the perfect, or essential ideal of social organization. In such a regime, all historical and philosophical analysis would seek to uncover the hidden correspondences between the past and the present in order to redeem the current hegemony by seeing it as a natural result of cosmic forces. In this understanding of historicism, it would seem we have found a parallel concept to Maravall's critique of the medievalizing thrust of baroque guided culture, as well as a symbolic practice homologous to Counter Reformation emblematics.

This nostalgia for a more perfect time and place where 'words mean what they say' has informed many influential studies of the *auto sacramental*. Parker, for example, takes rather literally the moniker for the Spanish Golden Age, believing he has found a time and an art form (in the *auto*) in which the respect for piety and the denigration of worldly goods survive through the material excesses of an incipient capitalistic mode of thought and the crisis-driven politics of the Hapsburg monarchy: 'That moral principles were universally held to be more important than an economic prosperity which could have been fostered by their abandonment, is one of the impressive features of Spanish life in the century of its "decadence"' (*Allegorical Drama* 150). Although I disagree with Parker's assessment, I do find his words to be a particularly potent description of how ideology overrides material considerations in early (and late) modernity. More recently, Bolívar Echeverría reiterates Parker's vision and resituates it within the politico-religious project of the Society of Jesus, which he celebrates as an attempt to construct an ecclesiastical utopia, albeit, one 'which, seen from the other side, is nothing more than one chapter in the history of the unstoppable ascent of capitalist modernity' ('Compañía' 59). Martin reframes both historicist fantasies by placing an ethno-nationalistic spin on the dialectic, calling the *auto* 'a hidden treasure of the purest culture to raise its head in Spain, and one of the most universal traditions of the West' (25). In every case, it is the way in which the *auto* blocks access to its material predicament that is seen to be the source of its aesthetic and, I would argue, ideological power. I think it is more productive to turn against this dematerializing strategy of religious theatre and descend into the maelstrom of historical change, although many critics would not agree.

In *Calderón: Los orígenes de la modernidad en la España del Siglo de Oro*, Antonio Regalado is quite upfront about the goals of his erudite and interwoven series of essays: 'It will be proven that the art of the *autos*, although rooted in the christian faith, is not reducible to a closed world, rather it is an open artistic paradigm, capable of awakening forgotten motifs, in which our need to orient ourselves by means of a symbolic order which makes present for us a dramatic image of the world stands out' (1:32). For Regalado, Calderón's art responds to a universal human need for drama. This is not a unique claim, but I would like to look more closely at the way in which Regalado's assertions are both upheld and undone by his own critical practice, which cannot help but remind one of Calderón's dramatic structure, especially the way in which the author attempts to head off skepticism concerning his assertions and, just as importantly, channel the apparent aesthetic and theological contradictions in Calderón's plays into the void of eucharistic presence. At the end of his Introduction, Regalado attempts to close off any discussion of the socio-political embeddedness of the *auto sacramental* by insisting on the aesthetic grounds of his essay, and he does so in a way that seems at first glance to be good-naturedly ecumenical: 'Let us abandon, then, the themes of the imperial, catholic, dogmatic, and inquisitorial Spain and allow ourselves to be touched by the art of the great poet and playwright, if we are capable of not being bovines, ruminants of that which has already been chewed, let us risk a moment in his world' (1: 96). A more generous reader might attribute Regalado's bestial characterization of materialist literary critics to a type of unconscious enthusiasm that spills over the edges of his passion for Calderón's genius. A second glance, however, unveils the same rhetorical fallacy with which Borja opens his Prologue, as the critic displaces questions concerning the political and social ramifications and functions of the *auto* towards a critique of materialist critics themselves, 'bovine ruminants of a pre chewed [dialectical materialism],' who perversely insist on reinserting this universal art into its specific processes and contexts of production. His construction and occupation of the role of the Good Shepherd attempts to mask the seemingly good-natured malice at the heart of his metaphorical side-step. But Calderón himself illuminates what is at stake, when *Culpa* declares, that 'the ignorant should not be given more than straw and hay' [porque no ha de darle al necio / más que la paja y cebada] (vv. 632–3). Even more contradictory is the view that by bracketing off the socio-political realities of Calderón's historical stage we are somehow given direct access to the poet's world. By situating his own drama in the marketplace, Calderón presents himself as being more attuned to the compromised nature of his art than his most ardent critical 'defenders' are willing to allow. As one proceeds through Regalado's essays, it becomes more and more apparent that he overcomes the limitations inherent in the historically contingent act of representation by articulating two interpretive models, one legitimate and one illegitimate. Moreover, the attempt to usher the reader into his utopian matrix of the Spanish baroque cannot be accomplished without first degrading contemporary culture and society, much as does Parker, by identifying it as symbolically 'raquitic' and 'impoverished.'

The most unfortunate effect of this reading, to my mind, is the uncritical repetition and propagation of the *auto*'s division of the world into Catholics and heretics. By redirecting baroque theatre's contingent symbolic practice away from the historical field of Counter Reformation political culture, Regalado avoids the complex relationship between the dramatic representation of apostasy, heresy, the Jew, the Lutheran, the non-believer, the sophist, etc., as well as the political, cultural, ethnic, and linguistic violence that surrounds and responds to such Manichean axiologies of Good and Evil. Or, perhaps we are seeing the marriage between the 'universal human need for drama' and a similar need to contain complex historical conflicts in simplified allegorical plots. By turning a blind eye to the marketplace, criticism neither recognizes nor is able to analyse how the *auto* plays with history in the same way it plays with allegorical meaning, through a sophisticated semiotic regime that emblematically uproots and reconfigures historical actors and their material relations according to a concrete political and ideological program for cultural guidance. If the *auto* is in fact an 'open artistic paradigm' capable of orienting us toward a dramatic experience of presence, one might ask what it is exactly that is made present in these dramas.

Recent historiographical work on the Spanish Inquisition and the social programs organized at the Council of Trent strongly suggests that the relationship between the *auto sacramental* and the historical reality of early modern Spain is much more complex than most literary criticism acknowledges. Jaime Contreras warns us that any historical documentation of *conversos* and judaizers has to be read with extreme care, since the primary sources of information, largely transcriptions of Inquisition trials, communicate a biased view of the actual social reality or even the historical existence of Spanish Jews and converts (129). Joseph Silverman goes even further, noting the complete incongruity between the theatrical terror produced by the figure of the Jew and their actual presence in Spanish society: 'By the time that Lope was writing for the theatre the Jew was only a phantasmagorical presence in his land, an imaginary threat to the catholic unity of the Spanish faith' (164). Sarah Nalle informs us that the spectacular trials and executions of Lutherans in Valladolid in 1559 are more the exception than the rule, as for all intents and purposes there were no Lutherans in Spain.[16] In matters of heresy, Richard Kagan's studies of *profetas de la plaza* conclude that the persecution and castigation of so-called false prophets was motivated more by specific and changeable political factors than by matters of doctrine ('Politics' 110). R. de la Flor summarizes: 'Ethnic minorities and groups of dissidents who live within the layers of an empire that is only superficially unified in its ideology employ deliberate concealment as a weapon against imperial hegemony, creating a blind spot that obscures strategies of infiltration and acculturation implemented by the imperial other' ('Sacrificial Politics' 243)

All of these observations beg the following question: If the dramatic representation of heretics is completely out of proportion to their historical presence and visibility, why do they play such a prominent role in sacred dramaturgy? The answer is provided in part by ritual scholars such as Bell, Bourdieu, and Grimes and their research on the importance in ritual practice of the 'motivation of bias.' As Victor Turner notes, 'Members of despised or outlawed ethnic minorities play major roles in myths and popular tales as representatives or expressions of universal human values' (110). Scapegoating, it appears, is also a universal human need. As we have seen with hieroglyphic symbols or authoritative *sentencias*, entire social, ethnic, or religious groups can be uprooted from their specific historical conditions and arranged according to the binary oppositions of ritual discourse. The following observation by Bell casts a curious light on the various purges of Jews, *conversos*, and *moriscos* that echo in the *autos* whenever the figure of the heretic is invoked: 'The historical record suggests that dramatic purges occur in inverse ratio to the presence of real enemies or policy failures. When analyzed more symbolically, these political performances appear to divide up the world into two absolute camps, the good and innocent on the one hand and the deviant and the reprehensible on the other' (*Ritual Perspectives* 163). According to these statements, the *auto sacramental* does not reflect an existing social animosity between Christians and non-Christians; it helps create it. The representation of eucharistic presence becomes a primary vehicle for motivating bias against a phantasmal figure of Otherness. In Benjamin's words: 'Knowledge of good and evil is, then, the opposite of all factual knowledge. Related as it is to the depths of the subjective, it is basically only knowledge of evil. It is "nonsense" [*Geschwätz*] in the profound sense in which Kierkegaard conceived the word' (*Origins* 233). The triumphalist staging of a Hispanic Counter Reformation hegemony cannot be accomplished without invoking a series of transgressive actions and antagonistic figures – such as the heretical statements and gestures of the Jew and the Protestant – which threaten the status quo, thus awakening the desire to eliminate the threats: theological sense and heterodox 'nonsense' are inextricably, i.e., dialectically, linked. Any attempt to question the monarchical or ecclesiastical right to rule based on the political failures or legislative excesses of these same bodies is subsequently characterized as demonic, perverse, unpatriotic, Other. Indeed, it is the imagined presence of the transgressive Other which triggers and drives the desire for the real presence of the symbolic and theatrical body of the State, including the most palpable gesture of its divine right to rule: State sanctioned violence.

With respect to the role of the emblem in this dynamic of ideological containment and guidance, Poppenberg notes that the 'difference between "image" and "itself," between theatrical presence and real eucharistic presence, between literary sign and sacramental sign remains problematical' (116). The solution to this problem in the *auto* appears to be the construction of a negative and theatrically unstable image that allows the spectator to locate and equivocally track a diabolical presence made responsible for the chaotic confusion of theatrical signs. All transgressive energy is channeled into this figure so that it can be isolated and eliminated in the denouement of the play. By the end of *El gran mercado* we have forgotten the words of *Mal Genio* when he is accused by his brother of harbouring a contradictory desire: 'If one cannot compete against oneself, don't place the Guilt on me, since we are all guilty' [Si el competir / no puede hacerlo uno solo, / no me des la Culpa a mí, / pues es de todos la culpa] (vv. 159–62). Although the poet solves this problem by having *Mal Genio* voluntarily elect *Culpa* as his traveling companion, the words remain in the body of the text, resisting its absolute closure, even if *Mal Genio*'s descent to hell necessarily colours all he has said previously.

To conclude, the answer to Díaz Balsera's question as to why the *auto* simultaneously incites the spectator to sin while punishing sinful desire is intimately related to Maravall's concept of cultural guidance, as it joins medieval theological dialectics to the modern paradigm of theatricality in the creation of a ritualistic theatricality. We are not really looking at a ritualistic making-present of the body of Christ and the ecclesiastical and social body of Counter Reformation society in the liturgical and medieval sense; rather, the *auto sacramental* is a modern, theatrical representation of a phantasmal, internal threat to a non-existent Spanish collectivity which acts to bring the desire for the presence of this collective into the psyche of the spectator, thus motivating the identification both with the threat and the castigation of that threat. Every subject is both the one and the other, a theatrical image and a changeable, hidden meaning, and the internal tension produced by this ideological-iconological structure is the very source of temporal power. When Benjamin and Paz speak of the baroque as a strategy in which the aesthetic and intellectual tropes used to move the spectator ultimately work against their own transcendence, we should also recognize that the ontological transience of baroque art can be translated into a mechanism which acts to establish the 'hyberbolic and universal solidity' – presence – of institutions that see themselves as subject to a constant threat of annihilation.[17] Similarly, when Calderón links the dramatic means of his artistic persuasion to the deceptive appearances and words of *Culpa* and *Mal Genio*, the power of art is both confirmed and masked in such a way that the only thing that remains in the end is the castigating gaze of the Father of the Law.

5 Calderón's *El alcalde de Zalamea*: Pedro Crespo as Literary Subject

> To penetrate every foreign will argues an eminence of wealth, and to know how to conceal one's own implies superiority.
>
> [Arguye eminencia de caudal penetrar toda voluntad ajena, y concluye superioridad saber celar la propia.]
>
> Baltasar Gracián, *El héroe*

In bringing philology to bear on the literary corpus of Pedro Calderón de la Barca, the editor-critic is faced with a series of lacunae, the most problematic of which is the effective lack of autograph manuscripts of the poet's plays. The manuscripts that do exist manifest significant revisions with respect to the published anthologies, even those authorized by the playwright himself. According to observations made by Arellano in *Calderón y su escuela dramática*, it is virtually impossible to approach, let alone 'fix,' the texts of Calderón's plays according to an archetype wherein the primordial intention of the author may be married to the moment of literary creation. The question becomes even murkier where historical performances are concerned. In a survey of the changes made to the manuscript of the play *El agua mansa* between the probable date of its composition in 1642–4 and its performance as part of the celebration of the marriage of Felipe IV to Mariana de Austria in 1649, Arellano writes: 'The length of the play obliges [Calderón] to cut passages, change the placement of some passages, and in the end, reconstruct the *comedia*' (*Calderón* 56). In a case like this, it is apparent that '"textual instability" is not a feature that shows the strangeness of literary texts but their ordinariness' (Gurd 5).

For an experienced playwright like Calderón, it seems unlikely that he would not have known that the original version of the play was too long for a performance. This, in combination with the many changes his texts manifest on their way to presses and bookshelves, suggests that writing the plays is every bit as important to their material function and meaning as performing them. Although all plays exhibit changes in their movement from the page to the stage, it seems worthwhile to consider for a moment the material and social functions of the text of the play as something other than a lifeless textual body, only brought to life through its ultimate realization as a dramatic performance. What I would like to consider in this chapter is how writing configures a communicative performance in and of itself.

Rather than bring the weight of philological science to bear on the assemblage and framing of monumental editions of early modern texts, especially dramatic texts, I would like to suggest, like Gurd, that it is more useful – and scientific – to foreground the endless process of rewriting and editorial intervention as a basic condition of the production of literature – and its editions. The textual challenge becomes particularly acute when dealing with something as ephemeral and undocumentable as theatrical performance. Due to the historical and cultural importance of mass spectacles and the theatre of the *corrales* in early modern Spain, critics of the *comedia nueva* have gone to great lengths to maintain their focus on the question of performance, even though the vast majority of studies rely on close readings of supposedly trustworthy texts. But as we have seen above, such faith in the text, especially in the case of Calderón, is out of step with the material history of those texts. At the root of this dilemma is the fact that early modern Spain is a culture in which writing becomes the preeminent bureaucratic, religious, and artistic institution. According to Godzich, writing and literacy, and especially published writing, are the main material supports for the linguistic universalism and imperial mimesis at the heart of both the political expansion of the empire and the humanist project. The two in fact are irremediably linked. For the literary subject of representation, '*language is the originally instituting institution*; it provides the framework within which the practice of the subject will be that of a self-positing of the Self in language. From this point of view, the modern subject, whom we saw earlier to be a consciousness of falsehood, becomes now the subject of inscription of Form, that is, the Artist' ('Language' 366–7). In light of Godzich's claim, one hypothesis for explaining the easy confidence with which the modern critic regards the critical edition would posit that the phenomenalization, or institutionalization, of the written text in early modernity itself produces a blind spot at the point at which the critic inscribes his or her own critical *caudal* into the textual economy of the institution of philology. If, as Gurd argues, 'the past is the currency in which the critical edition acquires its exchange value ... [and] becomes a commodity in a social relation with other commodified editions,' then the critic has no choice but to borrow against his or her own critical future by banking on the continued value of the edition (24). The constant complaints of writers like Cervantes, Gracián, and Calderón concerning the multiple perversions their texts suffered at the hands of copyists, typesetters, and publishers argue against such phenomenalization, but this is where the editorial practices of philology step in to correct, emend, amend, and comment on the text in order to stabilize the object of its own scientific practices and, by extension, its own findings and practices.

By foregrounding the foundational instability of text editing, I am not suggesting we abandon scientific rigour in the editing or analysis of texts. My own project is infinitely indebted to those scholars who have preceded me, even, or perhaps especially to those with whose opinions I differ. What I am suggesting is that we consider whether or not the archetype: 1) is an actual historical document, or a construction of the philologist whose goal is the making present of the primordial moment of insemination; and 2) brings us closer to or farther away from the historical and social conditions of artistic creation. If the material circumstances of Calderón's texts are their revisions, rewrites, excisions, additions, pirated copies of manuscripts, and anthologies that evidence the editorial intervention of actors other than the writer himself, then it stands to reason that writing and rewriting, drafting and correction are not prologues or postscripts to the establishment of the archetype but rather its very process of production and dissemination. As Gurd notes, the textual archetype is founded 'on the basis of a difference *internal* to its production,' since the philologist structures his or her practice according to the assumption that there are errors to correct, inconsistencies to smooth out, and lacunae to fill up with textual additions, footnotes, and commentaries: 'A critical edition, then, contains an internal and founding rift; like the remainder, the critical edition is split by an inner difference' (48). These splits, remainders, and differences should not be tidied up or rationalized in the attempt to stabilize and rationalize the text but should instead be redirected back toward the historical contingencies present and necessary in the act(s) of creation. In the words of Baena, 'To detain the process of error is to detain dissemination, point towards an "origin" before dissemination, before writing and reading, publishing and selling' (*Discordancias* 209). In the end, the archetype, a text which occupies no space in the material documents, points to a time out of time, before the imperfect quill touches the empty page and, as such, escapes time and history. It is, in other words, an *empresa* which communicates the intention of the philologist to objectify, essentialize, and historicize a mythical moment of authorial intention, i.e., presence, through the identification of fragments, the editing of manuscripts and anthologies, and the writing of commentaries.

One way around or through this impasse is to treat the text and its processes of production as a dynamic happening as opposed to an object of study (Iser 22). As we have seen in chapters 3 and 4, such an approach elucidates the movement from multiple receptive dispositions to a privileged point of reception by offering what Gurd calls 'a close textual reading with a plurality of texts, plural in form and spatio-temporal position' (21). It is dissemination which thus becomes the contingent and historically situated point of departure, rather than the ultimately unapproachable and unlocalizable moment of creation. Such will be the case in my analysis of Calderón's *El alcalde de Zalamea*, one of the most studied plays of Golden Age theatre. Obviously, a study of the emblem is neither the time nor the place for an extended consideration of the editorial history of the play. My intention, rather, is to understand the protagonist of the play, Pedro Crespo, as a fictional model and strategy for the creation of both a legitimate literary space and a 'literary subject' in baroque Spain. Although Crespo's most (in)famous act is the execution of a nobleman, his dramatic persona is produced in practice through his understanding and manipulation of discourse. Indeed, the archetypal act at the climax of the play takes place off stage, and its creative intention is purposefully shrouded in misunderstanding by the playwright and his protagonist. Thus, in addition to reading the small town mayor's execution of a nobleman and subsequent self-defense as a dramatic performance, I will also analyse it as a text, or *empresa*, whose editor-subject teaches us much about the emergence of literary stages and actors in the tempestuous arena of baroque Spain.

Fragments, Corpses, Emblems

According to Francisco Sánchez, early modern Spain witnesses the creation and institutionalization of a 'literary republic.' Within the consciousness of crisis that arose among the monarchical-seigniorial elites due to the 'substitution of an individual economic agent for feudal-religious determinations, ... [l]iterature was able to creatively mediate in this public concern by offering a fictional view of the state of an emerging civil society, its possibilities and its dangers' (Sánchez, *Early Bourgeois Literature* 55). As the mediator between historical change and the maintenance of the social and political prerogatives of the old regime, the literary subject represents a new, quasi-independent social agent, in whom 'the conscious articulation of self-interest with politically legitimate norms emerges as the means for social advancement' (Sánchez, *Early Bourgeois Literature* 64). We have already seen this humanist drive for social legitimacy in Lope's *Arte nuevo*, Horozco's *Emblemas morales*, and Calderón's complex treatment of theatricality; but the case of *El alcalde* offers a much more pointed historical and discursive staging of this social drama. Few plays present the historical, economic, social, and literary conflicts of the baroque with more urgency than *El alcalde*, which makes it an excellent laboratory in which to inspect the material forces at work in its fictional worlds.

The main point of dramatic – and critical – contention in *El alcalde* arises from the opaque ambivalence of Pedro Crespo's ingenious and awe-inspiring spectacle of vengeance/justice, in which a military officer is not merely executed but grotesquely and dishonourably garroted, making his death ignominious and problematic in both social and juridical terms. The uneasy closure of the play can be seen to respond to the social crises mentioned above by Sánchez and first theorized by Maravall in *El mundo social de* La Celestina. There is little disagreement concerning Don Álvaro's leading role in the kidnapping and rape of Crespo's daughter Isabel, or the immorality and violence of his crime. Rather, the problems stem from several challenges to the status quo produced by the structure of the play: Crespo's inferior social status; the apparently formalistic and superficial nature of his statements concerning his surreptitious attack on the blood hierarchy of baroque Spain; and the timing of the execution, which takes place off-stage and before the king can make a definitive judgment.[1] Compounding these difficulties are the incredulousness of Don Lope de

Figueroa, which is based on the aristocrat's prior knowledge of the mayor's theatrical guile, and the objections of the king concerning the mayor's violation of legal and, ultimately, social prerogatives.

An impenetrable cipher, Crespo's gruesome *invención* is open to multiple interpretations, as its hieroglyphic-like resistance to fully embody any one meaning is both source and limit of the play's perceived depth and ambivalence. By bringing emblem and ritual theory to bear on the problem, it becomes clear that this impasse arises from what Edward Said has called 'the practical worldliness of the text' (cited by Bell, *Ritual Theory* 81–2). Bell summarizes Said's notion: 'The practical worldliness of the text is not simply the socio historical context of the work or any type of irreducible essence within the work. [It is] its own practice of the strategies of social action inherent in texts and textualization' (*Ritual Theory* 113). In the case of Pedro Crespo, the practical worldliness of his difficult device is embodied in the highly ritualized nature of his social interaction with the other characters in the play, most especially with respect to the king. As William Blue observes with respect to Lope's Peribáñez, Crespo is 'a master of language's subtleties. He may dress like a farmer and use "farmerly" images, but only an innocent would be fooled' (50). The formal and formalized nature of his objections and interjections, his recurrence to tradition (even where no tradition exists),[2] his attention to rhetorical frames and juridical rules, and the convincing nature of his eminently theatrical performance are the very essence of his daring enterprise and the key to the king's seemingly resigned acceptance at the end of the play.

To this end, I will rely on Bell's notions of ritualized agents and ritual mastery, which she uses to cut through abstract discussions of symbolic meaning and intentionality. This shift allows the critic to focus on common actions that imply but never really achieve social and ideological resolution. I will also return to Egginton's definition of theatricality, which focuses on the movement from medieval corporate hierarchies and spectacles of presence to the modern State and its dependence on representation. This transformation is vital to the theatrical world of the absolutist State, in which a traditional world view characterized by unquestioned beliefs gives way to a modern period of consent wherein personal freedom, i.e., free will, becomes the source of political power, and where fragmentation becomes the basic condition of hegemonic domination. Similar to the way in which the theatrical representation of religious presence depends on the tension between legitimate and illegitimate *hábitos*, the dramatic conflict between hegemony and fragmentation is the condition out of which Felipe II's reluctant nod of consent arises to temporarily stabilize the chaotic *fronterizo* world of Zalamea.

One thing the play's critics can agree on is the chaotic nature of this rural *aldea* at the outset of the play.[3] As A. Robert Lauer observes, Calderón opens with a scene 'where the world moves in reverse, or better stated, where the peasants are rich and noble while the nobles are poor and wretched' ('*El Alcalde*' 137). Due to its conflictive and crisis-driven world, *El alcalde* is regarded as the most realistic of Calderón's plays, and many attempts have been made to locate it more precisely within one historical context or another. Rather than attempt to anchor the play in a concrete historical period, I prefer to consider its historiographical implications by privileging the anthropological nature of its structure. In effect, the urban tensions produced by the aforementioned erosion of social hierarchies brought about by rapid economic and political expansion are relocated to what can be characterized as a colonial space, where these tensions become embodied by frontier subjects who are seen to mimic yet not quite reproduce conflicting perspectives on honour. The first of these perspectives is an archaic view that redeploys the aesthetic conventions of chivalric and pastoral literature and which establishes the residual presence of what J.C. Rodríguez calls medieval organicism or substantialism: 'The crux of this ideology … is the notion of "blood," a notion that encompasses within itself both the category of organic life and the category of living substance' (*Theory* 94). The second, or emergent, frame of honour is Pedro Crespo's famous 'patrimonio del alma.' Rodríguez calls this modern form of ideology animism: 'in animism the *soul* no longer signifies one more qualification with respect to blood but, on the contrary, something radically opposed to it' (*Theory* 94). This second ideological matrix is the one that both contains and promotes the economic and social mobility of what Rodríguez and Sánchez call the bourgeois subject of the literary republic of early modernity, and which promotes the 'self-justification of literature as a socially relevant cultural product' (Sánchez, *An Early Bourgeois Literature* 117). For this reason, I have placed Crespo in the role of literary subject: it is not merely his execution of the aristocrat that creates an honourable space for him and family but, more importantly, his manipulation of a literary and juridical canon of 'texts.'

In the opening scene, the spectator is situated at the margins of a world characterized by fragmentation and conflict, both within and between the rural and imperial domains. Calderón uses this geographical dichotomy to translate the social tensions of the city into a territorial conflict at the margins of Castilian hegemony. It is a useful example of Maravall's concept of the baroque consciousness of crisis: 'It was an internal state of disarray, of discord. Its tensions affected the relation between nobles and commoners, rich and poor, old and new Christians, believers and nonbelievers, foreigners and subjects proper, men and women, central governments and peripheral townships, and so on' (*Culture* 45). Plagued by symptoms of fragmentation brought about by and resulting in conflicting interpretations of honour, duty, gender roles, political privilege, and so on, Zalamea stages a tightly framed representation of baroque urban tensions.

In spite of Crespo's picturesque *elogio del campo*, Zalamea does not experience a contamination of its pastoral innocence by the aggressive materiality of history, as arguably takes place in Lope's *Fuenteovejuna* (see Greenberg 54). The insistent march of historical time penetrates and divides the social landscape of Zalamea long before its maximum metaphor – the army of Felipe II – enters its social body. Don Mendo's caricaturesque courtship of Crespo's daughter Isabel offers no hope of honouring either party, while the *hidalgo*'s obvious lack of economic resources dishonours even his servant. 'Don' Mendo's acquisition of honour through the purchase of an *ejecutoria* reveals a gaping hole at the centre of his mimetic portrayal of organicist genealogical discourses concerning the relationship between 'alimentación' and the honourable *physis*. According to Bhabha, the mimicry of Mendo manifests a 'desire that, through the repetition of *partial presence*, which is the basis of mimicry, articulates those disturbances of cultural, racial and historical difference that menace the narcissistic demand of colonial authority' (126). If a colonial discourse, as Pratt argues, represents its subjugated Other to itself, in the case of Mendo we have a previously subjugated Other who, through economically legitimate and socially illegitimate means, threatens the ontological stability of the very discourse he deploys.[4] What is more, his organicist discourse ironically reflects Pedro Crespo's *elogio del campo* and its symptomatic paranoia with respect to contamination and ruin from without.[5] Maria Alberta Sacchetti calls this rhetorical structure 'the irony of self-betrayal,' and such irony taints the discourse of every character in the play, including Felipe II (47).

Few plays exemplify Gracián's sociological metaphor of casually and violently colliding *mónadas* better than this one. From the outset virtually every character holds to an independent worldview and imagines him- or herself in an autonomous and self-actualizing space. The question is not whether these alienated individuals are going to come into contact and, ultimately, conflict, but when and how they are going to respond when conflict occurs. As I have already suggested, the denouement of the play does not produce a Hegelian synthesis of antithetical postures with respect to duty, truth, obedience, etc., but offers instead an uneasy and unstable alliance, a contract if you will, between independent interests, signed on the text of Don Álvaro's corpse. Characteristic of this modern, incomplete synthesis is the tacit and theatrically staged consensus forged between Crespo and his daughter Isabel on the mountain, after she has been raped, he has been humiliated, and her brother provoked into attacking Don Álvaro, his superior.

When the spectator regards Pedro Crespo in his abject state on the mountain, the dishonoured father presents an even more pathetic spectacle than his defiled daughter, as he laments his fate and impotence, with his hands tied around an oak tree. By contrast, the relative mobility of Isabel suggests that even though she has suffered concrete physical and psychological violence, the crime affects her father more deeply. Modern sensibilities might be offended by this reading, but in Calderón's play, as in the honour system in general, the victim of rape is not the woman per se but her honour, which is another way to say the Name of the Father. More to the point, Isabel's furtive flight from her avenging brother and father reveals a split between her social interpellation and what can legitimately be called her *'patrimonio del alma.'* Her physical suffering and symbolic death unhinge her organicist social identification and transform her into a shiftless and formless spectre who secretly moves through the empty space on the frontier. This split between her social obligations and personal desire to save her own life and honour serves as a catalyst for Crespo's own transformation. Here we find a major difference between Crespo and other 'disgraced' Calderonian protagonists: Crespo has not merely imagined his dishonour; the symbolic survival of the Crespo family has been dealt a mortal blow.[6] (This is of course debatable, as is the legal status of Isabel's 'rape,' depending on which stratum of the caste system one occupies. Don Álvaro obviously believes he has committed no crime.) As a result, both characters begin Act 3 by speaking as if they were already dead, decrying the irremediable course of events and calling death down upon themselves to relieve them of the task of reconstituting their social and personal sense of honour.

But then a curious thing happens: first with Isabel and then with Pedro, discourse, in particular an emblematic literary language, steps in to reconfigure the meaning of their downfall from one of absolute annihilation to that of a temporary set-back. Daughter and father rewrite their tragedies from the margins of the symbolic order, plotting equally discursive paths to redemption. It is significant that Crespo's tutor in theatrical and literary performance is his own daughter, who models and performs the strategic, ritual use of emblematic discourse for her own ends. The manner in which the socially subordinate Isabel invites the interpellation of the Father into her individual project of redemption will be mimetically reproduced when Crespo confronts the king.

In the opening soliloquy, Isabel's discourse moves between two motives and possible reactions to her plight: her family obligation to submit to her brother, which would result in her death; and an individual declaration of innocence that opposes family honour to a more abstract, or spiritual, sense of justice. According to her own words, she already imagines herself a corpse; but from a theological point of view, she cannot simply offer herself up to her brother to be sacrificed, which would be tantamount to suicide. Peter N. Dunn's thesis concerning Calderón's juxtaposition of the pagan, or 'unchristian,' religion of honour to the 'Christian' ethic of forgiveness is a point well taken at this juncture ('Honour' 75–8). On the other hand, any attempt to save her honour independently by, say, pursuing Don Álvaro, runs the risk of making her misfortune public. Even her disappearance and silence would damage her family's standing due to the potential workings of *el qué dirán*. In other words, the conflicting ideologies of baroque Spain do not allow her to give way on either object of desire: her honour or her life. Something new will need to be produced here if she is to survive. That something begins to take shape after she spies her father.

When Isabel discovers her father in his immobilized state, the mutual alienation of father and daughter is temporarily mitigated by the unconsciously interlaced and pathetic *redondillas*. This poetic harmony is quickly undone, however, by Isabel's fear of patriarchal retribution.

ISABEL: *With his hands tied* behind a strong oak
CRESPO: Moving the heavens to pity with voices that call out
ISABEL: is my father.

CRESPO: my daughter comes.
ISABEL: Father and Lord!
CRESPO: My daughter, come here, and remove these bonds.
ISABEL: I don't dare: because *if my hands remove* the bonds that hold you prisoner, I dare not, sir, tell you my misfortunes, recount my grief; because if you see yourself *with hands freed and without honor,* your wrath will bring death down upon me; I want, before you see them, to recount to you my misfortunes.
CRESPO: Stop, Isabel, stop, do not continue; for to tell misfortunes, Isabel, it is not necessary to recount them.
ISABEL: There are many things you need to know, and when they are told, your courage will be moved, and you will want to avenge them before you hear them.

[ISABEL: Atadas atrás las manos
a una rigurosa encina
CRESPO: Enterneciendo los cielos
con las voces que apellida
ISABEL: ... mi padre está.
CRESPO: mi hija viene.
ISABEL: ¡Padre y señor!
CRESPO: Hija mía,
llégate, y quita estos lazos.
ISABEL: No me atrevo; que si quitan
los lazos que te aprisionan,
una vez las manos mías,
no me atreveré, señor,
a contarte mis desdichas,
a referirte mis penas;
porque si una vez te miras
con manos y sin honor,
me darán muerte tus iras;
y quiero, antes que las veas,
referirte mis fatigas.
CRESPO: Detente, Isabel, detente,
no prosigas; que desdichas,
Isabel, para contarlas,
no es menester referirlas.
ISABEL: Hay muchas cosas que sepas,

y es forzoso que al decirlas,
tu valor se irrite, y quieras
vengarlas antes de oírlas.]

(Act 3, vv. 85–110; my emphasis)

Before analysing this dialogue, Crespo's physical posture must be considered. Hands and eyes are among the most frequently represented images in emblem books: hands coming from the heavens, hands testing the value and truth of objects, open hands, closed hands, outstretched hands, the list goes on. Generally speaking, hands and eyes represent man's most important tools for measuring, judging, and shaping reality. As Gracián writes, 'Man without counsel, a darkened world. Advice and strength, eyes and hands; without courage wisdom is sterile' [Hombre sin noticias, mundo a escuras. Consejo y fuerças, ojos y manos; sin valor es estéril la sabiduría] (*Oráculo manual* 103).[7] In one of the most interesting emblematic images of this type, eyes look out from the fingers and palm of one of two hands that are about to embrace. Saavedra Fajardo comments on this image in his *empresa* 51, for which the inscription reads 'Trust and Distrust' [Fide et Diffide] (figure 7).

The subscription runs for several pages, but the central message appears early on: 'There is only one confidence that is sure, which is not to be subject to the judgment and will of another; because who can be sure about the human heart, withdrawn into the most hidden recess of the breast, whose designs the tongue cloaks and hides and the eyes belie, and the rest of the movements of the body contradict? [Solamente una confianza hay segura, que es no estar a arbitrio y voluntad de otro; porque ¿quién podrá asegurarse del corazón humano, retirado a lo más oculto del pecho, cuyos desinios encubre y disimula la lengua y desmienten los ojos y los demás movimientos del cuerpo?] (*Empresa* 51; 611). At issue in this *empresa* is the practical achievement of honour and power in the world without losing one's sovereignty and self-control. Lezra traces the spiritual anatomy of the hand back to Aristotle's *De Anima*: 'The soul, then, is analogous to the hand; for as the hand is an instrument [*organon*] which employs instruments [or 'an instrument of instruments'], in the same way the mind is a form which employs forms, and sense is a form which employs the forms of sensible objects [or 'the mind is the form of forms']' (108). The solution to acting in the world without endangering one's soul entails the figurative conversion of the hands and eyes into opaque signifiers in order

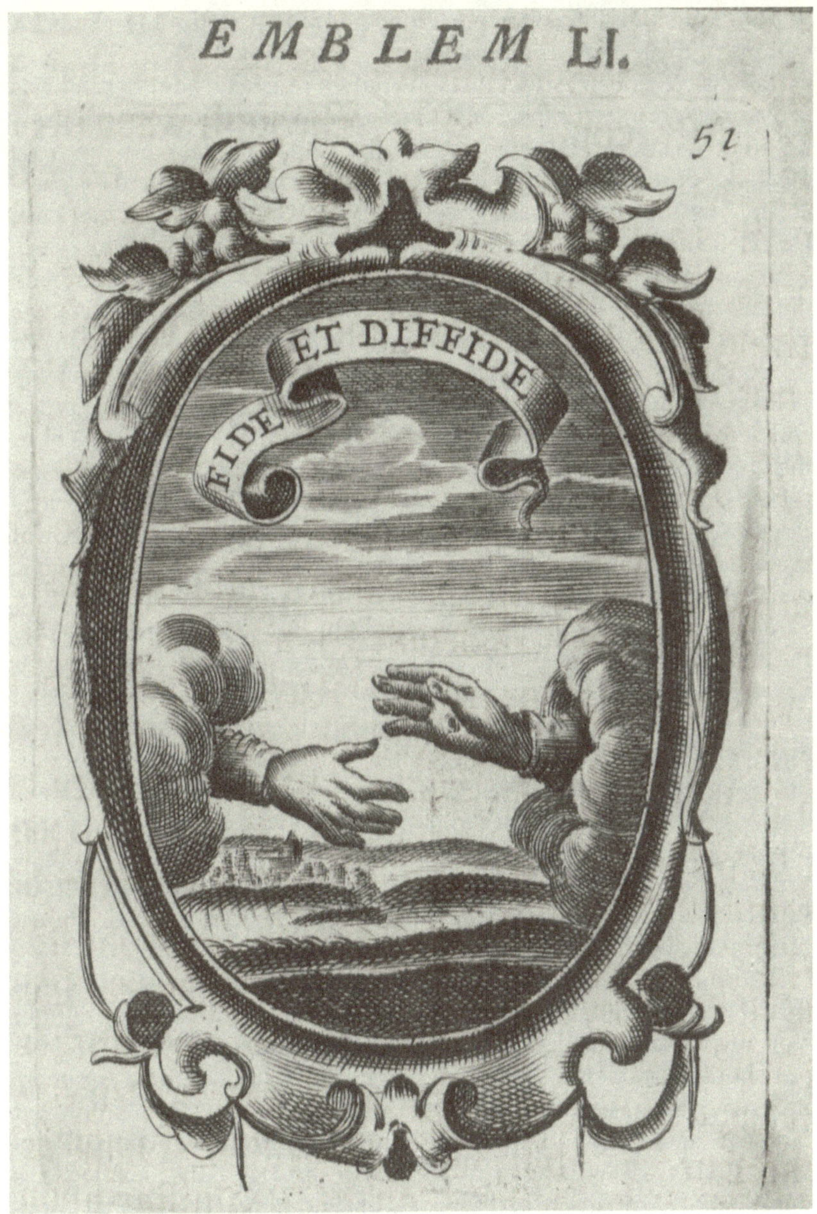

Figure 7 'Fide et diffide,' in Diego Saavedra Fajardo, *Empresas políticas* (1640), 364–5

to put others at a disadvantage, while not falling victim to the machinations of these same competitors.

Isabel's cautious gesture of reconciliation must consider her father's proven propensity for theatrical mimicry and deception, a social practice that frustrates the attempts of the Other to gaze on the 'true meaning' of his discourse and which adds menacing depth to his character. This mimicry characterizes every encounter Crespo has with Don Lope de Figueroa. Unlike Mendo, however, Crespo's mimicry is a self-conscious communicative strategy designed to both ingratiate himself with the aristocrat and hide the real intentions of his discourse. These mimetic abilities will prove vital later on in his encounter with the king, and can be related to Habermas's characterization of the political apprenticeship that leads to the domination of political discourse by cultural elites in the Enlightenment: 'The public sphere in the world of letters was not, of course, autochthonously bourgeois; it preserved a certain continuity with the publicity involved in the representation enacted at the prince's court. The bourgeois avant-garde of the educated middle class learned the art of critical-rational public debate through its contact with the "elegant world"' (cited in Sánchez, *Early Bourgeois Literature* 120). In this light, it becomes apparent that the rural-urban geography of the play can be read as a metaphor for the relationship between the monarchical-seigniorial elements of baroque society and those cultural agents who remained on the social margins of the court, even though their artistic and cultural commodities were deployed in the maintenance of this same society. Thus, Crespo's agricultural *caudal* can be read as a metaphor for the cultural capital that literary subjects such as Calderón strive to legitimize through their art. Even Isabel, herself, should be considered a literary subject, as the feminine representation of the poetic 'I' is a well-known literary device for seeking patrimonial favors.

Returning to the scene of the crime, Crespo's first request of Isabel is that she untie his hands. When she puts him off in order to tell her story, his violent reaction reminds us of Saavedra Fajardo's advice that one should not open oneself to another's will so as not to be deceived. It is in fact Isabel who exemplifies this lesson, as she will not allow her father to make any judgment without considering her own point of view, which she will attempt to impose on her father while he is deprived of a firm grasp on the world around him. Her personal application of the *Empresas políticas* will be characterized in Gracián's *Hero* as 'a reason of state for yourself,' which, as Sánchez argues, provides a 'normative model of conduct based on a description of a state of affairs in which every social exchange may result in damage for the person' (*Early Bourgeois Literature* 106). The actions of both characters demonstrate that the meaning of Isabel's disgrace is not immediate and universal but rather ambivalent and contingent and, as such, open to strategic manipulation. This ambiguity, along with the static nature of the scene – not to mention the naturalistic frame – corresponds to Cull's (and Horozco's) definition of an effective dramatic emblem: 'The dramatic emblem is most effective when it forms part of the staging of the play, so that the audience somehow sees the *picture* with their eyes while listening to the commentary in the dramatic dialogue' ('Emblematics' 121).

The here and now of the temporal and spatial disintegration of the mountain represent Isabel's one chance to make her claim – author her own text – and so, emboldened by her father's immobilized state, she slows the action down to a crawl in order to historicize her plight:

> ISABEL: Last night I was enjoying the peaceful security of your wise years, promised by my tender age, when those masked traitors – who deign that what honour defends, daring overcomes – kidnapped me; as when a hungry, bloodthirsty wolf rips the innocent lamb from the udder. That captain, that ungrateful guest who from the very first day introduced such an unexpected schism of treason and cunning, brawls and discord into the house, was the first to clutch me in his arms while the other traitors who march under his flag turned their backs. That confusing, hidden mountain over there, at the way out of this place, was his sanctuary.

> [ISABEL: Estaba anoche gozando
> la seguridad tranquila de tus canas,
> mis años me prometían,
> cuando aquellos embozados
> traidores – que determinan
> que lo que el honor defiende,
> el atrevimiento rinda –
> me robaron; bien así
> como de los pechos quita
> carnicero hambriento lobo
> a la simple corderilla.
> Aquel capitán, aquel
> huésped ingrato que el día

primero introdujo en casa
tan nunca esperada cisma
de traiciones y cautelas,
de pendencias y rencillas,
fue el primero que en sus brazos
me cogió mientras le hacían
espaldas otros traidores
que en su bandera militan.
Aqueste intricado, oculto
monte, que está a la salida
del lugar, fue su sagrado.] (Act 3, vv. 110–35)

The first image that Isabel evokes projects Crespo's self-fashioned patriarchal semblance onto his incapacitated state, mimetically empowering his imagination while playing on the life giving aspects of fatherhood. Nevertheless, the passive state of the father is reminiscent of Borja's motto: 'I will be satisfied when it appears.' Once Isabel resituates his wrathful gaze within this benevolent and protective frame, she assembles a small parade of emblems of beastly aggression and wanton violence into what can only be called a demonic and perverse sacrifice of innocence. To summarize, in spite of the careful watch of the vigilant shepherd, Isabel, the innocent lamb, was violently ripped from the breast of the ewe by bloody-mouthed, treasonous wolves. The suggestion of cannibalism, which emerges from the metaphorical conversion of the nobleman into a beast, unequivocally identifies Álvaro as the Other. In impeccably Aristotelian form, the rape itself is left out of the frame in order to allow the audience's (Crespo's) imagination to magnify its *terribilitá*.

We should note that Isabel offers no explicit solution to her plight, only a multiplication and magnification of its possible allegorical significance.[8] Nevertheless, as she dons the fleece of the innocent lamb, she places the staff of the *Señor* within reach of her father's hands, whose authority has been usurped by a monstrous being whose true nature can only be invoked by a language of total Otherness: 'Aquél, aquél.' The perversion of the politically and religiously 'stable' world of Zalamea is completed through the tragically ironic juxtaposition of rape and sacrifice, desolate mountain and sacred hermitage, transgression and military obligation. The rape is removed from the world of mundane sexual agression toward a universal plane where absolute perversion must be ritualistically and violently purged from the social body. Indeed, by avoiding any mention of the details of the rape and moving straight to allegory, her violation becomes emblematized, in the end, present in an extreme manner.

Isabel concludes her performance by returning to the scene of the mountain and recounting how her brother Juan entered after the rape and attacked the captain, before being overrun by his cohorts. Due to the injury caused by Juan's attack, Don Álvaro was brought back to Zalamea by his companions for medical treatment. At the conclusion of her simultaneously defiant and obedient discourse, at which point she offers up her life to the discretion of her father, she has displaced her own disgrace to the margins and redirected her father's self pity and anger onto Juan and Álvaro respectively. This subtle redirection of the gaze permits us to read the following comment by Bell in several ways: 'the ritual construction of power … involves dynamics whereby the power relations constituted by ritualization also empower those who may at first appear to be controlled by them' (*Ritual Theory* 207). It is immediately apparent that Isabel has exercised a particular type of power in order to save her own life. Just as importantly, she has empowered her father in several ways: her emblematization of their collective disgrace lessens his personal burden; she has redirected his gaze toward her brother, whose life and honour are both intact and, more importantly, in peril; finally, she has given Crespo a concrete means by which to pursue redress and redemption by informing him of the return of the captain to Crespo's home turf.

Before leaving Isabel and turning our attention to Pedro, it is worthwhile to consider how much information she has just provided. Isabel becomes in this scene the source of all the important historical details concerning the crime and, thus, a *cronista*. In this sense, her role is analogous to what we have seen with Lope's Rodrigo Terrazas and the allegory of *Culpa* in *El gran mercado del mundo*. Her framing and use of this history cannot be considered objective but rather form part of a personal enterprise. In the words of Sánchez, 'knowledge leads to reason according to [her] own personal investment in cultural goals' (*Early Bourgeois Literature* 115). The first movement of Sánchez's argument clearly pertains to Isabel; the second concerning cultural goals, however, turns our gaze towards Calderón's construction of the scene and his own goals in writing the play. Like Isabel – and Pedro (another Pedro) – he is an honourable if subordinate subject in the monarchical-seigniorial apparatus. My point is that his staging of the ways in which literary strategies rewrite history from individual points of view may be viewed as a bid for artistic and social legitimacy, which will be strengthened in the climax and denouement of the play.

The broad lessons of Isabel's ingenious self-defense will not be lost on her father. I say ingenious because, after her father reconsiders his desire to kill her, Isabel turns to the audience in an aside and says: 'My goodness, this is either prudence or cunning' [Fortuna mía, / o mucha cordura, o mucha / cautela es ésta] (Act 3, vv. 296–8) (note the reappearance of *Fortuna*). This is a very interesting and revealing comment on her father's words and behaviour, as *cordura* means prudence, while *cautela* can refer to prudence and caution, or artfulness and cunning.[9] Let us not forget that she also used *cautela* when referring to the hidden designs of the captain. Isabel's aside marks off a space of indetermination between the literal meaning of words and their practical worldliness vis à vis the ritual performance. Isabel is at once the powerless object of a familial conflict between Don Álvaro, her brother, and her father, and a prudent and artful actor who interpellates other readers and spectators into a particular way of interpreting her tragedy. Just as she earlier obliged Don Lope to give her a sign of his respect and love – the diamond *venera* with which the noble and the peasant girl are joined in a common bond of affection, as opposed to duty – she now obliges Crespo to free her from responsibility in his dishonour and to take action to restore her name. In each case, she exploits a dynamic that limits her own movement in order to position herself advantageously as both link and obligation. This sense of a calculated and strategic practice goes a long way towards explaining the behaviour of Crespo himself.

Literary Practice in Modernity

Like his daughter, Pedro Crespo will resolve his own dilemma by writing an emblematic spectacle in which his intentions are disguised and his personal agenda for vengeance abstracted into a ritualized performance of justice. In this performance, the dead body of the captain becomes infused with the presence of real power, i.e., the consent of the king. In '"Hablan poco y dicen mucho": The Function of Discovery Scenes in the Drama of Tirso de Molina,' Cull provides a platform for appreciating the iconic residue at work in the emblem as well as important keys for understanding how the doctrine of the real presence of the sacramental body is translated into the representational matrix of the *comedia*: 'The culminating moment of many Golden-Age dramas occurred, in fact, in one of these discovery scenes or "appearances" (*apariencias*), often (but not exclusively) towards the end of the play. A curtain was drawn to reveal a marvelous scene in one of the niches at the back of the stage, or an appearance of great visual impact was lowered into view by means of stage machinery. The combination of striking visual motifs (*pictura*) with commentary in the form of dramatic dialogue (*subscription*) imitated the structure of the emblem … These scenes, designed to provoke *admiratio* in the spectators, often embodied the play's central message, or moral' ('Hablan' 620). Egginton draws on this close relationship between sacred and secular drama in his concept of 'the crypt,' which he defines as a 'full space' on the modern theatrical stage where the constant transformations and transmutations made possible by the virtual space of modern perspective come to a halt. The crypt responds to the need of the audience to feel 'that one is in the presence, at last, of the real thing' (*How the World* 111).[10] The crypt, thus, is where the emblem, medieval allegories of presence, religious and political spectacles, and the *comedia* converge. Walter Benjamin was the first to point out the privileged role played by the corpse in emblematics and baroque allegory in general. We would do well to keep in mind, however, that for Benjamin the baroque corpse and its allegorical monumentalization do not bring about the effect of historical and semiotic presence but rather a sense of irremediable loss, melancholy, even nostalgia for something that was present but which is now absent. Thus, although the discovery of the corpse on the stage generally functions to bring the deceptive and fragmented movement of characters around and through the honour code to a halt, the sense of closure it imposes is always partial, problematic, and susceptible to the return of violence and further fragmentation.

Felipe II's *apariencia* on stage configures yet another emblematic moment in the *comedia*, in which the king embodies the presence of a transcendental deus ex machina who restores order by invoking a superior idea of what Parker has called 'poetic justice.'[11] In this case, however, the king is immediately stripped of his power to see and act when Crespo arrests his regal hand within a universal rhetoric of justice. Goaded by Don Lope, the king attempts to corner the peasant, who should be trembling at the physical presence of royal power. Like his daughter before him, Crespo anticipates the doubts and concerns of the king and deftly shifts the focus of the inquiry away from the way in which his own hand has surreptitiously guided events, and toward the heinousness of the crime, which is methodically and ritualistically opposed to the mayor's account of his measured application of due process.

> FELIPE II: And what excuse do you give me?
> CRESPO: This process, in which the crime is proven, deserving of death for having kidnapped a young lady, raped her in a deserted spot, and not wanting to marry her after her father begged him peaceably.
> DON LOPE: This is the mayor, and he is her father.
> CRESPO: None of that matters in such a case; because if a stranger came to plead, would justice not have to be done? Yes. So why should I not do the same for my daughter as I would for anyone else? Besides which, since I have imprisoned my own son, it's established that I would not listen to my daughter, as the blood is the same. See for yourselves if the prosecution is well done; look to see if there is anyone who says I have committed any malfeasance in the matter, if I have forced some witness, if there is anything written other than what I have said, and then put me to death.

[FELIPE II: ¿Y qué disculpa me dais?
CRESPO: Este proceso, en que bien
probado el delito está,
digno de muerte por ser
una doncella robar,
forzarla en un despoblado,
y no quererse casar
con ella, habiendo su padre
rogádole con la paz.
DON LOPE: Éste es el alcalde, y es
su padre.
CRESPO: No importa en tal
caso; porque, si un extraño
se viniera a querellar,
¿no había de hacer justicia?
Sí. ¿Pues qué más se me da
hacer por mi hija lo mismo
que hiciera por los demás?
Fuera de que, como he preso
un hijo mío, es verdad
que no escuchara a mi hija,
pues era la sangre igual.

Mírese, si está bien hecha
la causa; miren, si hay
quien diga que yo haya hecho
en ella alguna maldad,
si he inducido algún testigo,
si está algo escrito demás
de lo que he dicho, y entonces
me den muerte.] (Act 3, vv. 866–94)

When the king demands a reason (*disculpa*) for Crespo's refusal to obey Don Lope's orders, Crespo responds with 'this process.' In other words, there is no discrete, identifiable reason for his intransigence; rather, the entire *modus operandi* of the new mayor becomes his excuse and, eventually, his defense. By bringing the king's gaze away from his transgression and redirecting it towards his juridical process, Crespo converts the violent act of execution into a text, which the king should read in light of Crespo's objective presentation of the case. At the end of his declamation, Crespo moves even more forcefully into the literary republic by shifting the terms of his performance to writing: 'if there is anything *written* other than what I have said' (my emphasis). Like Isabel, he uses his knowledge of history to disarm and defy the king and his advisor, all the while insisting that he is placing himself under their power. As such, the king's authority no longer issues from his 'embodiment of regality' but must contend with an empirical and specific historical circumstance, of which he has no direct knowledge, as well as Crespo's 'more abstract calculation of power,' one rooted in the manipulation of language (see Pfeiffer, 'Dimensions of Literature' 58). Like Isabel, Crespo depersonalizes the crime by speaking as a detached observer and subsequently converting Álvaro's actions into an archetypal, emblematic example of transgression, not against Pedro Crespo but rather against a/the Father.

The king sanctions the means by which Crespo has investigated and substantiated the case. Nevertheless, the peasant's chronicle of his process is not verifiable in any absolute sense; thus the king cannot sanction the ends (the imprisonment of Don Álvaro), and so he orders the matter be handled by his own judicial body. Crespo has anticipated this attempt by the king to wield his absolute juridical prerogative. In fact, the mayor's whole plan is meaningless without this knowledge of how legal questions function at an institutional level. The fragmentation and skepticism produced by the unequal co-existence of a military court that answers only to its own legal prerogatives and a provincial space that attempts to do the same, both ostensibly yoked under a monarchy that seldom leaves the confines of the Court, are crystallized in Felipe II's rebuttal to Crespo's performance: 'Allá hay justicia.'[12] For Pedro Crespo and his rural family, there is no justice here in Zalamea.

It is at this moment that Crespo discovers the text of his investigation and judgment by handing over the 'prisoner' to the king. Felipe II is completely amazed by the gruesome spectacle of his captain's garroted body; more to the point, he is suddenly at a loss to make sense of the entire situation, which is, after all, his primary role in the play – and the empire. He attempts to take control with the rhetorical question 'How dare you?' [¿cómo así os atrevisteis?] (Act 3, vv. 900–1); but Crespo strategically takes the question literally rather than acquiesce to the power of the king. As the grim reality of Álvaro's dead body sets in, Crespo levels the playing field through an astute use of mimicry, referring to himself as the exclusive seat of legal justice in the territory, just as Felipe II is the only seat of justice in the imperial realm. To the king's assertion that there is justice 'over there,' Crespo retorts that there is adequate justice 'right here'! Through this invocation of competing and immobile centres of juridical practice, Crespo breaks the organicist link between the king, legal discourse, and the exercise of State-sanctioned violence. There are two possible solutions to this deadlock: either the king must punish Crespo and accept the juridical fragmentation of the empire and his monarchical body; or he must grant a previously excluded subject the power to act on his behalf according to his own understanding of the rules. In the second case, juridical language becomes at once universal and contingent, as its conversion into a practice, as opposed to a divine right, allows properly educated subjects to wield its language and power according to their personal objectives. The king, in effect, becomes subject to the universality of his own language. In the words of Louis Marin, 'if the monarch is absolute only in the official portrait that his subjects draw of him and that they present him in order to draw from him what they desire and what he alone possesses, if the king is only King in his portrait and in his secrecy … then this conjunction of portrait and secrecy[,] which is that of infinite representation and absolute power[,] signifies that the king in his portrait … is an empty monument' (238). Marin's point is that the moment the bodily presence of the king becomes deterritorialized in his representation is the moment he becomes subject to the leveling effect we have seen with respect to the visual image. He becomes one more image, or signifier, in an emergent symbolic economy. In this case, since Felipe II cannot fathom the relationship between the dead body (*pictura*) and the soul (*inscriptio*) of Crespo's *empresa,* he turns to the authority of the impresario for commentary, thus recognizing that there are limits to the king's knowledge of his realm. Fortunately for Crespo, this vacillation allows him to emphasize yet again the abstract and universal nature of the process and its execution. In this instance, however, he frames his act within a discourse of obedience to the king:

> All of your justice is no more than one body; if it has *many hands,* tell me, what does it matter if I kill this man that another would kill all the same? And what does it matter to err in minor things when the rest are on the mark?
>
> [Toda la justicia vuestra
> es sólo un cuerpo no más;
> si éste tiene *muchas manos,*
> decid, ¿qué más se me da
> matar con aquesta un hombre
> que esta otra había de matar?
> Y ¿qué importa errar lo menos,
> quien acertó lo demás?] (Act 3, vv. 937–46; my emphasis)

After previously reining in the king's hand with a discourse of universal justice, and then dividing the royal realm into distinct legal territories, Crespo now rearticulates the fragmented political body by turning himself and Don Lope into equally prudent and efficacious hands, equal extensions of a much larger corporate body whose soul is the nascent nation-state. In the end, Crespo's rhetorically interrogative *inscriptio* artfully places the responsibility for a correct reading of his emblem into the hands of a reader whom he has just disarmed: 'And what does it matter to err in minor things when the rest are on the mark?' It is now Crespo who wields the power of the rhetorical question.

At this point, the 'execution' moves from being the end of Crespo's actions to the means by which a universally just end is achieved. It has no actual meaning in and of itself; it is, rather, a strategic action of self-defense that emblematizes the entire juridical process. The fact that the king takes ownership over the device, and subsequently shares in the collective responsibility for Crespo's violent action, is demonstrated by his translation of Pedro Crespo's question into an affirmation of his own power: 'Don Lope, what's done is done, the death was well deserved: it does not matter to err in minor things when the rest are on the mark' [Don Lope, aquesto ya es hecho, / bien dada la muerte está: / no importa errar lo menos / quien acertó lo demás] (Act 3, vv. 937–46). In initiating his self-defense by mimicking the king's words back to him, Crespo has turned the tables: the king now mimics him.

Conclusion

Due to Pedro Crespo's manifest rage and guile, his violence and artfulness, there is no escaping the fact that Zalamea's newly appointed mayor uses his *fronterizo* power and discursive cunning to launch and legitimize a personal *empresa* of vigilante justice. We have seen this conversion of the personal *empresa* into an institutional *emblema* throughout this study, but in Calderón's play the resonance of this rhetorical manipulation is distinct, because the impetus for its movement and dissemination comes from a marginal subject, which creates a different kind of problem as far as reception is concerned. Due to the allegorical frame constructed around Don Álvaro's perverse crime, his arrogant refusal to accept that he has committed any kind of crime, and his rejection of Crespo's humble offer of Isabel's hand, the audience is not given the opportunity to condemn the peasant's actions in any substantive way. Put another way, any condemnation of Crespo's actions and/or denial of his literary and juridical legitimacy would first require the spectator to identify with the Other. Since the maximum representative of the monarchical-seigniorial elite recognizes Crespo's legitimacy, however haltingly, the aristocratic subject intent on perpetuating a blood-based ideology finds himself in the position of antagonist, as is the case in the *Poema del Cid* when the Infantes de Carrión are brought to the court of Alfonso VI to answer for their 'crimes' against Doña Elvira and Doña Sol. This does not mean, of course, that aristocratic spectators would accept the outcome of the play, nor that Calderón is subverting monarchical legitimacy. It is important to keep these different receptive dispositions in view when analysing the possible ideological impact of the play. Crespo is both the one – an honourable liege who listens, obeys, and is honoured for his subservience to the king – and the Other – a desiring and guilty subject who nevertheless 'gets away with it' by appropriating and rewriting juridical language. Given the long tradition of self-representation by playwrights through their pastoral characters, e.g., Juan del Encina, Lope de Vega, it is not inconceivable that Calderón is channeling his social and cultural aspirations through the small town mayor. It is my view that the poet redeems his literary practice as well as monarchical legitimacy by framing the king's gaze in a way that favours Crespo's performance with the creation of an independent yet legitimate space on the margins, but ultimately inside of, the absolutist court for those literary subjects who learn to dominate the discourses of empire.

The ambivalence of this solution should inform our consideration of the king's acceptance of Crespo's actions. Neither character can be said to embody their discourse in any substantial way. Both are artful, skeptical, and ultimately independent of the words and actions they speak and perform within the traditional forms of the legal discourse they wield. Roy Rappaport explains: 'First, to say that the performer accepts the authority of a liturgical order in performing it is not to say that he is necessarily doing anything very grave … Second, and more important, "acceptance" is not synonymous with belief. Belief I take to be some sort of inward state knowable subjectively, if at all. Acceptance, in contrast, is not a private state but a *public act*, visible to both the witness and the performer himself. Acceptance not only is not belief. It does not even imply belief' (186). The king and his subjects move in the space of modern theatricality among other subjects whose 'true' designs are simultaneously masked and communicated by their opaque gestures. As a result, the uneasy sense of closure that characterizes a symbolic field concerned with historical action, as opposed to an imaginative field of ideal contemplation, speaks to Calderón's consciousness of the irrecoverable loss that constitutes modernity and which lurks at the centre of ideological identification. For this very reason we cannot speak of the king as a deus ex machina in Calderonian theatre. Calderón's kings rarely impose order on the theatrical chaos in which they move; to the contrary, the most we ever find is diffident consent and uneasy compromise.

Still tied in many ways to nineteenth-century, romantic notions regarding heroism and victimization, modern criticism has had trouble reconciling such a complex and compromised understanding of human subjectivity and ideology. A well-known essay that explores the compromised world of honour in this play is Dunn's 'Honour and the Christian Background in Calderón.' Dunn begins his study with the following observation: 'If private vengeance were in fact cloaked in retributive justice, it is difficult to see how this play could escape the charge of being "fundamentally immoral"' ('Honour' 75). He goes on to argue that honour in Calderón constitutes a religion in and of itself that competes with and at times supersedes Christian faith: 'In short, *honor* as we see it in these plays entails a structure of ideas, ritual and symbolism which parodies the Christian pattern at each of these points. Honour's pattern and the Christian pattern cannot co-exist, because honour unbinds the destructive forces in nature and the human psyche which Christianity reconciles' ('Honour' 89). Put another way, the formal similarities between the divine punishment of *Mal Genio* and Pedro Crespo's ritual (and parodic?) execution of justice mark the latter's expression of honour and its dialectic of offence and vengeance as a 'perverse' reflection of perfect Christian unity.

If we were talking about two attempts to present perfectly integrated and harmonious worlds that sink their roots into a metaphysical doctrine of presence, then Dunn's thesis would probably hold. However, as we have seen with the emblem, in the baroque, the word itself becomes a stain that marks the fallen and historical existence of humankind. Similarly, honour, as ideology and not as an inalienable possession, must simultaneously encourage and contain the intransigent Otherness of subjects, manifested in their ideal desire for a social recognition not necessarily reflected by their membership in a traditional social caste. The only way for honour to become disseminated without destabilizing institutions of power is to follow what Calderón models on the stage: allow a limited and limiting space for subjects to construct their relationship with honour. In Sánchez's words, 'the society reinforces the subordination of social conduct to monarchical authority while assuming the need for a more calculated strategy for the linguistic expression of the person's goals' (*Early Bourgeois Literature* 104). Bell calls this dynamic redemptive hegemony. The subject consents to honour's social expediency while resisting its absolute pull on his freedom to act.

Pedro Crespo is not the dramatic vehicle for a possible subversion of the monarchical-seigniorial organization of honour. Nor does he reflect a proto-democratic impulse in seventeenth-century Spanish society. Rather, honour *qua 'patrimonio del alma'* is a necessary product of and condition for the consolidation and expansion of early modern ideologies of social organization and political power. Domingo Ynduráin notes that Crespo's actions demonstrate his obedience rather than his rebellion: 'a son has gone to the militia, the daughter to the

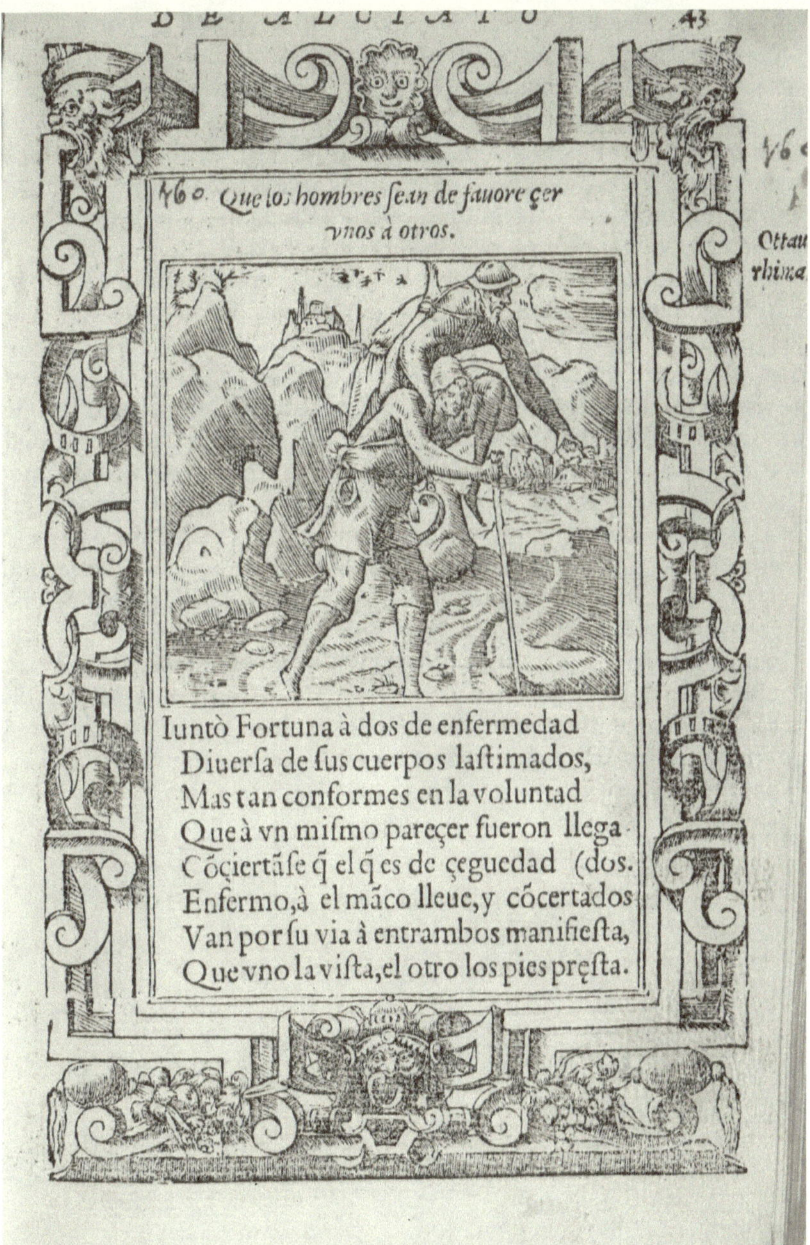

DE ALCIATO 43

Que los hombres ſean de fauoreçer vnos à otros.

Iuntò Fortuna à dos de enfermedad
Diuerſa de ſus cuerpos laſtimados,
Mas tan conformes en la voluntad
Que à vn miſmo pareçer fueron llega-
Cōçiertāſe q̄ el q̄ es de çeguedad (dos.
Enfermo, à el mãco lleue, y cōcertados
Van por ſu via à entrambos manifieſta,
Que vno la viſta, el otro los pies pręſta.

Figure 8 'Mutuum auxilium,' in Andrea Alciato, *Emblemas* (1549), 203

church ... in effect, P. Crespo is an admirable model' ('*El alcalde*' 311). More importantly, by successfully reifying his own honour from a subservient position he creates an ideological link with all those subjects marginalized by their material exclusion from social privilege and political power by configuring a 'less equal' but legitimate space for social practice. In this space, the meaning of his juridical text is much less important than what it does, just as the king's true feelings are immaterial where his nod of consent is concerned.

By way of a conclusion, allow me to offer an emblem from Alciato in which the peasant 'bestia de carga' is translated into a more ambivalent image. In the *pictura,* a blind man carries a lame man on his shoulders; the motto reads, 'Men should help each other' [Que los hombres se an de favorecer unos a otros]; the *subscriptio* elaborates, 'Fortune brought together two men with diverse maladies in their wounded bodies, but so similar in their will that they came to seem the same' [Juntó Fortuna a dos de enfermedad / Diversa de sus cuerpos lastimados, / Mas tan conformes en la voluntad / Que a un mismo parecer fueron llegados] (emblem 160, p. 203). As the army leaves Zalamea, Crespo's son Juan takes charge of Don Lope's *litera,* resituating the emblem as well as its commentary, which now might read: 'Fortune brought together two men of diverse wills, but so joined in the body (politic) that they came to seem the same' [Juntó Fortuna a dos de voluntad / Diversa de su honor lastimados, / Mas tan conformes en el cuerpo / Que a un mismo parecer fueron llegados] (figure 8).

PART THREE

Bodies and Signs

6 A Ritual Practice for Modernity: Baltasar Gracián's Organized Body of Taste

> Emblems, hieroglyphics, fables, devices, are the precious jewels in the gold of subtle invention.
>
> [Los emblemas, jeroglíficos, apólogos, empresas, son la pedrería preciosa al oro del fino discurrir.]
>
> Gracián, *Agudeza y arte de ingenio*

In his 2002 tour de force essay on the Hispanic baroque, *Barroco*, Fernando R. de la Flor introduces Juan de Borja's emblem *Hominem te esse cogita* (think that you are [only] a man) as evidence of a Hispanic counter-proposal to the Cartesian revolution instantiated by Descartes's emblematic motto for the modern subject: *Cogito ergo sum*. An emblematic reading in its own right, the Spanish scholar's lengthy dissertation on the historiographical commonplace of Spain's idiosyncratic relationship with European modernity deploys Borja's emblem as both point of departure and prolepsis for his definition of a specifically Hispanic definition of baroque culture. Charting an innovative philosophical course, R. de la Flor goes to great lengths to excavate what he sees as the (self-) destructive nihilism at the heart of Counter Reformation efforts to close off the Spanish empire from the progressive and instrumental definition of reason ostensibly at the heart of Descartes's attempt to define and legitimize the individual subject's encounter with and analysis of the real.

At the heart of R. de la Flor's desire to identify a specifically Spanish relationship with modernity – against that same modernity – is a rejection of Maravall's more instrumentalist definition of the Spanish baroque: 'I believe that the peculiarity of this hispanic baroque culture resides, precisely, in what Maravall denies from the beginning: that is, in the manifest capacity of its expressive system to move in the opposite direction to any established ends; in its ability to deconstruct and pervert, in the first place, that which we may think to be class interests, which in the end govern and to which paradoxically it is also subject, thus proclaiming a double adherence' (*Barroco* 19). R. de la Flor's face-to-the-wind navigation of Spanish mysticism, skeptical philosophy, and what he terms Calderón's 'theatre of cruelty' – a moniker which ironically places the Spanish playwright in close relation to Shakespeare – finally arrives at the anti-Cartesian summary of his reading of the Spanish baroque through Borja's emblem of *desengaño*: '[Borja] manages to give a precise body to a Counter Reformation *ethos*, profoundly contrary to what is revealed to be the growing material and process of self-sufficient individuation, attached to the expansive logic of capitalism. An axiom, of course, which we could certainly not call foundational, rather, to the contrary, profoundly delegitimizing, since above all it introduces the concept of contingency and decay, that which is precisely opposed to what, I'll say it once more, the proud Cartesian *cogito* and the *sum* and the *e*[r]*go* erect' (50). Here, the quixotic yet still modern drive of the Spanish baroque is produced in the very effort to seal Spain off from modernity, to override material and social decay through the creation of what R. de la Flor in another place calls the 'metaphysical peninsula.'[1] His thesis argues that the insistent and cruel ironization of the real – which I understand in this instance to be a phenomenological positing of historical or social reality – reduces social and economic hierarchies to dust and thereby open to derision. In this sense, the 'anarchical' tendencies of Hispanic baroque nihilism are seen to offer a perverse reflection of Cartesian scientific rationalism: where Descartes's indicative *cogito* rejects the neo-scholastic desubstantialization of the subject, Borja's imperative *cogita* reduces all hierarchical structures to the same nothingness at the heart of the confessional subject, thus preparing the ground for the liberating drive of modernity.

There are several problems with this characterization of the Spanish baroque, the most intractable of which arises from what has unfortunately become a commonplace and thus somewhat of a self-fulfilling prophecy of historiographical studies of Spain: the oft-lamented and/or celebrated difference as regards Spain's relationship to Europe. Another fissure in R. de la Flor's argument is the simplistic and at the same time very modern understanding of Descartes's place in modernity. As Lyle Massey points out, Descartes's attempts to legitimize an empirical approach to natural philosophy are plagued by the same interdictions arising from the finitude and fallibility of human faculties and bodies that R. de la Flor associates with a Counter Reformation understanding of human (un)reason. Jacques Lezra reminds us that most commentators of Descartes since Etienne Gilson's original thesis recognize the formal and substantial debt of the *Meditations* to Ignatius's *Spiritual Exercises*: 'Imagined as an exercise analogous to Descartes's own represented experience, a reading of the *Meditations* would, then, link its epistemology to a phenomenology of perception that leads from error or "difficulty" to the truth by stages or by exercises – one reading after the next, marking in the margin where one has hesitated' (89). Once Descartes is resituated in an early modern, as opposed to late modern, context, we are able to see that it is not the Spanish baroque which offers a perverse or deformed reflection of Cartesian rationalism; rather, it is Descartes who (unconsciously) offers a deformed reflection of religious interdictions on scientific rationalism.

I have begun this chapter with R. de la Flor's emblematic reading of Descartes through Borja's emblem for a number of reasons: in the first place, unlike previous chapters, my discussion of Gracián is not strictly based on his use of emblems but rather seeks to imitate R. de la Flor's method in that the emblematic mode will serve as a point of departure and reference for a discussion that is more theoretical than philological; and in the second, like R. de la Flor, the subject of the following discussion is modernity. However, rather than focus on what he terms the 'negative ontology' which arises from the tortured artistic and literary jousts and expressions of the Spanish baroque, I will argue that Gracián's modernity finds empowerment in the very nihilism which, for R. de la Flor, hobbles Spain's movement into the modern world.

Although he never produced what we would call an emblem book, no texts are more emblematic of the baroque, courtly subject of representation than those penned under the name of Lorenzo Gracián, Baltasar Gracián's unconvincingly pseudonymous 'brother.' Jesuit priest, popular preacher, confessor of nobles, alternately favoured and chastised by his own religious order, Gracián's aesthetic and philosophical crystallizations embody the culminating moment of the baroque taste for allusive, witty, conceptual, and difficult verbal gymnastics. Emblem scholars gravitate towards *El oráculo manual y arte de pruden-*

cia, *Agudeza y arte de ingenio*, and *El criticón* much like adepts are driven to perform the most challenging rites of passage, as Gracián's navigation of aesthetic, philosophical, and courtly arenas of theory and practice allow for the mapping of the broad scope of emblematic-allegorical practices in early modern Spain.

Karl Selig has suggested that Gracián's interest in emblems can be traced to his association with the literary circle assembled and maintained by the Aragonese aristocrat Don Vicencio Juan de Lastanosa, whose vast library included at least fifty emblem books ('Gracián'). In broader cultural terms, Sagrario López reminds us that emblem reading and composition were also an important part of the intellectual and rhetorical apprenticeship of Jesuits in the sixteenth and seventeenth centuries.[2] Whether for these reasons, or due to the fact that early modernity is, as Russell argues, the 'age of the emblem,' emblems and emblematic modes of communication are at the centre of Gracián's aesthetic program for the discrete persona of the court. Alciato's emblems appear no less than sixteen times in *Agudeza y arte de ingenio*, but it is in Gracián's assemblage of a genealogy of writers of 'philosophical truths' where emblematics takes its proper place at the centre of baroque aesthetics:[3]

> All wise men took aim at the same target of philosophical truth, although by different paths of invention and wit. Homer with his *Epics*, Aesop with his *Fables*, Seneca with his *Sentences*, Ovid with his *Metamorphosis*, Juvenal with his *Satires*, Alciato with his *Emblems*, Erasmus with his *Adages*, Bocalino with his *Allegories* and the prince Don Juan Manuel with his *Stories*. Semblance is the foundation of all feigned invention, and the translation of falseness into truth is the soul of this wit.[4]

> [A un mismo blanco de la filosófica verdad, asestaron todos los sabios, aunque por diferentes rumbos de la invención y agudeza. Homero con sus *Epopeyas*, Esopo con sus *Fábulas*, Séneca con sus *Sentencias*, Ovidio con sus *Metamorfosis*, Juvenal con sus *Sátiras*, Alciato con sus *Emblemas*, Erasmo con sus *Refranes*, el Bocalino con sus *Alegorías* y el príncipe don Juan Manuel con sus *Cuentos*. La semejanza es el fundamento de toda la invención fingida, y la traslación de lo mentido a lo verdadero es el alma de esta agudeza.] (425)

There is much that could and should be said about this innovative assemblage of a literary and cultural canon, which establishes new meanings and relationships between widely varying aesthetic, moral, and philosophical enterprises around the concept of philosophical truth. I will limit my focus to two issues. The first is the way in which aesthetics and philosophy are held to be inextricably related, an early modern commonplace which, nevertheless, is too often missed by those modern critics who seek to bracket off literary creation from social or 'more properly' theoretical spheres of practice. As Sánchez points out, any separation of aesthetics or philosophy from the socio-ontological predicament of artists and thinkers in modernity obfuscates important aspects of symbolic practice and reception: 'A literary culture ... provides a distinctive intellectual practice for the individuals who see themselves as members of a *república*, an exchange of art and artifice, and a competition of virtuous – that is profitable – conduct' (*Early Bourgeois Literature* 117). The second issue concerns the fact that what all of these genres have in common is the oblique and connotative manner in which they assemble and communicate their truths. By taking an indirect, 'literary' position with regard to the validity of discourse in general, Gracián implicitly and peremptorily invalidates the incipient modern split between the referential discourses of science and the aesthetic world of the imagination. All discourse falls under the rubric of what he terms 'ficciones' in some places and 'mentiras' in others, as he situates aesthetic-philosophical practice at the centre of 'a system of moral and epistemological rigour ... Truth, in short, becomes a function of learned judgment, not of the material itself, which in time seems to owe even its existence to the [literary subject]' (Said, *Orientalism* 67). Due to the self-conscious way in which they foreground their fictional status, allegories, epics, maxims, parables, mythological metamorphoses, and emblems unmask and problematize the unstable and tenuous relationship between language, history, truth, and subjectivity. In Massey's words, 'it is in the moment when skeptical doubt is strongest and most overwhelming that a glimpse of the truth or certainty of being is possible' (1163). The religious explanation for this philosophical predicament is based on a universal notion of 'theological guilt' (Buck-Morss 172); nevertheless, Gracián, like Calderón, seems to take advantage of this epistemological instability in order to open up a space of indeterminacy for the strategic intervention of the literary subject.

What makes Gracián's writing the epitome of emblematic wit thus also signals a limit at which the emblem's evocation of presence and claims to truth crash to earth in the dust of their own signifying apparatuses; and yet this 'crisis of representation' is precisely where the literary subject finds its freedom and power. In Gracián, and analogous to Gurd's notion of radical philology, 'the specificity of ancient literature is not based on any geographical, chronological, or linguistic delimitation but rather on a particular relationship with the modernity that possesses, produces, and invokes antiquity endlessly in its own processes of self-definition' (34). It is the subject of representation who now collects accumulated 'knowledge' and places it into circulation for his own ends. In *El Criticón*, the character *el Discreto* shows off his library to Andrenio and Critilo and declares: 'What dish is more delicious to the taste of the wise man than a refined museum, where the understanding is amused, the memory enriched and the will nourished, the heart opened and the spirit satisfied?' [¿Qué convite más delicioso para el gusto de un discreto como un culto museo, donde se recrea el entendimiento, se enriqueze la memoria, y se alimenta la voluntad, se dilata el coraçón y el espíritu se satisfaze?] (II, 4.356). Writing is the nourishment and lifeblood of the modern *persona*, and its meanings, functions and value are performatively determined through its circulation on the stage of the absolutist court.

Where Calderón's *auto sacramental* deploys the emblem in an attempt to preserve the residual sense of presence suggested by iconic or hieroglyphic symbols, in Gracián we touch the opposite pole, according to Russell's understanding of emblematics as a 'transitional form between the reign of the natural sign, and the coming dominance of the arbitrariness of language' (*Emblematic Structures* 242). In spite of the efforts of Borja and Horozco y Covarrubias to contain the practices and functions of emblematic literature, the changeable nature of the troublesome relationship between the figural body and discursive soul evolves in the baroque into a seeming chaos of ever expanding multiplicity. Neither the 'triplex' form nor the emblem's prominence within the Jesuit program of moral education provides an adequate structure with which to contain its heterogeneity according to either aesthetic or ideological frameworks. A quick survey of Spanish emblem books shows that the visual image is not regarded as necessary to the recognition of emblematic tropes; it is the allusion to images and concepts that drives emblematic thought, which weakens the iconicity of emblematic modes even further. Gracián's oeuvre is exemplary in this sense, as one gets the impression that an actual visual image would unnecessarily restrain his flights of allegorical invention. What is needed in a study of the emblem, then, is a flexible notion of genre in general, one capable of dealing with the contingencies and textual flux we have seen to this point. Gumbrecht suggests we define genres as institutions: 'a conception of genre based on the theory of institutions implies the assumption that the genesis, stabilization, modification, and dissolution of genres are mainly (not exclusively, to be sure, but all the same) dependent on their functions' (*Making Sense* 43). We have just seen Gracián create a genre of allegorical literature by framing a heterogeneous body of texts according to the concept of philosophical truth. In the following discussion, we will see that the Jesuit thinker is much more ambitious than that, as he ties all discursive production to the emergent institution of taste.

Analogous to what we have witnessed in *El alcalde*, Gracián redirects a share of the signifying supplement of emblematic modes from the symbolic augmentation of the Counter Reformation Church and the absolutist State toward individual success (*éxito*), an emergent phenomenon that Sánchez has similarly called 'an ontological supplement' ('Cultura' 277). In ritual discourse this surplus of meaning is perceived as issuing from another place to which the ritual performance allows the participant temporary access: the aura of the hieroglyphic is divinely inspired; the presence of God comes to infuse the host through the ritual dramatization of the Eucharist, etc. This supplement is both theorized and experienced as the transubstantiation of an Other, more permanent and universal (extensive) body into the holy host, which then penetrates the bodies of the participants in the sacred dramatization of the Eucharist. As I stated in chapter 4, in the post-Trent world, this sacrament becomes the only legitimate method for evoking and experiencing the real presence of an otherwise irremediably absent God.

Gracián reveals his modernity when he displaces the trope of taste as it relates to eucharistic transubstantiation and redirects it towards the social performance of aesthetic taste, deterritorializing, in effect, the ritual 'surplus.' In Discurso XXIII in *Agudeza y arte de ingenio*, titled 'On paradoxical wit,' Gracián introduces a short citation from his brother Felipe which draws a curious but explicit analogy between the sacred *manjar* of the Eucharist and the notion of aesthetic taste: 'It had (this ingenious priest says) this Eucharistic dish had [sic] all the flavors (*gustos*), and pleasures that could be desired; it seems, that it only lacked that great delight, which is to be stolen' [Tenía (dice este ingenioso padre) tenía este manjar Eucarístico todos los gustos, y delicias que se podían desear; sólo parece, que le faltaba aquel sainete que lo es grande, del ser hurtado] (220). The same trope appears in Meditación XL of *El comulgatorio*: 'Buy it, good soul, at any price, and eat it like bread you have purchased, which is more savory, or as if you had *stolen* it, which is sweeter' [Cómprale, alma, por cualquier precio, y cómele como pan comprado, que es más sabroso, o como *hurtado*, que es más dulce] (156; my emphasis).[5] Gracián is not suggesting that the Eucharist itself is lacking anything in its perfection, but rather that the imperfect taste of man is incapable of completely enjoying this sacred dish without adding something to it. And what is added corresponds to man's ontological and epistemological shortcomings, which converts a perfect morsel into something imperfect, or incomplete, yet infinitely more satisfying to an imperfect and incomplete palate. In an imperfect microcosm, taste, even transubstantiated taste, must be moved by a transgressive – or pathological – void, or slip, which functions as a mysterious addition. By taking an uncompromising stance on the theological truth of man's fall from grace, the Jesuit thinker reformulates important aspects of emblematic presence in an effort to configure an alternate, ritual body of power, one based not on presence but on absence, not on surplus but on lack.

The theological-philosophical keystone of Gracián's relentless attack on presence and its invocation of ontological and epistemological certitude is the notion of *desengaño*. I have argued, as have scholars and critics such as Maravall and J.C. Rodríguez, that *desengaño* is a transitional ideology that seeks to mediate the movement between the residual, univocal cosmological hierarchies of the Middle Ages and the socio-political, religious, and artistic transformations that accompany the onset of modernity. Due to its iconic residue as well as its allegorical malleability, the emblem is situated at the nexus of these conflictive encounters between competing matrices of symbolic activity. In Juan de Borja, the emblem is deployed in an effort to forestall all historical transformation by underlining the evanescent nature of temporal existence, a tactic that unveils the tendency of Counter Reformation ideology to, in R. de la Flor's words, 'annihilate' all human endeavors (*Barroco* 46–76). What better way to redeem the status quo than by characterizing all human initiatives and the changes they imply as a willful move away from the most perfect model of society? In Borja and Horozco, the meaning of a past conjured up by divinely inspired hieroglyphics is fixed – de-radicalized – by suturing the signifying surplus of these natural signs within a baroque *fábrica* of allegorical composition. Such a move contains, castrates as it were, humanist attempts to destabilize Scholastic and/or neo-Scholastic edifices of meaning by wrenching ancient pagan and Christian symbols out of their medieval allegories and rehistoricizing them through ingenious philological explorations and recontextualizations. In *desengaño*, the human condition is portrayed as constitutively finite, condemned by and limited to its temporal-corporeal nothingness: in essence, its fallen condition is translated into insuperable ontological and epistemological limitations which terrify and paralyze what R. de la Flor calls the confessional subject. A closer look at the allegorical practices of Spanish emblematists reveals, however, that their attempts to contain the flux of language and meaning are materially communicated through these same early modern philological practices and, thus, constitutively precarious.

Recognizing the active role of the writer in constructing and maintaining these symbolic edifices, Gracián seems to ask: What if this human lack were regarded in a different way, and instead of a sign of absolute interdiction, it suddenly appeared as a positive possibility? What if the very validity of human activity – political, artistic, and historical – were seen to arise from its categorically immanent condition? The basic premise of *desengaño* concerning the imperfection and finitude of mundane existence would still hold, but a change in perspective would change the meaning of, precisely, everything. In *Organs without Bodies*, Žižek describes Kant's 'transcendental turn' in the following way: 'In the standard Leibnizian ontology, we, finite subjects, can act freely *in spite of* our finitude, since freedom is the spark that unites us with the infinite God; in Kant, this finitude, our separation from the Absolute, is the POSITIVE [*sic*] condition of our freedom. In short, the condition of impossibility is the condition of possibility' (43).[6] Žižek's description of the shift from the theological doctrine of free will toward a philosophical paradigm of free intellectual activity provides, in my view, a valid framework within which to consider the works of the last two authors in this study: Gracián and Cervantes. It also provides a compelling platform from which to challenge R. de la Flor's nihilistic reading of the Hispanic baroque. If we replace Leibniz with Descartes, and Kant with Gracián, we encounter a dialectical relationship and historical evolution homologous to the one sketched by Žižek: where Descartes attempts to overcome radical doubt, Gracián moves his subject to take possession of it. I do not mean to suggest that Gracián and Cervantes come to similar conclusions concerning the proper uses of this new freedom; however, both authors do configure positive notions of (wo)man's agency by anchoring ethical activity in modern articulations of the human body. Similar to Žižek's description of Kant's 'folding' of Leibniz against himself, Cervantes and Gracián redeem human activity and knowledge in the face of *desengaño* by making their 'condition of impossibility' the very basis for legitimate practice: 'Human means must strive as if there were no divine means, and the divine as if there were no human ones' [Hanse de procurar los medios humanos como si no huviesse divinos, y los divinos como si no huviesse humanos] (Gracián, *Oráculo* 237). By taking *desengaño* to its logical conclusions, both writers deal a definitive blow to organicist, presence-based notions of social hierarchies and their role in the legitimization of political privilege and power. In the words of Alban Forcione, 'the process of *desengaño* is redirected away from its conventional Christian goals of eliciting the deep terror of the formless and emptying out the illusory substances and structures of the world and simultaneously re-cognized as a paradoxical source of world-affirming energy' ('At the Threshold' 28–9). Rather than lamenting man's negative ontological status, Cervantes and Gracián positively regard reality as a dialogic construction in a constant state of *becoming*.

Corporeal Frames

In order to clearly differentiate between the corporeal reorganizations offered by these two writers, I will deploy distinct concepts of realism to guide my analysis: for Cervantes, I have borrowed the term coined by Bakhtin in his study of the carnivalesque, *grotesque realism*; in the case of Gracián, I will use the term *political realism*, taking my cue from his various allegorical characterizations of truth. The (rhetorical) terrain on which I will compare and contrast these two models is the body, a term that stands in for the iconic matter of emblematic discourse. Both writers privilege images and tropes of a corporeal nature, but where Cervantes, whom I will study in chapter 7, constantly grounds the imaginative and utopian inclinations of his characters in the grotesque body of becoming, Gracián assembles what I call the organized ritual body of taste. My hypothesis is that where Gracián configures a series of machine-like, intellectualized organs of taste designed to tactfully attract, provoke, and manipulate the desire of other subjects in the public representation of the 'hombre con fondos,' Cervantes constantly returns to corporeal matter, what Bakhtin calls the grotesque body of becoming, in order to rescue the body and its organs from the Augustinian soul-body dialectic and, in so doing, redeem individual histories and the truths they hold.

What is striking about Gracián's treatment of the emblematic split between body and soul is the way in which corporeal figures begin to play an ever more central role in what Hayden White might call a 'tropics of taste.' Gracián resolves the dichotomy between figure and discourse, body and soul, by translating bodily organs into political, discursive machines: as Malcolm Read states, 'The solution, inevitably, is to collapse the body into the spirit' (*Visions* 9). Philosophers and critics such as Hans Georg Gadamer and Anthony Cascardi have long recognized and duly analysed this 'passage from sensuous to social body,' as procreative and degustative metaphors become the linguistic and conceptual building blocks for Enlightenment notions of artistic creation and sensibility (see Cascardi, 'Gracián' 257). However, Gracián's writings not only can be used as a springboard towards modernity; they should also be studied for how they achieve the ultimate disembodiment, or dismemberment, of the carnivalesque body of physical enjoyment. By converting the intellect into so many procreative, receptive, penetrating, and penetrated 'organs,' the material bodily excrescence and its organic drives are domesticated, or sublimated, becoming subsystems of an intellectualized machinery. A consideration of Bakhtin's notion of grotesque realism will lead us to a better understanding of Gracián's completely modern notion of political realism, and towards a modernity which reveals its historical tensions and aspirations in the corporeal organization of a machine-like body of power.

Beginning with his description of erudition as a 'banquete de entendimientos' in *El Discreto*, Gracián repeatedly returns to apparently carnivalesque themes of enjoyment (207). *El oráculo manual* serves a 'banquet for wise men' [banquete de sabios] featuring 'sensible dishes' [platos prudenciales] (97), while *Arte de ingenio* presents a wide variety of dishes attuned to the 'variety of tastes for whom they are seasoned' [diversidad de gustos para quienes sazonó] (133); finally, in *El Criticón* the author seeks to deliver a balanced diet, 'always leaving the palate piqued, not overwhelmed' [dexando siempre picado el gusto, no molido] (63). Gracián is of course talking about intellectual enjoyment rather than a carnivalesque privileging of the grotesque body, but in light of the emblem's persistent relegation of the body and, more importantly, pleasure to the lower, vulgar sphere of the senses, this privileging of the creative libido represents a significant departure. The constant invocation of limitations, on the other hand, tends to universalize the fallen condition, converting it into a possibility for reconsidering and subtly altering, not so much the need for social hierarchies and their monopoly on power, but rather the ways, the discourses through which these hierarchies are organized and maintained: 'although he is a prince, if he knows nothing of the things he wants to talk about, or casts his vote in something he neither knows nor understands, he immediately reveals himself to be vulgar and plebian' [que aunque sea un príncipe, en no sabiendo las cosas y quererse meter a hablar de ellas, a dar su voto en lo que no sabe ni entiende, al punto se declara hombre vulgar y plebeyo] (*El Criticón* II, 5.388).

An interesting place to begin this discussion is with the body of Gracián himself. As Benito Pelegrin has so eloquently summarized, the biographical reconstructions of Gracián – the writer and the man – have concerned themselves in large part with the placement of his persona and works inside or outside of Jesuit thought, Spanish nationalism, or Aragonese 'nationalism,' for that matter (*Ethique*). Like an anamorphic portrait, Gracián is seen to embody the best and the worst, the most arcane and most postmodern tendencies of Counter Reformation culture and power. Since he left few clues concerning what we moderns might call his personal views or opinions, biographers have had to reconstruct Gracián's life by following his movements, his appointments, his writings, and the writings of others about him. To quote E. Correa Calderón, 'To provide a copy of the life of Baltasar Gracián, one would have to write a tenuous biography, in gray and darkened tones' (11).

Among the more peculiar primary documents cited by biographers are the assessments of Gracián's humourous imbalances written by the *Society* in its periodic visits to monitor the health and behaviour of its members. I say 'imbalances' because, according to the most widely-read treatise on the subject, Juan Huarte de San Juan's *Examen de ingenios*, every subject is unique in his or her particular *destemplanza*, but all subjects are, in the end, distempered (see Read, *Juan Huarte* 111). Church officials alternately diagnosed Gracián's imbalance as bilious and sanguine, or melancholic and choleric, but the point I would like to make is that these reports reflect and propagate an essentialist understanding of the mind-body connection, yet another residue of organicist discourse.[7] As Read notes, 'Huarte came to formulate a theory of biological determinism which was in essential respects a scientific counterpart of Luther's theology of predestination' (*Juan Huarte* 19). In this sense, the *Examen* faithfully reflects the inherent limitations and contradictions of an organicist understanding of society – and its obsession with notions of blood purity and miscegenation – even as it propagates a 'rational' program for altering the social make-up of the nation.[8] If our knowledge of the world is categorically imperfect due to our fallen nature, if the *ingenio* is condemned to receive imperfect external impulses by means of unstable bodily organs and humours, and if the taste of food depends more on the tongue than on the properties of the food, then how do we propose to change the world?[9] For Huarte, one way to regulate and remedy these imbalances is by focusing on an alternate locus of procreation, the aforementioned *ingenio*, which is then impregnated, or fertilized, by the *entendimiento*. This intellectual double of the corporeal excrescence functions through the marriage of separate but similar faculties (organs), both of which are seen as active, or (pro)creative: the understanding (*entendimiento*)[10] and the *ingenio*.[11]

Gracián takes these same intellectual organs and organizes them around a new social body, which he calls *taste*. Since all representations of reality are conditioned by an irremediable absence of uncontaminated essence, taste becomes the ideological field in which all subjects, or potential subjects, either achieve a temporal semblance – *persona* – or fail in the attempt: 'Those with whom no dealings are carried out are not present, nor are those who communicate in writing ever absent' [No están presentes los que no se tratan, ni ausentes los que por escrito se comunican] (*El Criticón* I, 1.69). Returning to the question of truth, I will consider Gracián's translation of Mateo Alemán's parable of how truth came to employ the masks of *engaño* in order to mitigate the direct unveiling of her terrible visage. Before doing so, however, it is worthwhile to consider some emblems of Truth. If we look to Borja, we find references to truth's brevity and clarity. In the second part of his collection, an emblem shows a circle with a line running through the middle of it, and it carries the motto, 'Veritas Brevis' [Truth is short (a shortcut)] (figure 9).

Below, the author writes: 'the truth ... is brief and straight, and for this reason they compare it to a straight line, because as from one point to another there can be no shorter road than that of the straight line, handling the truth in this same way is the straightest road there is; on the contrary, the lie, and falsehood, is the greatest detour of all' [la verdad ... es breve, y derecha, y assi la comparan à la linea recta,

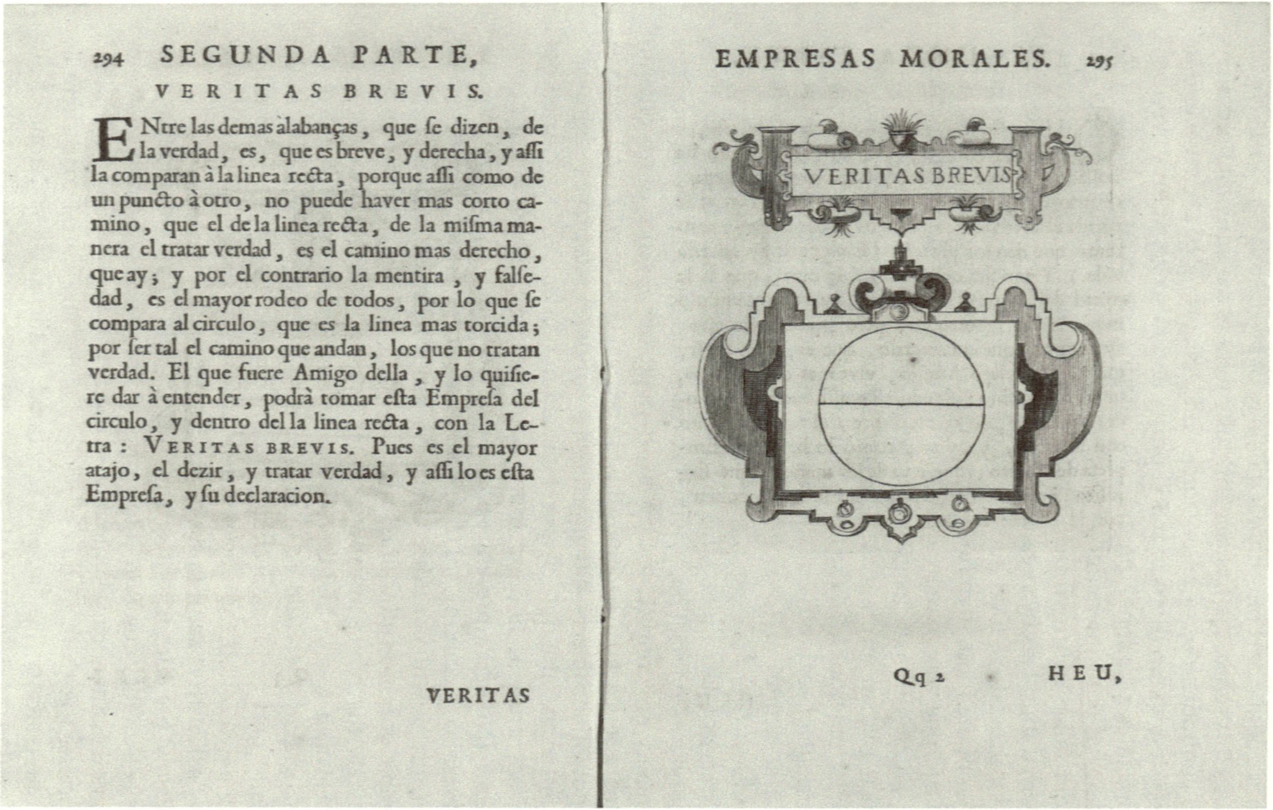

294 SEGUNDA PARTE,

VERITAS BREVIS.

ENtre las demas alabanças, que se dizen, de la verdad, es, que es breve, y derecha, y assi la comparan à la linea recta, porque assi como de un puncto à otro, no puede haver mas corto camino, que el de la linea recta, de la misma manera el tratar verdad, es el camino mas derecho, que ay; y por el contrario la mentira, y falsedad, es el mayor rodeo de todos, por lo que se compara al circulo, que es la linea mas torcida; por ser tal el camino que andan, los que no tratan verdad. El que fuere Amigo della, y lo quisiere dar à entender, podrà tomar esta Empresa del circulo, y dentro del la linea recta, con la Letra: VERITAS BREVIS. Pues es el mayor atajo, el dezir, y tratar verdad, y assi lo es esta Empresa, y su declaracion.

VERITAS

EMPRESAS MORALES. 295

VERITAS BREVIS

Qq 2 HEU,

Figure 9 'Veritas brevis,' in Juan de Borja, *Empresas morales*, part 2 (1680), 294–5

porque assi como de un puncto à otro, no puede haver mas corto camino, que el de la linea recta, de la misma manera el tratar verdad, es el camino mas derecho que hay; y por el contrario la mentira, y falsedad, es el mayor rodeo de todos] (294–5). An emblem from part 1 is even more succinct (figure 10): the motto reads 'Veritas,' and the commentary states: 'The light that truth brings is so great that one can see through the darkness and falseness of lies with it' [La luz, que la verdad tiene, y trae consigo, es tan grande, que con ella luego se hechan de ver las tinieblas, y falsedad de la mentira] (124–5).

Apart from this clever attempt to frame an emergent scientific discourse within the spiritual program of the Counter Reformation, what stands out in Borja's treatment of truth is his unproblematic acceptance of its existence and the ability of the properly trained and motivated reader to find it. This position contradicts the emblem by Borja with which this chapter opens, which holds that the human vessel is too imperfect to ever arrive at God's truth by its own means. Writing about Gracián's contemporary Descartes, Massey points out, 'This puts him in a paradoxical position in which certitude of God's infinite nature and perfection emanates from the mind, which itself is imperfect and finite' (1154).

Three decades later, Sebastián de Covarrubias y Horozco (1609) shades these positive assertions in an emblem with the motto 'Shadows are born from the truth' [Sombras son de la verdad] (figure 11). The figure shows a chess board with a single piece in the middle that throws shadows in every direction. On the wall behind the table, a giant pair of spectacles with lenses that are prismatic in appearance is suspended (*con lunas cuadreadas*). In spite of the anamorphic possibilities of the image, the main idea of the poetic *subscriptio* and following commentary is similar to Gracián's understanding of truth; however, in Covarrubias, truth is married to religion, which effectively removes her to another plane of signification, one not considered in Gracián's allegory. It is for this reason that 'the truth has but one face, it is always the same, and it is steadfast even though it suffers a thousand setbacks, which libel and lies bring to it' [La verdad no tiene más de una cara, siempre es una, y está firme aunque padezca mil adversidades, que le acarrean la calumnia y la mentira] (43). In the end, truth is only perceptible if one looks through the gaze of religion.

Finally, we come to Gracián's contemporary, Saavedra Fajardo. As with Covarrubias, the similarities between the baroque diplomat's

124 PRIMERA PARTE,

VERITAS.

LA luz, que la verdad tiene, y trae conſigo, es tan grande, que con ella luego ſe hechan de ver las tinieblas, y falſedad de la mentira, la qual por mucho que ſe esfuerçe, à contradezir à la verdad, aunque ella adelgaze, no quiebra, antes con ſu luz haze callar à la falſedad; que es lo que ſe dà à entender por eſta Empreſa de las ranas con la lampara encendida, (por eſcrivirſe, y tenerſe por cierto, que es remedio muy ſeguro, para hazerlas callar de noche en ſus charcos, ponerles alguna luz) con la Letra, que dize. VERITAS. Que quiere dezir. *Verdad.* El que quiſiere dar à entender, que es amigo della, y del efeto, que haze (que es hazer callar à todos los que no la tratan) puedeſe valer deſta Empreſa.

VERI-

EMPRESAS MORALES. 125

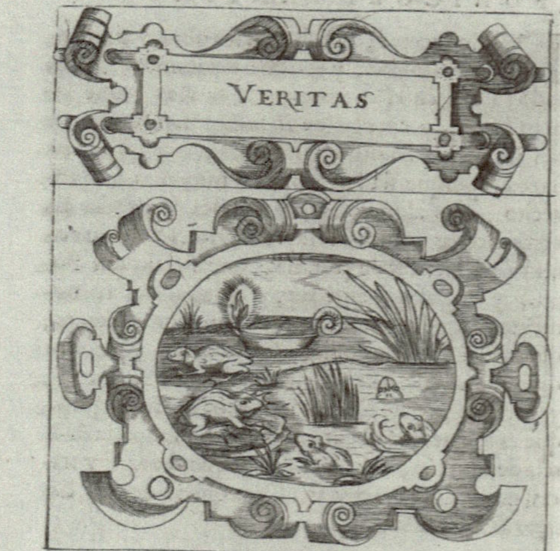

S FUNI-

Figure 10 ‘Veritas,’ in Juan de Borja, *Empresas morales*, part 1 (1680), 124–5

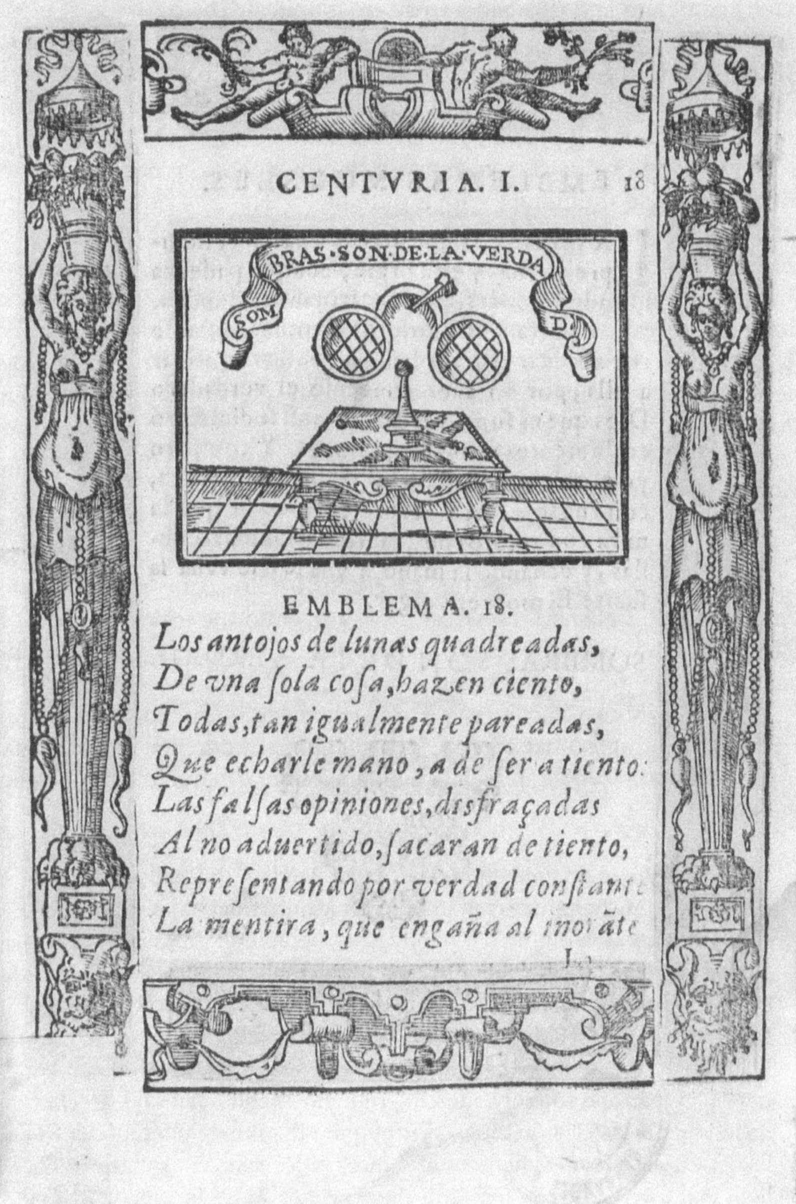

CENTVRIA. I. 18

EMBLEMA. 18.

Los antojos de lunas quadreadas,
De vna ſola coſa, hazen ciento,
Todas, tan igualmente pareadas,
Que echarle mano, a de ſer a tiento:
Las falſas opiniones, diſfraçadas
Al no aduertido, ſacaran de tiento,
Repreſentando por verdad conſtant
La mentira, que engaña al inorãte

Figure 11 'Sombras son de la verdad,' in Sebastián de Covarrubias y Orozco, *Emblemas morales* (1610), 43

twelfth emblem and Gracián's story are manifest. The figure is a celestial image in which the sun embraces half of the earth with its rays while leaving the other half in darkness. The motto reads, 'Excaveat Candor' [brilliance blinds]. In the commentary Saavedra tells us that the Romans and Egyptians symbolized honesty and truth by hanging a gold or sapphire heart from the necks of their children or princes: the idea is that one should act with a pure heart. This is a notion Gracián takes up in the *Oráculo* when he ridicules the naïveté of Momo, who thought that it would be a good idea for men to have glass torsos so that everyone could see their true intentions (224). Although Saavedra does not recommend that the prince be transparent, he adamantly defends that he should always have truth on his side: 'To destroy deceit with ingenuity and lies with the truth is a triumph worthy of a prince. Lying is a vile act of slaves and unworthy of the magnanimous heart of a prince, which more than any other should strive to resemble God, who is truth itself' [Digno triunfo de un príncipe deshacer los engaños con ingenuidad y la mentira con la verdad. Mentir es acción vil de esclavos y indigna del magnánimo corazón de un príncipe, que más que todos debe procurar parecerse a Dios, que es la misma verdad] (288). Later on, however, he wades into the murky waters of Reason of State with the tenet that the prince should allow other subjects to believe non-truths when it suits him.

What is new in Gracián is his refusal to see mundane or political truths as anything other than a dialogic game of perspective. The following quotation is Gracián's transliteration of a parable from Mateo Alemán:

> Truth was the legitimate spouse of understanding, but Falsehood, her great rival, took it upon herself to exile her [Truth] from her wedding bed, and knock her down from her happy state; because of this, what scheme did she not design? what frauds did she not commit? ... She cast Taste as her go-between, so that in very little time she achieved so much that she tyrannized for herself the great King of all the powers. Seeing herself disdained, and even persecuted, [Truth] sought refuge with Wit, shared her trials with her, and sought counsel. 'Truth, my friend – Wit said – there is no food more tasteless in these corrupt times than cold undeception. Did I say tasteless? There is no mouthful more bitter than a naked truth. The light that travels directly torments the power of an Eagle, of a lynx, how much more so the power of he who becomes dispirited! For this reason the wise Physicians of the soul invented the art of gilding truths, sweet-

ening disillusions. What I mean to say – and observe this lesson well, esteem this piece of advice – is that you should become political; dress yourself like deception herself, disguise yourself with her adornments, and in that way I assure you victory.' Truth opened her eyes, and began to move with artifices; since then she has used inventions; she presents herself in a roundabout way, triumphs through strategems, paints far away what is very close, proposes things in a foreign subject that she seeks to condemn in her own, points at one thing to arrive at another, dazzles the passions, refutes the affects, and through ingenious circumlocution always comes to rest at the point of her intention.

[Era la Verdad legítima esposa del entendimiento, pero la Mentira su gran émula, emprendió desterrarla de su tálamo, y derribarla de su felicidad: para esto ¿qué embustes no traçó?, ¿qué supercherías no hizo? ... Echó por tercero al Gusto, con que en poco tiempo obró tanto, que tiraniçó para sí el Rey de las potencias. Viéndose la Verdad despreciada, y aun perseguida, acogióse a la Agudeza, comunicóla su trabajo y consultóla su remedio. 'Verdad amiga – dijo la Agudeza – no ay manjar más desabrido en estos estragados tiempos que un desengaño a secas. ¡Qué digo desabrido!, no ay bocado más amargo que una verdad desnuda. La luz que derechamente termina atormenta la potencia de una Águila, de un lince, ¡quánto más la que flaquea! Para esto inventaron los sagazes Médicos del ánimo el arte de dorar las verdades, de açucarar los desengaños. Quiero decir – y observar bien esta lición, estimadme este consejo – que os hagáis política; vestíos al uso del mismo engaño, disfraçaos con sus mismos arreos, que con esso yo os asseguro la vitoria.' Abrió los ojos la verdad, dio en andar con artificio; usa desde entonces las invenciones, introdúzese por rodeos, vence con estratagemas, pinta lexos lo que está muy cerca, propone en un estraño sujeto lo que quiere condenar en el propio, apunta a uno para dar en otro, deslumbra las passiones, desmiente los afectos, y por ingenioso circunloquio viene siempre a parar en el punto de su intención.] (395–6)

I have cited the text from *Arte de ingenio, tratado de la Agudeza*, published in 1642. The more commonly cited text is the 1648 (expanded) version, *Agudeza y arte de ingenio*. I point this out because in the 1648 version, the term *desengaño* replaces *engaño* when describing how Truth began to dress herself. It will be apparent to the reader that the earlier version is more useful for my understanding of Gracián than the second. Just as interesting is how the discrepancy between the two versions opens up the question of intentionality and underlines the impossibility of determining with any certainty who actually made the editorial choice and why.

Returning to the allegory, Truth was the legitimate spouse of Understanding until Falsehood exiled her from the marriage bed and threw her down from her state of happiness. As a result of this adulterous affair, Truth tries to win back her errant spouse, who now belongs to Falsehood. Isolated, she turns to Wit, whose description of the relationship between man and Truth begins with the language of taste: 'no dish is more harsh, no morsel so bitter, as the plain, naked truth.'[12] To overcome the limitations of the human palate, Wit advises Truth to become 'political'; toward this end she should dress herself in the garments of *engaño*.[13] Truth opens her eyes at this point, but not to her own substantial being; to the contrary, what she 'sees,' or what her 'political' insight reveals, is a negative reflection of her lack of being in the trappings of the world: 'Things do not pass for what they are, but for what they resemble' [Las cosas no passan por lo que son, sino por lo que parecen] (*Oráculo* 156). Being, then, only has value when it can be (deceptively) perceived. Ontology depends on representability and not on substance, and, as such, Truth's existence now becomes a game of position, perspective, discursive feints, and visual trompes l'œil. Not content with the intellectual game, Wit extends the power of deceit to the passions and affects; thus Truth must be sought not only in a visual game of mirrors, she also influences and is influenced by an emotional and affective game of deception. The possibilities she now has to re present herself in the finite world thus become infinite: 'finítamente infinito.'

This dialogic understanding of the relationship between representation and desired meaning reaches a climax when Gracián introduces his version of Don Juan Manuel's exemplum, 'The Emperor's New Clothes.' According to the version in *El Conde Lucanor*, the condition that determines the subject's ability to see the cloth is limited to whether or not he is truly the son of his father, which is based on a feudal, or organicist, understanding of legitimate ownership. In Gracián's transduction, caste (*mala raza*), genealogical purity (*bastardo*), and the woman's loyalty to her *Señor* (*agraviado de su mujer*) indicate that we have moved to baroque Spain and its obsessions with purity of blood and the honour code. The modern translation of the story, however, unveils the lack behind the desire for absolute guarantors of these impossible-to-(tran)substantiate class and ethnic markers. It also reveals the dependence of royal power on public opinion while disclosing, in Forcione's words, 'Gracián's insights into the disconnection of the foundation of the political order from an evident natural order, the inadequacy of traditional organicist metaphors as explanations of its cohesion, the hiddenness of its origin and source of control, and its reliance on illusion and a "technology of power" for legitimation and self-perpetuation' ('At the Threshold' 45).

Much like the voluntary blindness of the *aldeanos* in Cervantes' 'El retablo de las maravillas,' the king's most egregious error is giving in to his desire to overcome his mundane finitude by seeking an otherworldly guarantee for his socially contingent dignity in this world. According to Marin, 'No one knows that, on the contrary, the king is only his image, and that behind or beyond the portrait there is no king, but a man. No one knows this secret, and the king less than everyone else perhaps' (218): no one except the literary subject, that is, and his parabolic avatars, the two carpetbaggers. By agreeing to the contractual conditions of the two con artists, the king places his power and prestige in the orchestrating hands of clever artificers. They, not he, now define and frame the gaze of power, which converts the king from an actor-director into a spectator of his own desire. He literally does not know himself – as a lack, that is. If he did, he would know that his 'certification' depends on his ability to dialogically maintain others in suspense: 'The wise man avoids being sounded to the bottom of his being, whether in his knowledge, or his worth, if he wants all to venerate him. Acquaintance is permitted, but not comprehension' [Excuse el varón atento sondarle el fondo, ya al saber, ya al valer, si quiere que le veneren todos. Permítase al conocimiento, no a la comprehensión] (*Oráculo* 154). Not only does Gracián's king allow the tailors to pull the strings of his desire for power, he places additional barriers between his perspective and the truth by sending his ministers for reconnaissance instead of going himself. The relation of this ruse to the allegory of Truth is direct in the sense that both examples conclude with the non-presence of the protagonists in question: the king and Truth herself. As in the case of Truth, once the hypostatic marriage between monarchical power and the king's body is deceitfully – yet truthfully – undone, and once the king is reduced to playacting on the same discursive stage as everyone else, he begins to 'represent' his political power. In being, as in truth, lack becomes the positive condition of limited ontological possibilities: embodied power becomes political, representing what it is not. In the end, the king's tragedy, or parody, arises from his failure to act as a charlatan of power in his own interest: 'The king in his portrait, the king as portrait, the portrait-king, the truth of the infinite representation of political power and the absolute monarch as representation, is a parody of the Eucharistic mystery, the mystic body and the real presence' (Marin 230). The ultimate effect of this deconstruction of embodied power is the empowerment of the disembodied subject of language.

Crisi 4 in part 1 of *El Criticón* begins with a conversation between Fortune and Love in which the two allegories lament how humans blame them for their fall from grace and their resulting impotence in the face of love. At the outset, the representation of the pagan gods is classical, and the mortals flail blindly in the face of mortality. In Crisi 6 of part 2, however, Fortune returns to defend herself by redefining her relationship to the world and to men. Unlike the traditional portrait in which she is blind and unpredictable, now her vision is as sharp as an eagle's, and her intervention in the world is framed within a providential Christian view: 'I protest, first of all, as I am the daughter of Good parents, of God and his divine providence, and so obedient to their commands, that neither a single leaf in a tree nor a straw on the floor moves without his wisdom' [Protesto, lo primero, que soy hija de Buenos, pues de Dios y de su divina providencia, y tan obediente a sus órdenes, que no se mueve una hoja de un árbol ni una paja del suelo sin su sabiduría] (II, 6.409). Even more striking is the reorganization of her relationship to human actions and history. All of the ills of mundane existence are now understood to be the direct consequence of the perverted desires and actions of humanity: 'I always give things through the hands of men themselves, as I have no others' [yo siempre doy las cosas por manos de los mismos hombres, ni tengo otras] (II, 6.410). And like Pedro Crespo's orchestrating hands, a select group of men is seen as more powerful than Providence herself: 'those who are truly wise men, which are the prudent and virtuous ones, are higher than the stars' [los verdaderos sabios, que son los prudentes y los virtuosos, son superiores a las estrellas] (II, 6.415). Returning to the story of the 'Emperor's New Clothes,' the real protagonists of the parable are the artificers, as the king gradually becomes dependent on them in his efforts to uphold his fantasy. Their self-obfuscation and manipulation of aristocratic subjects provides a model for the representation of the power of the State.

The Organized Body of Taste

The Gracianesque *fábrica*, or *empresa* of strategic and witty concepts is a living, breathing, eating, and begetting corpus that penetrates and is in turn penetrated by other bodies on the political stage of the court. Like the physical body, the *persona* has its 'sweet' and 'kingly' defects, and is fecund in its conceptually procreative act; moreover, its goal is to become the object of desire under the foreign, admiring gaze, which it attracts and amazes with the impression of substantial depth. Although humanity itself is categorically rejected as a 'sack of filth,' the language of taste is overdetermined by corporeal metaphors and analogies, which reveal that we are looking at a social or politically informed body. Pierre Bourdieu explains that the ritual creation of the socially informed body involves much more than the five conventional senses: '[T]his principle is nothing other than the *socially informed body*, with its tastes and distastes, its compulsions and repulsions, with, in a word, all its *senses*, that is to say, not only the traditional five senses – which never escape the structuring action of social determinisms – but also the sense of necessity and the sense of duty, the sense of direction and the sense of reality, the sense of balance and the sense of beauty, common sense and the sense of the sacred, tactical sense and the sense of responsibility, business sense and the sense of propriety, the sense of humor and the sense of absurdity, moral sense and the sense of practicality, and so on' (*Outline* 124).[14] What we see throughout Gracián's oeuvre is the conversion of bodily organs into a spiritual and aesthetic body of tropical machinery, one which produces and judges conceptual creations in the movement of time and space. As both Read and Rodríguez have noted, this body reflects the new 'freedom' of labour in modernity, as the subject is freed from his material body in order to remake himself according to the demands of the marketplace. What we are talking about, in other words, is the commodification of the modern subject, whose value is determined by its circulation, which, according to Susan Buck-Morss, brings us back to the emblem: 'Commodities relate to their value in the marketplace just as arbitrarily as things relate to their meanings within Baroque emblematics. "The emblems return as commodities." Their abstract and arbitrary meaning is their price' (179). The advantage of this new body for the decadent political class of the Spanish State is that it is infinitely replicable by those subjects who possess the material and intellectual requisites for redeeming the status quo, subjects who are then denied a substantive legitimacy on which to base a project for real social change by the selfsame limitations.[15] The disembodiment of power means that it can be everywhere and nowhere all at once.

In *The Fold*, Gilles Deleuze adroitly observes that the folding of the bodily organs into the spiritual faculties is not a linear process; the self-conceived organs are themselves endlessly folded into one another. Gracián exemplifies Deleuze's metaphor: 'eyes inside the same eyes, in order to look at how they are looking; eyes and more eyes and glances, aspiring to be the overseer in such an advanced age' [ojos en los mismos ojos, para mirar cómo miran; ojos y más ojos y reojos, procurando ser el mirante en un siglo tan adelantado] (*El Criticón* II, 1.294). Wit is 'a whole body' [un cuerpo entero], but it is also 'food for the soul' [pasto del alma] and 'sustenance for the spirit' [alimento del espíritu] (*Agudeza* 27). Witty conceits feed the soul and the spirit, but in other places they pass for life and spirit themselves: 'Conceits are the life of style, the spirit of speech and have as much perfection as they do subtlety' [Son los conceptos, vida del estilo, espíritu del decir y tanto tiene de perfección, cuanto de sutileza] (*Agudeza* 510). In the end, the interplay between aesthetic, intellectual, and bodily organs is impossible to disentangle, as, like the emblematic image, the connotative potential of the carnivalesque tropes is open to infinite recontextualization. For Bell, this embodiment of expedient schemes and practices is the key to understanding the workings of ritual: 'Ritualization is embedded within the dynamics of the body defined within a symbolically structured environment' (*Ritual Theory* 93).

In *El Criticón*, each of the three books meticulously describes the remaking of the social body, i.e., persona, beginning with Andrenio's grotesque account of his bestial birth in nature (*madrastra del hombre*), which is juxtaposed to Critilo's remaking of himself after he is shipwrecked: 'Seeing myself with no living friends, I hailed the dead, I immersed myself in reading, I began to know and to be a *persona* (as up until then I had not lived the rational life, but the animal life)' [Viéndome sin amigos vivos, apelé a los muertos, di en leer, comencé a saber y ser persona (que hasta entonces no había vivido la vida racional, sino la bestial)] (I, 4.109). Bodily death becomes not an end but rather the beginning of the 'universal reform' of man into an intellectual being (II, 1.287). This process begins in earnest in Crisi 8 of part 1: 'Art is the complement of nature and another second being that greatly improves her and even aspires to exceed her in its own works.

It holds itself in high regard for having added another artificial world to the first; it habitually disguises the oversights of nature, perfecting it in everything: as without this help from artifice, it [nature] would remain unrefined and coarse' [Es el arte complemento de la naturaleza y un otro segundo ser que por estremo la hermosea y aun pretende excederla en sus obras. Préciase de haber añadido un otro mundo artificial al primero; suple de ordinario los descuidos de la naturaleza, perfeccionándola en todo: que sin este socorro del artificio, quedara inculta y grosera] (I, 8.171). This description of a nature that is lacking might seem surprising until we remember that Gracián is talking about human nature. Consequently, the first steps toward personhood consist of a series of recognitions of the eminently 'deceived' and lacking nature of man. All of the senses, starting with sight, are dematerialized and interiorized, turned away from sensual delights and the physical world in order to begin the transformation towards being in the political world: 'he puts an end to pleasure and makes of life a means for taste' [haze fin del deleite y de la vida haze medio para el gusto] (I, 8.195). Note how pleasure and taste become dialectically opposed in this imperative. The eyes must learn how to see everything in the world *al revés*, or even through 'estranged eyes' [ojos ajenos] (II, 1.293). The ear becomes an intellectual organ by playing deaf, while the sense of smell is painstakingly attuned to more spiritual emanations: 'it discerns the good smell from the bad and it understands that a good reputation is the breath of the spirit' [discierne el buen olor del malo y percibe que la buena fama es el aliento del ánimo] (I, 8.197).

Unlike Bakhtin's grotesque body of becoming, the persona in the state of political becoming must convert his sensual organs into a site of perpetual unbecoming, whose perfection, i.e., completion, coincides with the physical death of the subject: 'Man dies when he should have started to live, when most successful … thus he is born a beast and dies very rational' [Muere el hombre cuando había de començar a vivir, cuando más persona…assí que nace bestia y muere muy persona] (*El Criticón* III, 11.763). Gracián's works repeatedly and meticulously – ritualistically – erase any positivistic notions concerning truth and the subjective 'content' of the courtly actor in order to arrive at a completely immaterial, absent, or Other form of subjectivity and artistic activity, one exclusively interested in arranging and occupying courtly stages of representation. As Egginton argues in *How the World Became a Stage*, this modern subject is not a substantive entity but rather a spatial relation: 'This "subject" is the intellectual manifestation of a new way of experiencing the self in space, a way of experiencing that depends on the ability, for example, to distinguish actors from characters and the space of the one from that of the other' (6). Even colours lose their substance due to their origins in the same dust out of which the nothingness of man emerges: 'green is not green, nor is red red, rather everything consists of different dispositions of surfaces and of the light that bathes them' [el verde no es verde, ni el colorado colorado, sino que todo consiste en las diferentes disposiciones de las superficies y en la luz que las baña] (III, 6.652). Gracián thus configures a series of machine-like, intellectualized organs of taste designed to attract, provoke, and manipulate the desire of other subjects in the public representation of the 'the profound man' [hombre con fondos] in the changeable space of the absolutist court.

A more difficult problem is presented by the nature and location of what Calderón might call the *genio* or *inclinación* of the subject of taste with respect to the organized social body. If, on the one hand, it is clear that the intellectual and sensible faculties are constantly interacting with and penetrating each other and the ingenious performances of other subjects, the point of origin of all this activity is decidedly obscure and decentred by comparison. Spadaccini and Talens describe Gracián's courtly subjects as 'those who practice a strategy and technique of prudence, of hiding their *true selves* ... [and] control[ling] their own destinies' (Introduction xi; my emphasis). This Cartesian-based concept of the true self is problematic in Gracián, as he translates the human subject into a locus for positive activity, not by rejecting the pessimistic view of human agency and the institutions that employ it for repressive (even nihilistic) ends, but by seeing the possibilities in *desengaño*'s constitutive negativity that allow the individual subject of the court to advance and triumph in the world of appearances. If it is true that 'things are nothing more than what they are taken to be' [No son las cosas más de como se toman] (*El Criticón* III, 5.652), then the search for truth – and true subjectivity – becomes a contingent and illusory game of artistic appearances. In the words of Jorge Checa, 'It is one thing to be false and another to be unable to be true' [Una cosa es ser falso y otra no poder ser verdadero] ('Alegoría' 118). What has generally been lamented as man's difference with respect to God's once immaculate and now fallen creation is celebrated here as the source of a new anti-body of creation: as Žižek explains, '"subject" is nothing but the void, the gap, opened up by the failure of reflection' ('Cartesian Subject' 263). If the State is seen to occupy such a void, its incompleteness mirrors that of the subject, and any move towards plenitude estranges the subject from the dialogic relation produced by the evocation of redemptive hegemony. This is pure perspective, or what Mitchell calls a 'rigorous relativism,' in which truth is a rhetorical effect produced and disseminated thanks to the power with which the symbolic enterprise amazes and holds the gaze of this spatially conceived subject (*Iconology* 38).

In the last chapter of *Agudeza y arte de ingenio,* Gracián approaches what can be described as postmodern theories of subjectivity when he looks to Seneca for an explanation of what he means by an 'anomalous' subject: '[E]very great genius has a measure of madness. It tends to change with the day and the hour, in such a way that it misrecognizes itself; it is altered by extrinsic and even material impressions; it resides towards the margins of the affect, towards the radius of the will and is poorly accompanied by the passions' [todo ingenio grande tiene un grado de demencia. Suele estar de día, y tener vez, de modo que él mismo se desconoce; altérase con las extrínsecas y aún materiales impresiones; vive a los confines del afecto, a la raya de la voluntad y es mal avecindado el de las pasiones] (537). This is the most precise definition of the *ingenio* that Gracián formulates, and it hinges on the demented nature of the greatest thinkers, which would include those listed in his genealogy of authors of philosophical truths. Seneca returns in *El Criticón,* declaring that 'there is no understanding without inspiration' [no hay entendimiento grande sin vena] (II, 13.526). Santos Alonso clarifies Gracián's meaning by noting, 'A mad fancy, it is understood' [Vena de loco, se entiende] (526n39). The echoes of Huarte de San Juan's *ingenio caprichoso* are hard to miss, but we must note the alterations that Gracián introduces.[16]

In his reading of ingenious madness, the *ingenio* never coincides with itself; it is always Other to its affect, its will, and its passions; in the end, 'it misrecognizes itself.' Even its greatest powers were taken from another faculty: judgment. In an emblem by Juan de Borja, the *ingenio* is represented by a 'machine,' or 'crane,' which lifts a heavy weight (figure 12). The motto of the emblem reads, 'Genius overcomes force' [Ingenium vires superat] (102–3).

In the *pictura,* the *ingenio* is only present in the tools it employs and the weight it lifts, while its ultimate location is veiled, coinciding with an invisible and indirect intention that drives the machinery in the performance of the event. The effect of the wit's influence is found in the movement of the weight, while wit itself remains veiled. We get a similar image of 'Art' from the second *empresa* of Diego Saavedra Fajardo, which shows a blank canvas erected in a landscape of seemingly infinite proportions (figure 13).

102 PRIMERA PARTE,

INGENIUM VIRES SUPERAT.

EL que quiſiere emprender, y penſare acabar grandes coſas, confiado en ſolo ſu poder, y fuerça, aunque la tengamos grande, ſe hallarà burlado, porque ſerà facil coſa hallar otro, que con menos fuerça, y mas ingenio le ſobrepuje, y vença, por ſer tanto mas, lo que puede el ingenio con mediana fuerça, que ſolo el poder de la fuerça, quanto ſon mayores, y mas de eſtimar las potencias del alma, que los ſentidos del cuerpo. El que quiſiere dar à entender, que eſtima mas entendimiento con mediano poder, que mucha fuerça ſin èl, puedelo declarar por eſta Empreſa de la maquina, con la qual levanta un hombre muy mayor peſo, del que podria levantar con ſola ſu fuerça, con la Letra, que dize. INGENIVM VIRES SVPERAT. Que quiere dezir, *El ingenio vence à la fuerça.* Porque de la miſma manera, lo que por ſola fuerça no ſe podria alcançar, con ingenio, y entendimiento ſe alcançarà.

INGE-

EMPRESAS MORALES. 103

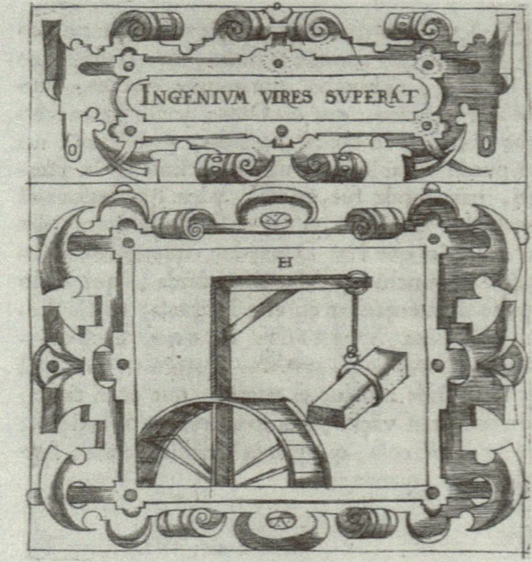

P 2 STE-

Figure 12 'Ingenium vires superat,' in Juan de Borja, *Empresas morales*, part 1 (1680), 102–3

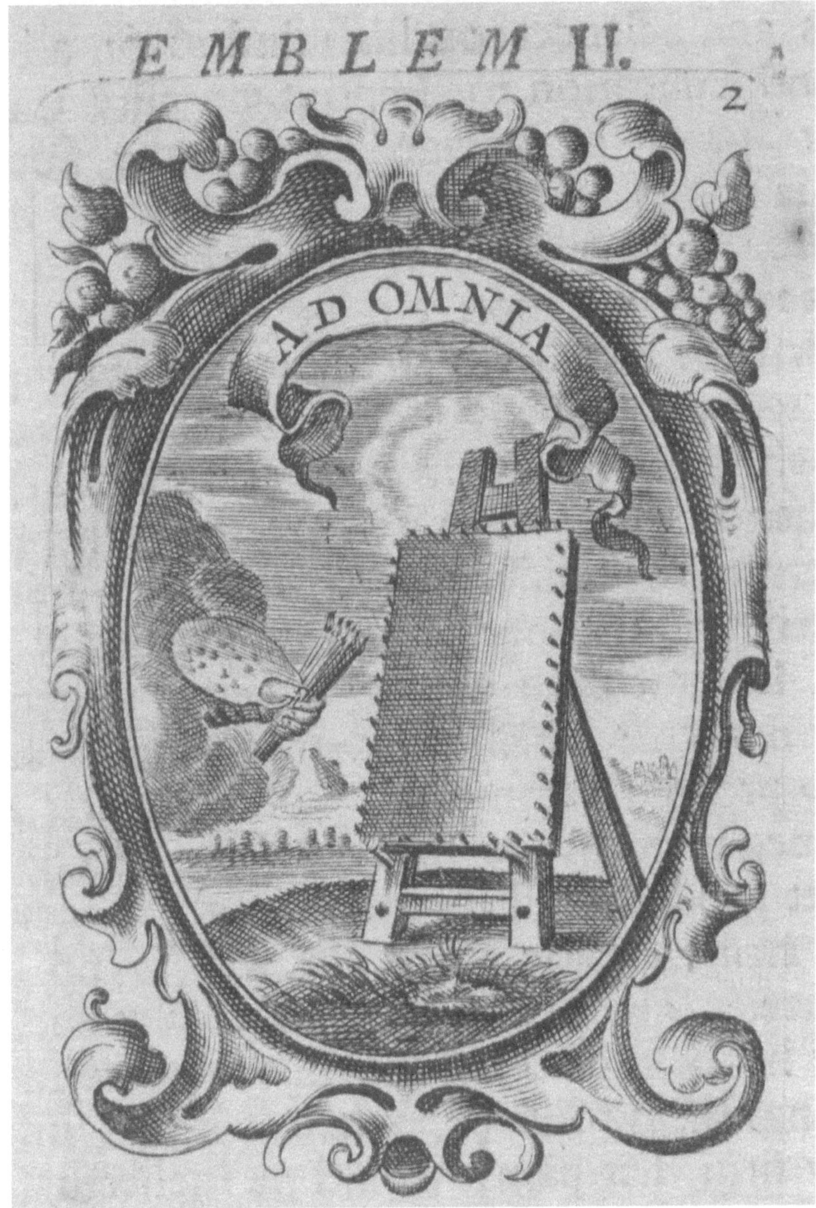

Figure 13 'Ad omnia,' in Diego Saavedra Fajardo, *Empresas políticas* (1640), 202

On the left hand side is a cloud, and from the cloud a hand emerges holding a palette and several brushes. The *inscriptio* reads, 'For all things' [Ad omnia], while the first line of the commentary states: 'With paintbrush and colors, art displays its power in all things' [Con el pincel y los colores muestra en todas las cosas su poder el arte] (202). When placed alongside Borja's emblem, the structural relationship between *ingenio*, art, and power becomes apparent, as the force and ultimate truths that produce and are produced by the mechanism of taste remain veiled.

What is striking here is not the secrecy concerning the source of power behind its representation, but rather the foreignness of the *ingenio* with respect to the subject himself, which becomes not so much an effect as an imperative for the courtly persona. The persona is a permanently self-estranged subject, which results in a subject of power who shares a constitutive trait with the State and, ultimately, God himself. In the words of Jean-Luc Nancy, 'the christian god, and the catholic god more than any other, will have been the god of the death of god, the god who retires from all religion (from every link to a divine presence) and who begins from his own absence … the same thing distinguished in its sameness' (28). Just as God fabricates a human body in order to negatively reflect himself (through his absence) and be recognized in the substantial lack behind his corporeal reflection, so too does Gracián's persona require a socially informed body in order to exercise its obscure will. This decentred, or redoubled, point of enunciation endows the subject with a certain independence and self-consciousness through which it may manipulate language and perception to its own advantage. On the other hand, the courtly avatar is also subject to foreign and penetrating, and possibly erroneous, readings, just as God's will is darkly perceived, if at all, behind the words of his earthly artefacts. This linguistic freedom, then, does not necessarily lead to substantive changes in baroque society, but acts instead to isolate the subject from all other subjects and necessitates the individual encounter with ideology and power.

The following advice that Critilo gives to Andrenio demonstrates that baroque 'freedom' is not to be understood as a positive movement into the world but rather as a cautious and closed resistance to 'being in the world':[17] 'Strive to proceed cautiously in what you see, hear, and above all in what you say; hear everyone and trust no one; all will be your friends, but guard yourself from everyone as if they were your enemies' [Procura de ir con cautela en el ver, en el oír y mucho más en el hablar; oye a todos y de ninguno te fíes; tendrás a todos por amigos, pero guardarte has de todos como de enemigos] (*El Criticón* I, 3.100). In part 2, this idea is universalized by *el Valeroso*: 'the greatest valor of man consists of not committing himself nor of seeing himself obligated to use it [his valor]' [la mayor valentía de un hombre consiste en no empeñarse ni verse obligado a sacarla] (II, 8.445). As with Pedro and Isabel Crespo, freedom is understood as a negative resistance to complete identification; indeed, this gap is necessary to the subject's very ability to consent to his utilitarian and inferior role within the hegemony of the State. Or as Maravall puts it, 'choice was the equivalent of choosing one's own behavior or at least freely attempting to direct one's behavior physically, following the line established by one's own will' (*Culture* 171).

In the ritual embodiment of schemes of social positioning, Gracián creates a practice through which individual subjects may amass personal power and prestige without directly threatening the existing sociopolitical organization, all of which works to achieve Bell's notion of redemptive hegemony by shifting the exercise of power toward the individual. Bell's model of ritualization does not separate freedom from the workings of power; rather, the two are mutually constitutive and informative. Like clockwork, Andrenio's voluntary, material disembodiment becomes constitutive of his re-embodiment as a subject of power and fame: 'No one appears until he disappears' [Ninguno parece hasta que desaparece] (III, 12.787). Moreover, the constantly folding and unfolding hierarchy of *ingenio, entendimiento, alma, espíritu,* etc., is placed in perpetual motion so that the subject can activate a sense of universal totality, 'finitely infinite': 'In God everything is infinite, all is immense; thus in a Hero everything should be grand and majestic, in such a way that all his actions, and even his reasons, go forth adorned by a transcendent and grandiose majesty' [En Dios todo es infinito, todo inmenso; assí en un Héroe todo ha de ser grande y magestuoso, de suerte que todas sus acciones, y aun razones, vayan revestidas de una trascendente grandiosa magestad] (*Oráculo* 258).

As we have seen in the emblems of 'art' and '*ingenio*,' this immanent majesty functions through self-difference, always leading the adoring or circumspect gaze to where it is not: 'so manifest in his creatures and so hidden in himself … That being said, this great God is so hidden, that he is known and not seen, hidden and manifest, so far away and yet so near; that is why I am beside myself' [tan manifiesto en sus criaturas y tan escondido en sí … Con todo esso, está tan oculto este gran

Dios, que es conocido y no visto, escondido y manifiesto, tan lexos y tan cerca; esso es lo que me tiene fuera de mí] (*El Criticón* I, 3.94). The common ground that Gracián establishes between God and man is that of the relationship between immaterial – or absent – substance and external representations. Critilo 'finds himself' not in himself but in an absent God, just as those who surround the prudent subject are amazed (suspended) and guided by a calculating political Hero who gauges their 'palates,' 'inclinations,' and 'wills,' and in so doing convincingly performs 'learned' roles with the learned and 'saintly' roles with the saintly: a 'discrete Proteus,' who represents all things for all subjects (*Oráculo* 145). In the end, the Hero is as absent as God himself: 'the great beauty is not to be and yet to appear to be, that is indeed wisdom' [el gran primor es no ser y parecerlo, esso sí que es saber] (*El Criticón* II, 6.433).

The reasons for the Church's discomfort with Gracián's thought become clear here, as his radically orthodox treatment of *desengaño* underlines a heretical yet empowering nihilism at its dogmatic centre. In such a desubstantialized world, art is not the reflection of the subject's positive yet hidden truth; nor can we separate its technical aspects from the achieved effect of political success; rather, art *is* the system of politically motivated self-representation. Consequently, taste is the name given to a ritually structured eco-system (Rappaport) in which individual bodies of taste, or agents, sustain and are in turn sustained by a social body whose primary ontological and epistemological product is not truth or substance, but power. If we replace 'Ritual' with 'Art,' we get the following statement from Bell: '*Art* is the thing itself. It is power; it acts and it actuates' (*Ritual Theory* 195).

Conclusion

At the end of *El Criticón*, Critilo and Andrenio, accompanied by *el Peregrino*, cross over to the Island of Immortality, where Merit asks the pilgrim for his manifest ('patente': understood here as a pass or 'papers'). 'Manifest' on the manifest is the entire history of their journey, which is also the journey of the reader through the three books. When the two heroes step onto the isle, however, the reader is left stranded on the shore. For those readers who want to see how the story ends, the narrator leaves the following advice: 'What they saw there, and all they achieved, whoever wants to know these things and experience them should follow the path of famous virtue, and he will arrive at the theatre of fame, to the throne of esteem and to the center of immortality' [Lo que allí vieron, lo mucho que lograron, quien quisiere saberlo y experimentarlo, tome el rumbo de la virtud insigne, del valor heroico, y llegará a parar al teatro de la fama, al trono de la estimación y al centro de la inmortalidad] (III, 12.812). The only way to follow the fictional heroes over the threshold of ignominy to fame is to actively take up – embody – Gracián's text, which becomes a guide no less imposing and all-encompassing than Ignatius's *Spiritual Exercises*.[18] Both texts seek the active and voluntary engagement of the reader, and neither is complete without the ritualized embodiment of the practicant, whose goal in each case is immortality.

This brings me to my last point: What could be more god-like than leaving the dependent other with an infinite desire for satisfaction? In political terms, this is the strongest arm of Gracián's apparatus: '*Leave them wanting more*. One must leave a little nectar on the lips. Desire is the measure of esteem; even with material thirst, it is a trick of good taste to incite it, but not to satisfy it' [*Dexar con hambre*. Hase de dexar en los labios aun con el néctar. Es el deseo medida de la estimación; hasta la material sed es treta del buen gusto picarla, pero no acabarla] (*Oráculo* 260). We find a corollary passage in the religious text *El comulgatorio*: 'drink insatiably from his wounds and fill yourself, oh soul, with God' [bebe hidrópica de sus llagas y llénate, alma, de Dios] (61). We return, in the end, to the trope of the Eucharist, as the next and last aphorism of the *Oráculo* signals the end of the apprenticeship and the commencement of the saintly life of the hero. But we should not be fooled by this religious language into thinking that Gracián is upholding the essentialist dogma of the monarchical-seigniorial elites and their genealogical organicism. By taking baroque ideology to its limits, he prepares the State to overcome its constitutive contradictions by setting it free from medieval, organicist myths of divine presence. In this sense, Bolívar Echeverría is correct when he argues that the Counter Reformation is a bridge to modernity, but not because theology is used to reconfigure early capitalism. Read explains in his critique of Max Weber what Maravall and J.C. Rodríguez have argued with respect to Counter Reformation ideology: 'it is the bourgeois ideological unconscious that impacts upon the sphere of religion, not "Protestantism" that impacts upon the "spirit of capitalism"' ('The Modernity of the Subject' 474). In the case of Counter Reformation *desengaño*, once all earthly phenomena are marked by the same lack of transcendental significance – commodified – the State turns to the psychic and symbolic investment of the subject of representation to establish its earthly presence.

Gracián's saint, like Truth, Wisdom, and the *ingenio*, is an artistic creation whose substance and power emanate from the gaze of the enthralled Other and not from the blood of its sacrifice. 'Desire is the measure of esteem,' meaning the hero's superiority lies not in himself but in the effectiveness of his artistic labour, an effectiveness that comes into existence through the desire of an Other. At this point we reach the absolute evacuation of meaning from the body, which, in emblematic terms, means that we have arrived at the culmination of the Counter Reformation initiative to void any and all iconological manifestations outside of its control. Whereas previous emblematists deploy and perpetuate an organicist residue of iconic 'representation' in order to make present the universal legitimacy of Spain's Catholic monarchy, Gracián brings out the inherent contradictions that arise when sacred symbols circulate in a secularized symbolic economy in order to unhinge the State from aristocratic resacralization. Only when power is produced by and through immanently conceived social relations does it become absolute in any real sense. Only when truth is subject to the same immanent conditions of judgment can it be tied absolutely to power. The masters of this new sphere of political activity are those subjects who master the production and reception of semblances: artists.

7 Bodies and Corpses, Voices and Silence: Grotesque Presence in *Los trabajos de Persiles y Sigismunda*

> He thought each memory recalled must do some violence to its origins. As in a party game. Say the word and pass it on. So be sparing. What you alter in the remembering has yet a reality, known or not.
>
> Cormac McCarthy, *The Road*

Los trabajos de Persiles y Sigismunda occupies a unique place in Cervantes studies in that the distinct critical postures brought to bear on the text and its troublesome ambiguities are so radically contradictory, on the one hand, and so insistently present, on the other. The highly contested terrain of this text has arguably produced more totalizing interpretations than all of his other works combined, as on all ends of the critical spectrum we find readings that can be classified as emblematic in their attempts to sweep the complex worlds and stories contained in the work into totalizing and all-encompassing images or visions of and for the author's unstated intention(s). Many of these readings seek to explain (away) what Marcelino Menéndez Pelayo characterized as Cervantes' 'senile debility' [debilidad senil] when confronted with what seemed to the founding father of Spanish philology a lamentable aesthetic failure (cited in Nerlich, *El* Persiles 15). We have just seen similar attempts by Gracián scholars to perform similar, biologically informed readings of the Jesuit's artistic corpus.[1]

An instructive example of this critical ambivalence can be taken from the two seminal books written by Alban Forcione: *Cervantes, Aristotle and the 'Persiles,'* and *Cervantes' Christian Romance: A Study of 'Persiles y Sigismunda.'* In the first instance, Forcione articulates a forceful theoretical and textual argument to show how Cervantes carries out a systematic attack on baroque aesthetic precepts in the interest of the creative freedom of the artist. This book marked a turning point in *Persiles* criticism by reassessing the work from a point of view that did not seek to apply preconceived novelistic and/or religious paradigms to the textual complexities of the work. In the second study, however, Forcione defends almost the opposite position in his claim that Cervantes yokes his creative impulses to an overarching narrative of religious transcendence.[2] Such critical ambiguity abounds in the world of *Persiles* studies, although many critics, rather than carry the burden of their 'corrective' readings, prefer to place the burden for their self-confessed disorientation squarely on the shoulders of the author, thus mimicking Menéndez Pelayo's attempt to bury the work forever under the weight of his negative judgment of Cervantes' declining talents.

Such are the readings of Carlos Romero Muñoz and Stephen Harrison, the first of whom seeks to provide a definitive philological reading by dismissing the many 'omissions,' 'errors,' and the overall 'carelessness' in the work as signs of Cervantes' impatience due to his drive to finish the text before his death. In his punctilious edition of the work, and even more so in his belaboured 'reconstruction' of the meaning of the text, Romero's goal is nothing less than the rendering of an imagined *Urtext*: 'It is easy (and – let us understand – always legitimate) to establish the parallel between the *real* masterpiece and the work that is somehow "flawed"' (Introducción 14).

Harrison, for his part, assembles a complex narrative of Cervantes' creative process in which many of the same contradictions and apparent errors and oversights are used to build a case for the critic's hypothesis concerning the largely interpolated and/or abortive creative processes behind a work that in the view of both critics fails to reach aesthetic fruition. Julio Baena's sardonic critique of similar philological liberties taken with the *Quixote* underlines the great leaps required in any attempt to reconstruct a quixotic *Urtext*: 'What has been done up to now is to hide the poverty of the *Quixote*, or, worse yet, *repair it*, coming up with a supposed *Quixote* "that Cervantes wanted," as if every act of signification were not always already a *meaning to say*' (*Discordancias* xiv). At one point, Romero suggests that Cervantes did not completely understand his own creation: 'Periandro and Auristela point towards a difficult path, not manageable for everyone. Cervantes admires (is filled with wonder at) them, but perhaps he understands them less than the other characters in his novel' (43). Following the discussion of Gracián's irremediably split subject, it is reasonable to assume that no modern author completely understands his or her own creation, or the intention behind it, but this is not Romero's point. Taking Regalado's division of the reading public into the enlightened and unenlightened one step further, Romero places the aged author alongside his unenlightened readers, a move which clears the way for the critic's insistent correction/dismissal of discursive ambiguity in favor of a monocular reading of the early modern Greek 'epic.' In Foucault's words, 'The author is therefore the ideological figure by which one marks the manner in which we fear the proliferation of meaning' ('What Is an Author?' 230). Such readings place Barthes's pronouncement of the death of the author in a curious light, as for both Romero and Harrison, Cervantes' imminent death is the only explanation for what they see as the many careless mistakes and contradictions in an otherwise brilliantly conceived, if poorly executed, text.

Both critics are correct in saying that Cervantes does not completely understand his own work, but not because the dying writer rushed it to press before taking the time to edit out the 'errors' or 'inconsistencies'; rather, their work on Cervantes points toward the more general linguistic and historical predicament of the modern subject of language. Let us look at the following word-emblems of the narrator of the *Persiles*: 'We see effects in nature whose causes we do not know; one person's teeth go numb or are deadened when he sees a knife cut through cloth; a man perhaps shivers at the sight of a mouse, and I have seen one man tremble at the sight of slicing a radish, and another get up from the table out of respect for setting out some olives' [Efetos vemos en la naturaleza de quien ignoramos las causas; adormécense o entorpécense a uno los dientes de ver cortar con un cuchillo un paño; tiembla tal vez un hombre de un ratón, y yo le he visto temblar de ver cortar un rábano, y a otro he visto levantarse de una mesa de respeto por ver poner unas aceitunas] (II, 5.302).[3] In the attempt to clear out a space for their textual supplements, both Romero and Harrison go beyond Cervantes' recognition of self-estrangement by focusing on what they see as specifically lacking – and therefore excessive – in the text of the *Persiles*, an approach which reveals a number of truths about interpretation. According to the Lachmannian philological tradition, the *Urtext* is approached by assembling a genealogical relationship between different editions of a text through the identification of different family stems of editorial errors, and then tracing the errata back to where the contamination originated. Through this corrective labour, in which a presupposed original text is purged of its errors, a philological science based on the documentation of errors more or less mechanically postulates an errorless text that would ideally present the unadulterated intention of the author. In Altschul's words, 'this tree provides the means to correct the text in a mechanical fashion, without requiring the judgment or the interpretation (*iudicum*) of the editor' (14). In the cases of Romero and Harrison, we could even characterize their analytical work in psychoanalytical terms, since their goal is to go beyond the material manifestations of the text in order to reach what we might call the unconscious of the *Persiles* and, more importantly, its author. In the words of Jacques Lezra, their corrective readings constitute 'linguistic events' in and of themselves. Lezra's model, which subjects such critical enterprises to a practice he calls 'eventful readings,' holds that any event that refers to something 'beyond itself … must be thought of as both exceeding and falling short of "itself" – as bearing, in short, always and necessarily an allegorical relation to a referent constantly dispersed across a field that it cannot encompass' (42). The way out of this critical loop, 'in which every "cut" cuts (only) a thread linking a subject (or an object *to itself*),' which is to say, a thread that links the posited *Urtext* to the desire of the philologist, is the aforementioned practice of eventful reading (73): '*Eventful reading* is the name I give to this *practice* of material poetics, this necessary tendency of desublimation. This practice is only in appearance quietistic: it posits that etiologies or genealogies of the eventful emergence of power are always phenomenalized according to regressive patterns, and that the event *as such* is also the name we give to the mystification of the origin of ideology and to the relation between ideology and effect' (33). The readings of Romero and Harrison constitute a double regression in that, on the one hand, the inherited, imperfect text is used to posit a supposedly perfect, or real, text, which effects a temporal leap or regression into the past to a moment of insemination, before pen was put to paper; on the other hand, the ideological framework for this imagined text constitutes a temporal regression in the opposite direction, which brings the unconscious desire of the philologist back to the contemporary moment of his or her articulation, or high modernity. As in the case of Borja's *tau*, the textual artefact is wrenched out of its material context in order to place it within a meaning structure compatible with modern philological imperatives.

In spite of the apparent logic behind Romero's and Harrison's scientific method, this eventful reading uncovers several potential problems, many of which can be found in the origins of emblematic practice in the Renaissance. As just described, two temporal structures are produced by the new historical consciousness of the Renaissance humanist/philologist. In the first case, any historical manifestation of the classical, or biblical, text is taken for an imperfect version of the eternally stable but unattainable original. Returning to Gumbrecht, this philological practice is directed towards the making present of the permanent, which is to say, transcendental meaning of the text, thereby evoking the voice of the absent Author. A second problem is that both the text and the critic are irreparably caught in the historical moment of both their own emergence into language and their concrete encounter in the act of interpretation. This ambiguity is reproduced in early modern texts such as *Lazarillo de Tormes* and both books of *Don Quixote*, wherein the narrator(s) is situated on a different plane from both the text he ostensibly inhabits and the reader, who is prevented from reaching a definitive understanding of the text by the structural ambiguities in which the argument, or narrative content, is inextricably caught. In Lezra's words, '*Don Quixote* dwells allegorically on such novelistic effects in a manner that constitutes them both as objects of knowledge understandable to a method of reading that the novel produces *and* as *events* forever troubling the horizon of that internal epistemology' (137). In other words, there is a 'blind spot' both in the gaze of the text itself and in the eye of the reader: one produced by the opaque materiality of the text to the gaze of the reader; and the other by the impenetrable materiality of the critic to himself.

There is also a third problem, which can be traced through the editorial energies directed at hypothesizing the 'text that Cervantes really wanted,' as well as the sundry attempts to create a substantial link between the life of the author and his work. If we begin with Romero's and Harrison's laments for the errors, inconsistencies, formal contradictions, and general carelessness that seemingly plague the *editio princeps*, a structure emerges in which a difference is established between the material manifestation of the text and what both critics claim should be regarded as the *true* text. As Gurd points out, this difference is internal to the text itself. Whether we are talking about Romero's deployment of Américo Castro's theory concerning the different periods of Cervantes' religious evolution, or Harrison's linking of different fragments of the *Persiles* to different creative periods of the author's life, what becomes apparent is that this same minimal and, I would argue, constitutive difference is posited between the author and himself. In the Introduction to this book, I referred to Carlos Gutiérrez's framework for considering this problem in his study of the complex and contradictory figure of Quevedo. Here is the full quotation from *La espada, la pluma y el rayo*: '[I] believe it is necessary to enlarge the focus of the [literary] field dynamic and from there the relation with the field of power, in order to give an account of what we might call "QUEVEDO." Within this concept, beneath which is unified the analytical division that traditional studies made between the work and the biography of the author, a distinction must be made between the *microquevedo* (an intratextual staking out of positions) and the *macroquevedo* (a space of sociopolitical and literary possibilities; *habitus* and ensemble of takings-of-position, definitively)' (20). One of the points that Gutiérrez makes is that the truth of any text is not found in the unified voice of the author but rather in the processes of social, political, ideological, and aesthetic mediation in which the text both negotiates with inherited practices and traditions and, through that negotiation, offers new positions that markedly alter the literary field. We have already seen this point made from a different theoretical approach in Gurd's definition of a radical philology.

In light of these theories, the question I would pose is not where Cervantes' intent lies in relation to the interpretation of his text but rather where the text itself lies. Since the text is both limit and source, object and subject, of critical endeavors, it is not unreasonable to treat it as a hieroglyphic, or emblematic body, whose multiple and contradictory stories and structures both provoke and frustrate the reader's search for meaning. What this means is that the textual arborescence, like the hieroglyphic *tau*, provokes multiple readings not because of its positively charged ambiguities (although that, too) but rather due to the void that persists at the very horizon of any perceived authorial intent. One place to begin to understand this problem and its implications for textual criticism is Žižek's notion of a 'parallax view,' which describes 'the *apparent* displacement of an object (the shift of its position against a background), caused by a change in observational position that provides a new line of sight' (*Parallax* 17; my emphasis). I have emphasized the word 'apparent' because, according to the psychoanalytical reading of the relation between subject and object, neither the one nor the other positively exists as an identifiable entity; rather, traces of the changing relationship between the one and the Other allow us to perceive a relationship that, of necessity, requires two points of reference. The text thus perceived becomes a medium that includes both the artefact and the archeologist, but neither variable is real in the phenomenological sense. Rather, the movement and negotiation between them provides outlines of their positions without filling in their 'spaces' with any stable content, much like Gracián's colliding billiard balls.

By taking this position, I am following in the path laid down by critics such as David Castillo and William Childers, who both emphasize the strategic opacity of Cervantes' text where authorial intent is concerned. For it is one thing to say that all texts are plagued by the same structural obstacles where authorial intent is concerned; it is quite another to argue that an author includes such dynamics in the discursive design of his or her text. Castillo argues that Cervantes' anamorphic play with Counter Reformation symbols simultaneously opens up conservative and liberating readings; more importantly, the mere existence of such anamorphic mechanisms makes the former inclination susceptible to constant rupture by the latter, especially since the guidance provided by the narrator(s) is so insistently equivocal (*(A)wry Views*, chapter 5). Similarly, Childers introduces the concept of the 'ambivalent marvelous' to describe the unsettling effect of Cervantes' unresolved movement between 'rational' and supernatural explanations for portentous events throughout his writings: 'The texts have in common the element of ontological ambiguity, that is, a lack of clarity concerning exactly what has happened, or how it has happened. Is this a supernatural event or does it obey natural causality? How can we tell?' (58). According to Childers, the 'ambivalent marvelous' grounds human attempts to take symbolic control over their world in their constitutive contradictions. Moreover, his use of the term 'event' brings us close to Lezra's subversive paradigm of eventful reading, which 'can only succeed where it becomes the practical disposition toward an understanding of what will have occurred neither as what properly had to occur, nor as what took place adventitiously, but as what remains from or resists that distinction "before" it is aestheticized as an event that afflicts a subject whose advent it marks' (33). According to an eventful reading, the sign is estranged from its signified, the body is estranged from its subject, and, finally, the text is estranged from its author. What remains of the Real of the text of the *Persiles*, then, is the very shift from perspective to perspective: 'ultimately, the status of the Real is purely parallactic and, as such, non-substantial: it has no substantial density in itself, it is just a gap between two points of perspective, perceptible only in the shift from the one to the other ... the parallax Real is ... that which accounts for the very *multiplicity* of appearances' (Žižek, *Parallax* 26). Unlike the prefabricated reception of emblematic allegories, which projects and phenomenalizes a 'before,' what we find in the *Persiles* are simultaneous and conflictive semantic possibilities that make the reader aware of his or her own intervention in the world of the text.

Literary Fields and Emblematic Reception

Recent historiographical work on literacy in early modern Spain has changed the way scholars regard the relative importance and historical impact of the Golden Age canon. Keith Whinnom's inventory and analysis of the literature in circulation in the sixteenth and seventeenth centuries challenges the assumption that Spanish subjects were avid readers of the works that have occupied the centre of Golden Age studies in the last two centuries.[4] This view is supported by Sara T. Nalle's analysis of printing press inventories and Inquisition interviews with people accused of various religious deviations in the region of Cuenca during the same period. Nalle finds that the inventories of titles found in both printing presses and the inquisitorial records are dominated by religious books, with works of imaginative literature, mainly chivalric romances, occupying a distant third place behind professional volumes of the self-help variety ('Literacy' 87). On the other hand, Nalle's work, in combination with Richard Kagan's study of the growth in post-secondary education, increases substantially the number of readers in Castile compared to earlier estimates.[5] According to both Nalle and Gutiérrez, this marked growth in the number of readers is treated with great suspicion by religious and political authorities, who attempted to exert control over the circulation of printed materials through censorship and legislation (Gutiérrez 47). Reading thus becomes a highly contested site for ideological control – and personal empowerment – due to what Childers calls the 'internal colonization' of Spain, and in particular Castile, which gains momentum after the Council of Trent (3–14). As a result of the attempts of the Spanish church to standardize religious belief and practice in its own territory, underground communities of readers begin to form around all sorts of internally colonized Others, be they Moriscos, Conversos, or subjects otherwise excluded from the institutional or economic privileges afforded those who were better able to prove their genealogical purity and political utility, as we have seen with Juan de Horozco and his brother Sebastián de Covarrubias (Childers 14–23). With such a wide range of reading practices, the critic is hard pressed to offer a 'typical' reading of the *Persiles*, as it becomes ever more apparent that a valid historicized reading of the text would necessarily be partial and limited to an identifiable material matrix, which brings me, once more, to the emblem.

Throughout this study I have argued that, due to its centrality to philosophical, aesthetic, and political developments in early modern Spain, the emblematic mode provides both the rhetorical specificity and breadth of intellectual thought demanded by a work like the *Persiles*. Indeed, many studies have observed that the book contains a significant number and wide variety of emblematic structures and motifs.[6] An abbreviated catalogue would include: the frequent use of actual emblems, such as Alciato's emblem of eloquence in which the chains of Hercules stretch from his mouth to the ears of his enthralled audience; the emblem of excessive ambition, featuring a winged ant; the humility that the proud peacock feels when he looks down at his ugly feet; Borja's representation of repressed desire, symbolized by a smoldering volcano; the wheel of fortune; the clock of *entendimiento*; oft-used emblematic images such *grullas, rémoras, víboras, águilas,* and the ubiquitous *Ocasión* and *Fortuna;*[7] allegories of pilgrimage as well as the numerous scenes that take place on ships, boats, *leños, maderos,* and other metaphors for life's journey towards death and/or redemption; the constant play between voices and silence;[8] the use of allegory in Periandro's dream;[9] the central role played by portraits;[10] and, finally, the itinerant author of the *Flor de peregrinos aforismos.*[11]

This proliferation of traditional symbols and ideals would seem to add weight to allegorical readings of the novel, yet Cervantes' curious deployment of these ritualistic devices takes us far from the hieroglyphic evocation of divine presence. It is for this reason that my study has anachronistically given Cervantes the last word on the emblem. If the *Persiles* had limited itself to a Lopean-like deployment of emblematic structures, I could have placed this chapter much earlier in the book; and if we were looking at a strictly eventful deconstruction of emblems, according to Lezra's model, I'm not sure the *Persiles* would merit its own chapter. What we will see, however, is that Cervantes does both things, or neither, in that the emblems that will be analysed here can be classified as linguistic events, but ones which resist the closure and presence effects typical of the emblematic operation. They are, in other words, eventful emblems.

In order to understand what Cervantes does with the emblem, I will begin with Gumbrecht's articulation of an alternative staging of presence, which is based on art's ability to challenge meaning-based interpretations through the evocation of emotion, or affect. In *Production of Presence*, Gumbrecht associates an experience of embodied, as opposed to disembodied – immanent as opposed to transcendental – presence of Being: 'Aesthetic experience is an oscillation between presence and meaning effects,' which performs the 'movement between losing and regaining intellectual control' (*Production* 128). This strategy of material presence thus sets up a dialectical structure in which presence of Being is opposed to the presence of Meaning found at the heart of traditional philological practices. Several recent readings of the *Persiles* move in this same direction, including those of Baena and Jesús Maestro, who find that the ironic staging of discursive ambiguity is one of the strategies that Cervantes uses to ground Counter Reformation ideology in its historical and discursive contradictions. As Maestro puts it, in the *Persiles* one finds 'no slippage in the (orthodox) forms but not a single innocent intention' (114). According to these critics, the *Persiles* offers an alternative, materially-based experience of presence by unveiling the inherent contradictions of Counter Reformation, emblematic-allegorical practice even as it exemplifies a new method for deploying what we might call a 'historicized iconicity,' a term I use to refer to the way in which the scars and imperfections in cultural artefacts trigger multiple readings arising from the disjunctive processes of their concrete articulation and reception. I offer historicized iconicity as a translation of Žižek's parallax view for this study of the emblem, since any historicization of an icon produces a 'short circuit' in the conventional function of the icon: in Žižek's words, such an action 'bring[s] to light its "unthought," … its disavowed presuppositions' (*Parallax* ix). The short-circuiting of the emblem's allegorical drive towards transcendence is produced in the *Persiles*, as it is throughout the Cervantine oeuvre, through the evocation of that which the emblem tries so hard to control: the grotesque nature of historically anchored, dynamic, and speaking bodies and/or signs. In direct contradiction to Gracián's silence concerning the scandal of the physical body, Cervantes places the body and its material reality in the foreground as the very condition by which meaning and knowledge come into being.

This strategy inexorably disrupts the dialectical movement between being and interpretation by exposing the conventional, emblematic relationship between the human body and the symbolic order and, by extension, the relation between art and an over-determined moral order. From the first sentence of the *Persiles*, Cervantes achieves a startling synthesis of image and commentary that surpasses the most striking examples from the emblem in both complexity and ambiguity: 'Corsicurbo the barbarian shouted into the narrow mouth of a deep dungeon, more tomb than prison for the many living bodies there entombed' [Voces daba el bárbaro Corsicurbo a la estrecha boca de una profunda mazmorra, antes sepultura que prisión de muchos cuerpos vivos que en ella estaban sepultados] (I, 1.17). This explosive knot of voices and mouths, bodies and prisons, and, finally, tombs, which both projects and stifles its cacophonous possibilities, situates the reader within the broad aesthetic and thematic field of emblematics; yet, it is no accident that this chaotic scene stubbornly resists a reasonable solution. Throughout the *Persiles*, Cervantes contrasts the closed, moralizing allegories of the emblematic mode with a series of vital and uncontrollable impulses that spring from the lives and narratives of both protagonists and minor characters.

The textual birth of the novel is itelf embodied in the physical 'dar a luz' of Periandro from the bowels of the earth, as after removing the youth from the aforementioned *mazmorra* with a 'thick hemp rope' [gruesa cuerda de cáñamo], the barbarians 'shook out his hair, which covered his head with countless rings of pure gold. When they had cleaned his face, which was covered with dust, such marvelous beauty was revealed that it amazed and softened the hearts of those who were to be his executioners' [le sacudieron los cabellos, que como infinitos anillos de puro oro, la cabeza le cubrían. Limpiáronle el rostro, que cubierto de polvo tenía, y descubrió una tan maravillosa hermosura que suspendió y enterneció los pechos de aquellos que para ser sus verdugos le llevaban] (*The Trials* I, 1.17; *Los trabajos* I, 11.128). In *El círculo y la flecha*, Baena notes that almost every image in this passage, from the thick 'umbilical' cord tying Periandro's hands, to the cleaning of the face and hair, and the vocal explosion that immediately follows, alludes to the rituals that accompany the moment of birth (144). In the words of Luis Avilés, 'the narrative starts from the bowels of the earth,' emphasizing the material – that is, the carnal and common – condition of the human being and, by extension, the textual body that attempts to contain and communicate human existence ('To the Frontier' 144).

Upon being freed from the hole in the ground, Periandro vociferously thanks the heavens that he is alive. The barbarians, who do not understand this unexpected speech, respond to his utterance by closing off the dungeon with a big rock and threatening the youth with an 'enormous arrow' [desmesurada flecha]. The parallelism between the living tomb and the human body becomes manifest when the protagonist responds to the threat by shrugging his shoulders and closing his mouth; his arching eyebrows lend a patently architectural aspect to his posture: '[he] drew up his shoulders, pressed his lips together, arched his eyebrows, and in the profound silence of his heart asked Heaven, not that he be saved from that danger so cruel and close at hand, but that he be given strength to bear it' [encogía los hombros, apretaba los labios, enarcaba las cejas y, con silencio profundo, dentro en su corazón pedía al cielo, no que le librase de aquel tan cercano como cruel peligro, sino que le diese ánimo para sufrillo] (*The Trials* I, 1.18; *Los trabajos* I, 1.130). The exaggerated size of the symbolic elements in this scene – rock, arrow, lips, arching eyebrows – is indicative of emblematic perspective, as the narrator guides the reader towards that which is most significant or expressive in the statuesque image of the hero.

What happens next is even more surprising, as the *barbarian* is overcome by the beauty of the boy and throws away the bow: 'the barbarous archer, whose hardness of heart had been softened by the youth's beauty, chose not to prolong the threat of death by keeping the arrow aimed at his chest. He threw the bow aside and approached the youth, making it known as best he could by signs that he didn't wish to kill him' [el bárbaro flechero ... hallando la belleza del mozo piedad en la dureza de su corazón ... arrojó de sí el arco y, llegándose a él, por señas como mejor pudo, le dio a entender que no quería matarle] (*The Trials* I, 1.18; *Los trabajos* I, 1.130–1). The beauty of the boy successfully short-circuits the relationship and function of power in this scene and sets bodies in motion once again. In a gesture that foreshadows the amorous hand play of the Spanish castaway Antonio and his barbarian bride Ricla, Periandro's captor attempts to communicate his peaceful intentions through *señas*.[12]

This is a significant departure from the emblematic use of hands in Calderón and Gracián, as Cervantes takes a bodily member normally used to symbolize prudence and power, and deploys it instead to convert an adversarial relationship into an attempt to communicate through a common language rooted in the body.[13] It also illustrates Gumbrecht's idea concerning the power of art to resist all attempts to domesticate its ambivalent and ambiguous presence effects.[14] As stated in the Introduction, power for Gumbrecht is defined by 'the potential of occupying or blocking spaces with bodies' (*Powers* 5). In this case, the barbarians have pulled Periandro through a hole in the earth, cleaned the earth from his face (and mouth), filled the space in the earth with a boulder, and closed the space of Periandro's mouth with the large and pyramid-shaped stone at the end of a huge arrow. Periandro's beauty upsets this relationship, and instead of an unequal relationship of power based on the threat of violence, we end this scene with the barbarian anxiously performing his dexterous hand *orchesta* under the gaze of beauty incarnate.[15] Just as importantly, we are presented with a parallax view of the barbarian that upsets the civilized-barbarian dialectic with its staging of a 'barbaric' attempt to communicate in a foreign 'tongue.' It is in fact the barbarian Other who attempts to break through the linguistic barrier separating two distinct ontological spaces in his attempt to constitute a new language. Unlike Lope's *indios*, there is no fictitious linguistic bridge erected between them in order to mitigate either the strangeness of the Other or their common corporeal 'language.'

The appearance of Auristela is no less striking in its potential for violence, and yet its significance is different from Periandro's narrative 'birth' in important ways. Duped into believing she is a man, the barbarians are about to sacrifice her, as they do with all young male strangers, in their ritual search for a king to rule over them:[16] 'Several barbarians immediately took hold of the youth and with no more ceremony than blindfolding him, made him kneel down, tying his hands behind him. Not saying a word and like a gentle lamb, the young man waited for the blow to take his life' [Asieron al momento del mancebo muchos bárbaros, sin más ceremonia que atarle un lienzo por los ojos; le hicieron hincar de rodillas, atándole por atrás las manos, el cual sin hablar palabra, como un manso cordero, esperaba el golpe que le había de quitar la vida] (*The Trials* I, 4.28; *Los trabajos* I, 4.152).[17] Kneeling like a martyr (in another statuesque posture), Auristela is threatened with death, just as Periandro had been. Both are also male victims, but what is striking about this scene is that Auristela could save herself by revealing to her executioners that she is a woman. However, because she is more afraid of revealing her identity than losing her life, she does not speak – a decision that condemns her to immobility and bodily death. Moreover, since Cervantes has already upset the natural order between civilized and barbarian subjects, the meaning of her speechlessness is framed in a compelling manner. In the words of Maria Alberta Sacchetti, 'A revealing insight into Auristela's over-anxious and defeatist nature is the fact that she had volunteered to be sacrificed to put an end to her troubles' (44). Auristela's compulsion to seek definitive closure throughout the *Persiles* has also been noticed by De Armas Wilson, and its insistent reappearance provides important clues to the relationship between meaning and being in the work as a whole.

Returning to the emblem, the fact that Auristela's actions (or inactivity) and words (or silences) are motivated by symbolic interdictions rather than by the physical threat of death brings us into the world of the emblem and its specific treatment of voices and bodies. In these moments, Cervantes offers a critique of the way emblematics organizes and allegorizes human experience, in particular, the voluntary extinction of life in the interest of a transcendental narrative that drains any specific or historical meaning from the story of the individual. In the words of Bernat Vistarini, 'the action of a certain moral relativism in Cervantes would make a poor marriage with the apodictic severity of emblematic moral maxims' ('Algunos motives' 84). What we discover in Cervantes is a staging of bodies that stalls or exceeds the quest for definitive allegorical readings and, therefore, challenges emblematic interdictions that convert the body into disposable, if significant, waste.[18] His carnivalesque use of bodies models new ritual strategies for representation and communication by favoring the creative and procreative energies of the human bodily material – what he calls in the *Persiles* 'a single mass' [una misma masa] – over what is generally taken in the Augustinian vein for an execrable sign of man's fallen nature: mere matter (I, 18.243). The body becomes more than a sign of an absence, a move which has the curious effect of turning signs themselves into living entities.

Feliciana de la Voz (y Cuerpo): Grotesque Presence

In summarizing her emblematic reading of the hymn that serves as *subscriptio* to Feliciana de la Voz's harrowing story of forbidden love, Aurora Egido concludes that the platonic trajectory established by this not-quite-virgin's hymn to the Virgin Mary 'sublimates' human motherhood 'frente a la virginidad perfecta' ('Poesía' 23). In a similar reading, Patrizia Micozzi states that the hymn 'redeems [the knowledge] of fleshliness and redresses it with dignifying grace and charm' (721). Both critics see the trajectory of this story as unidirectional and vertical, starting from the humble act of expiation of Feliciana's guilt and culminating in her redemption as a married mother. This same progression is at the heart of Casalduero's, Avalle-Arce's, and Forcione's allegorical readings of the *Persiles'* redemption of, respectively, Counter Reformation history, the Great Chain of Being, and Christian romance.[19] The displacement of the specific towards the abstract universal – which is the structural common denominator of these readings – is characteristic of the emblem, especially in baroque theatre. If the *Persiles* were a work that aspired to religious allegory, what we might call the straight emblematic reading of the plot – in which the heterodox lovers make a pilgrimage to Rome in order to purify their Catholic faith and consecrate their unconsummated marriage – would provide a convincing interpretation. If, on the other hand, the work 'lacks consistency and any depth … as a celebration of catholicism,' as Mercedes Blanco concludes, then a different trajectory must be plotted by the critic (633). This second path is the one I will follow in the following pages.

The most problematic aspect of Feliciana's story, with respect to the emblematic reading, is that the young woman's acknowledgment and confession of guilt never actually take place. When she tells the story of her 'fall from grace' to the group of pilgrims, Feliciana repeatedly protests against a moral code that condemns what she takes to be her legitimate marriage to Rosanio. Let us recall that the episode begins when a mysterious man hands over a 'gift' to the pilgrims, who have stopped for the night on a hill covered in 'infinite oaks and other rustic trees' [infinitas encinas y de otros rústicos árboles] (III, 2.447). The gift turns out to be a newborn whom the pilgrims are charged to deliver to the night visitor's friends in the nearby town of Trujillo. The man leaves as quickly as he appeared, but he is followed by a very young woman, who stumbles into the foreground: 'as beautiful as she was young, just as young as she was beautiful' [tan hermosa como niña y tan niña como hermosa] (*The Trials* III, 2.204; *Los trabajos* III, 2.449). When asked if she needs help, she replies: 'The first thing, señores, you must do, is put me underground; I mean, hide me so anyone hunting for me can't find me. Secondly, you must give me something to eat, for I am dying of exhaustion' [Lo primero, señores, que habéis de hacer, es ponerme debajo de la tierra; quiero decir, que me encubráis de modo que no me halle quien me buscare. Lo segundo, que me deis algún sustento, porque desmayos me van acabando la vida.] (*The Trials* III, 2.204; *Los trabajos* III, 2.450). The opening request situates the harried exile within the hyperbolic and violent world of honour; but what at first seems to be a desperate death drive is immediately contradicted by the less epic request that they hide her. The change in tone becomes clearer when she asks for food because she feels weak. The movement is decidedly downward: earth, food, body. And this is not the closed, idealized body of Renaissance art, which, according to Bakhtin, stands out due to its finished, perfected condition, in which 'all the signs of unfinished character … [,] growth and proliferation were eliminated; protuberances and offshoots … removed, convexities (signs of new sprouts and buds) smoothed out, apertures closed' (*Rabelais* 29). To the contrary, the body in Cervantes is constantly marked by its material biological processes, its proximity to other open bodies, and the wounds and scars of its passage through space and time: indications all of its dynamic and 'grotesque becoming.' Throughout the *Persiles* these grotesque, open, and unfinished bodies are repeatedly juxtaposed to the seemingly supernatural perfection of the protagonists, until the protagonists themselves are brought to earth at the very end of the novel: 'Sigismunda was beautiful before this misfortune befell her, but after it she was extremely so; often one of the side effects of pain is that it increases beauty' [hermosa era Sigismunda antes de su desgracia, pero hermosísima estaba después de haber caído en ella, que tal vez los accidentes del dolor suelen acrecentar la belleza] (*The Trials* IV, 14.349; *Los trabajos* IV, 14.711). What stands out in the descriptions of both women is how the ravages of time increase their beauty. This ennobling of the body through its scars and faults provides another example of historical iconicity: bodily perfection and presence are constituted in and by the grotesque body's passage through time.

This earthy tone continues in the opening scene of book III, chapter 3, when the narrator personifies the hollow tree in which a shepherd has hidden the woman as 'pregnant.' In this unemblematic image it is difficult to discern where the tree ends and the woman begins, since they are joined in a complex relation of synthesis.[20] Continuing in this same vein, the child nurses from the udders of a goat, while the woman, who will not be able to recognize her own son until her husband appears at the end of the episode, is nourished on 'peasant food' [rústico sustento] (III, 3.451). Still, to this point, Cervantes seems to deploy the traditional structure of romance, in which the portentous birth of the child leads to the heir's temporary exile from his legitimate home. That being said, the question of identity is not really solved according to the feudal genealogical necessity that drives romantic plots. This ambiguity is significant, since, according to Lezra, 'Naming is intuitive knowledge tying body to subject, act to representation, form to matter' (155). One could argue that the fact that Cervantes does not give a name to the child sheds an oblique ray of light on how his characters insist on controlling the terms of their own social recognition. In this sense, the fact that Auristela seems so out of touch with the gap separating how she desires to be seen from how the narrator repeatedly questions this object of her desire is indicative of a Cervantine 'critique of the aesthetics of self-recognition' (Lezra 137). In the present case, the mystery of the reunited yet still estranged mother and child penetrates the minds of the protagonists, driving them to hasten the woman's recovery: 'they took her out of the tree to give her some air and to learn from her what they wanted to know' [la sacaron del árbol para que le diese el aire y para saber della lo que deseaban] (*The Trials* III, 3.206; *Los trabajos* III, 3.452). The echoes of the opening scene of the novel resonate as the pilgrims subject the 'prisoner of the tree' [prisionera del árbol] to their insistent questions and desire for knowledge (III, 3.451).

When Feliciana's narration begins, the tension and violence between the honour code and her procreative, grotesque body of becoming provide the conflictive medium for the narration of the episode. She tells the pilgrims of her noble origins and apologizes for her present state of faded beauty. Her beauty had already been compared favorably to that of Auristela and Constanza upon her arrival, so her humility serves to reintroduce Cervantes' insistence on the positive effects of time on human beauty and understanding. In like fashion, her narration deepens our understanding of the relationship between beauty and the accidents of history, while critiquing the violence produced by social and moral imperatives, through the lyrical and playful portrayal of her secret courtship and marriage to a man her father forbade her to marry. She narrates their secret encounters ('we often saw each other alone' [vímonos muchas veces solos y juntos]) and unintended consequences in a way that stages the *becoming* of bodies and their material transformation: 'Because of these meetings and loving thefts, my dress was shortened and my infamy grew, if the conversation of betrothed lovers can be called infamous' [Destas juntas y destos hurtos amorosos se acortó mi vestido y creció mi infamia, si es que se puede llamar infamia la conversación de los desposados amantes] (III, 3.454). In the end, her love story is symbolized through the concept of 'conversación,' an irreducibly anamorphic image which synthesizes bodily and verbal communication while establishing the body as both source and medium of the lovers' dialogue. This passage also corroborates the view that Feliciana's story defies the dialectic of guilt and innocence in several ways. In the same way that her body rejects baroque standards of beauty, the narrative places conventional, institutional morality in an antagonistic position as regards her love story. Her defense of the legitimacy of her desire and its effects prevents the reduction of this concept to a moral lesson.

What follows is an ambivalently marvelous story, whose conflicts are staged for an impertinently curious audience through a series of vivid and suspenseful images: the desolation Feliciana feels when she is informed by her father that the fiancé he has chosen for her is waiting downstairs to marry her; her fear that her husband might be discovered while he waits for her in the garden; finally, the unexpected appearance of the child that she 'hurled ... to the floor' [arrojé ... en el suelo], while her father shouts and pounds at her door (III, 3.455). In a more conventional context the climactic image might serve as an emblematic warning against any number of 'illegitimate' desires, but here there is nothing but suspense, or intensity, according to Gumbrecht's definition of presence: '[it] so blinded my ability to think, not knowing what to do, I waited for my father or my brothers to come in and take me not to get married, but to my grave' [a mí me cegó el discurso de manera que sin saber qué hacer, estuve esperando a que mi padre o mis hermanos entrasen, y en lugar de sacarme a desposar, me sacasen a la sepultura] (*The Trials* III, 3.207; *Los trabajos* III, 3.455). Once again the opening scene of the novel is anamorphically alluded to, destabilizing the civilized-barbarian dialectic. The diegetic tension in the story is heightened even more by the extra-diegetic signals that suddenly come from the 'centinelas' posted by the pilgrims, warning of the approach of other unexpected visitors. Might we call this reminder of the staged, or metafictional, nature of these marvels metasuspense? The distance opened up by the intervention of the narrator is not completely ironic, as the unexpected visitors on the scene resituate the group of protagonists within the personal history of Feliciana and her own abysmal experience. They are no longer observers but participants, accomplices, as is the reader, who may be led to consciously take note of his or her enjoyment and emotional investment in the ambivalently framed honour play.

Gumbrecht uses the term *Erlebnis* to describe 'an object of perception on which a consciousness focuses without having made sense of it.' This open-ended moment of wonder, in which meaning is destabilized by the appearance of 'objects that have no practical use … leaving them *present to hand* without making them *ready to hand*,' is the essence of Gumbrecht's attempt to displace the phenomenon of presence towards an anti-ideological and anti-utopian conception of art (*Production* 77). According to Lezra, 'On the one side [*present to hand*] would be found the stubborn pathology of a set of more or less resistant symptoms giving rise to an effort to make sense out of them, and on the other [*ready to hand*] would be found the equally stubborn institutional necessity of representing the relation between pathology and its description as a referential narrative' (55). In any emblem it is imperative for the emblematist to 'discover' a soul for the iconic and thus resistant body he places in the foreground; just as important, he must convincingly demonstrate how the new, ingenious relationship between the two is the 'natural' or institutional meaning for the object. As we saw in the chapter on Lope de Vega's emblematic *indios*, Žižek compares this operation to the movement in the Hegelian dialectic that creates the effect that the object, or subject, always-already meant what we are just now discovering through the act of interpretation, as well as a forgetting of the interpretive activity of the reader. In short, the emblematist's goal is to make the object-image *ready to hand*, which means that its meaning becomes overdetermined to such an extent that the material object disappears into the allegorical fabric of meaning: body signifies sin; birth signifies death, etc. *Present to hand*, on the other hand, is what one encounters, for example, in Don Quixote's *baciyelmo*, where the meaning of the object vacillates between at least two possible uses, two possible ways of becoming *ready to hand*. For if the basin-helmet has two meanings and therefore two uses, might it not have an infinite number of possible uses depending on its material experience of what J.C. Rodríguez calls 'radical historicity' (*El escritor* 72)? Are we not then completely estranged from its specific, which is to say, socially determined use value? The 'thingness' of this curiously shaped, metal object overrides our ability to say with certainty what it is, or what its real or natural purpose might be.

A similar situation occurs when Feliciana unexpectedly 'hurls' the sexless and nameless 'creature' out of her body onto the floor of her room. What could be more indicative of the grotesque nature of human existence, its brute power as well as its fragility, than unconsciously giving birth while being threatened with death? What could be more antithetical to the divine presence conjured up in the politically charged world of the *auto sacramental* than the presence of a vibrant and slippery mass of newly arrived flesh whose meaning is infinite? At this moment, when Feliciana is frozen with fear, threatened from seemingly every side, the natural meaning of her child, born either inside or outside of wedlock, depending on one's point of view, cannot be established (a fact underlined several times in the episode, as we never learn his name). If we recall the opening scene of the book when Periandro is at least cleaned up by the barbarians before being threatened with the arrow, a disturbingly barbaric frame begins to shade the honour code that threatens the life of both mother and child throughout this episode.

At this high point in the narrative, it is significant that Cervantes turns to Auristela, who interjects the following commentary: 'It is a case that can serve as an example for shy ladies who want to make a good account of their lives' [es un caso que puede servir de ejemplo a las recogidas doncellas que quisieren dar bueno de sus vidas] (III, 4.458). This emblematic aside wrecks the high suspense of Feliciana's narrative by converting it, with a dizzying turn of perspective, into an exemplary 'case study.' The change is so abrupt that it forces us to consider its source. The moralistic tone of the sententious metacommentary is completely out of step with the ambivalent timbre of the narrative, and yet, the reader can at least smile, if not laugh outright, at the irony that arises from the realization that Auristela is precisely this type of 'exemplary' character: a young woman who travels around the world with her husband/lover after having fled her home to avoid marrying the man chosen by her family. Imminent tragedy turns to hilarious (self-)parody at Auristela's narcissitic pointing of the finger at her own mirror image and subsequent inability to recognize the similarity between herself and the willful Feliciana. This is only one of many examples of what Sacchetti calls the 'irony of self-betrayal,' in which Auristela's actions or words unmask her own questionable motives and conduct (47).

As Auristela's emblem quickly falls apart, Feliciana picks up the thread of her story and tells how she ran out of the house, leaving her family, newborn child, and husband behind. One would be hard pressed to say what her family really is at this point, since the alienation is so complete that she even fails to recognize her child upon being reunited with it: 'This token must belong to another, it is not mine' [De otra debe ser esta prenda, que no mía] (III, 4.460). All of the bloody rituals in the *Persiles* that De Armas Wilson has convincingly associated with the paternal paranoia at the heart of symbolic constructs of genealogical certainty are undone by this wriggling and nursing kernel of absolute Otherness: neither blood nor hidden sentiments serve to clarify its point of origin or its intended meaning. If the maternal signature can be erased by the same symbolic structures meant to fix the offspring's place under a paternal signifier, what does this say about patriarchal identity itself? Once again, the biblical echoes (*this sign must belong to another*) are contextualized in a completely unexpected way, especially if we consider the similarities between Feliciana's flight and that of Mary and Joseph in the wake of Herod's infanticidal furor. For that matter, we might also consider the problematic paternity of Christ himself. Let us recall that Mary was also already engaged when the archangel secretly came to *converse* with her. Or scandalously put, God sends the archangel to arrange his nocturnal visit with a betrothed virgin, which lends a mysterious and sacramental light to Rosanio's secret visits to Feliciana's garden.[21] Seen yet another way, the continued intertwining of tragedy and parody threatens the central mysteries of the Christian faith altogether.

The subversion continues when Auristela asks Feliciana if she feels well enough to take part in the pilgrimage. The old shepherd who hid Feliciana assures them that the girl-mother is stronger than any of them thinks, as he compares her to an ewe that wanders off to give birth and then almost immediately returns to the flock. To complete his *exemplum*, the shepherd adds a commentary on Eve and the improbability that she gave birth in a bed or even under a roof. In an arrangement that is structurally identical to the composition of an emblem, Feliciana's plight is re(con)textualized within a three-sided mosaic composed of an ewe (mother of the lamb [of God]), Eve (mother of human kind), and Feliciana herself (mother of an unnamed child). The tone of this assemblage has little or nothing to do with the allegorical and transcendental discourses of emblematics; instead, we are presented with something closer to the famous paintings by Diego Velázquez of Bacchus and Mars. Much as occurs when Velázquez dresses the Roman gods in earthly flesh and garb, the placement of the allegories of the Virgin and Eve in the mouth of the old shepherd subjects them to a grotesque materialization, or process of earthly becoming, through which religious allegories morph into blurry, proto-sketches of vividly real and highly personal *historias*. As Maravall puts it, '[Velázquez] in no way wants to paint psychology; what he is searching for is to resolve the engrossing problem of painting existence, life, in its dramatic and concrete singularity' (*Velázquez* 100).

Feliciana's story comes to a climax in the monastery of the Virgin of Guadalupe, where the pilgrims decide to stop on their way to Rome. Once again, the body occupies the foreground of the story when the pilgrims enter the church and find innumerable wax eyes, crutches, walking sticks, a large number of crude prosthetic devices, and shrouds adorning the temple walls, where they expected to see luxurious and costly adornments.[22] Maestro finds this scene to be a hilarious parody of religious ceremony and imagery, while Nerlich compares the tableau to the dark fantasies of Hieronymus Bosch. As I read this scene, however, the grotesque nature of the *ex votos* helps to strengthen the thematic descent toward materiality that characterizes the whole episode, symbolizing the Virgin's intervention in the most basic, grotesque concerns of the pilgrims who visit the shrine.

When Feliciana enters the sanctuary she assumes an imploring posture, becoming a 'living statue,' and 'without moving her lips or making any other sign or movement that would indicate she was a living creature, released her voice to the wind' [sin mover los labios ni hacer otra demostración de movimiento que diese señal de ser viva criatura, soltó la voz a los vientos] (*The Trials* III, 5.217; *Los trabajos* III, 5.473). Her voice becomes a pure instrument of heavenly praise even as her bodily movement is frozen in time, recalling the statuesque portraits of the protagonists at the beginning of the book. As in the case of Periandro, her voice brings the threat of physical death when her father and brother recognize her singing: 'she who will not be, if this blow from my arm does not err' [la que no será si no yerra el golpe de este mi brazo] (III, 5.474). The father checks the son's violent gesture more out of piety for the religious space than out of concern for his daughter's life; thus the blasphemous and immoral taint adheres to both kinsmen as they leave the church with Feliciana in tow. In Childers's words, 'The text inscribes them as desecrators, both when they seek to capture and kill her, and when the brother attempts specifically to avenge his honour in church, before the altar of Our Lady of Guadalupe' (98).

At this climax, Rosanio arrives with his clan to defend his wife and his marriage. In the end, Feliciana's father relents, and the last image of the episode is of the new grandfather, who, 'taking [the child] in his arms, bathed his face in tears, then dried them with kisses and wiped them clean with his gray hair' [tomándolo en sus brazos, tiernamente le bañó el rostro con lágrimas, y se las enjugó con besos y las limpió con sus canas] (*The Trials* III, 5.220; *Los trabajos* III, 5.477). This 'anti-emblem' juxtaposes life and death, the frailty of youth and the understanding of old age, in an image that promises the continuation of life and a transformation of the symbolic rather than the mortification of the flesh according to an allegorical imperative. The sudden outpouring of tears from Feliciana's father serves to baptize the grandson even as it allows the aged visage of the grandfather to be reborn. Lest we be completely overcome by the emotion of the scene, the following words – spoken by the grandfather – serve as an ambivalent inscription for the tender image and reintroduce the motif of the body of the mother and the sensual and playful nature of creation: 'May the mother who bore you and the father who conceived you have all the happiness in the world' [¡Que mil bienes haya la madre que te parió y el padre que te engendró] (*The Trials* III, 5.220; *Los trabajos* III, 5.477). In a barely perceptible nod to Tomé Cecial's 'elogio' of Sancho Panza's daughter Sanchica – '¡Oh hideputa, puta, y qué rejo debe de tener la bellaca!' (*Don Quixote de la Mancha* II, 13.512) – Feliciana's father transforms the conventional insult 'la madre que te parió' into a blessing, thus exemplifying the ambiguity and versatility of language, an effect Bakhtin associates with the blazon: 'The blazon preserved the duality of its tone in its appreciation; in other words, it could render praise ironical and flatter that which was usually not to be flattered' (*Rabelais* 427). Just as the child's body eludes complete codification, the word also comes to life, refusing to correspond completely with one meaning or the other.

Critics as diverse as R. de la Flor, J.C. Rodríguez, and David Castillo have studied Cervantes' tendency to foreground the grotesque throughout his oeuvre. The grotesque is by no means antithetical to Counter Reformation aesthetics and morality, but Cervantes' use of it challenges its conventional function. Malcolm Read's *Visions in Exile* convincingly argues that the baroque grotesque body generally functions within an Augustinian understanding of the 'Great Chain of Being': 'The Chain of Being dramatizes the basic conflict of mind/spirit against body, with mankind delicately poised between these realms' (3). This is the same structure we have seen in Calderón's allegorical characters *Buen Genio* and *Mal Genio*. Read goes on to observe that this concept is also philosophically and morally consonant with predominant schools of thought in the Renaissance, including the Erasmian flight from the body, Huarte de San Juan's association of the body with the *vulgo*, and Platonic attempts to spiritualize the body (11–23).[23] Read and J.C. Rodríguez are therefore in agreement when they connect the cruelly burlesque and satirical use of the body to an organicist ideology that establishes the moral superiority of the ruling elites through the association of grotesque motifs and expressions with the 'lesser' humanity of lower social strata. What we see in Cervantes, on the contrary, responds to what Rodríguez calls 'the animist or capitalist grotesque' [lo grotesco animista o capitalista] (*El escritor* 352). As Maestro notes, 'In Cervantes, the comical is completely dissociated from social humility' (36), which leads to the conclusions of Spadaccini and Talens, Amy Williamsen, David Castillo, and Childers concerning the primary thrust of Cervantes' aesthetics: to wit, his parodic and anti-utopian deconstruction of Counter Reformation dogma. In Cervantes' positive reading of the grotesque, the human body and its inexorable processes of becoming cannot be contained by allegory. Presence in this scheme becomes a radically historicized experience of being as opposed to the expression of an original, transcendental meaning out of time. Human knowledge is gained through experience in time, which leads to understanding, but which leads also to the material effects of time, or scarring. The scars of time, in fact, are constitutive of human understanding. This does not mean that the body and voice of Feliciana achieve a comfortable synthesis with the meaning of her story. The ultimate meaning of her text only exists in the constantly shifting perspectives brought to bear on it, just as the meaning of the appearance of the child's flesh is placed beyond any significant discourse. As Lezra concludes in his reading of *Don Quixote*, 'Every *occasion* – every *event* – that afflicts the Knight, that he encounters or decisively takes up, doubles explicitly and implicitly as an instance of reading and writing, and his thoughts, the narrator's, and Sancho's on these plot events are also instances of metacommentary about the peculiarities of *reading-events* and *writing-events*' (12). The insistent corrosion of linguistic events by a metacommentary that moves between their writing and reading, without allowing the reader to establish meaning in a way that would allow an objective distance, is at the heart of Cervantes' innovative use of emblematics.

Fortune and Occasion: Cervantes' Reformation of Emblematics

There are many occasions in the *Persiles* where Cervantes deploys specific and very recognizable emblematic motifs. Both Feliciana's narrative and Auristela's personal (mis)interpretation of the exile's tale begin with what appear to be conventional allusions to very popular emblem motifs: Fortune and Occasion. What Cervantes does with these emblematic structures, however, is anti-emblematic and can be used to develop my thesis with regard to Gumbrecht's definition of immanent presence. After Feliciana's narration of her trials, Auristela prefaces yet another pathetic complaint to Periandro with a classical and quite conventional reference to the vicissitudes of Fortune:

> 'It seems to me, dear brother,' said Auristela to Periandro, 'that trials and dangers have jurisdictions not only over the sea but over all the land as well ... This woman they call "Fortune," whom I've sometimes heard talked about and who they say takes away and gives good things when, how, and to whomever she pleases, must certainly be blind and capricious, because it seems to me she raises up those who should be on the ground and brings low those who are on the mountains of the moon.'
>
> [– Pareceme, hermano mío – dijo Auristela a Periandro – , que los trabajos y los peligros no solamente tienen jurisdicción en el mar, sino en toda la tierra ... Esta que llaman fortuna (de quien yo he oído hablar algunas veces, de la cual se dice que quita y da los bienes cuando, como y a quien quiere) sin duda alguna debe de ser ciega y antojadiza, pues, a nuestro parecer, levanta los que habían de estar por el suelo y derriba los que están sobre los montes de la luna.] (*The Trials* III, 4.209; *Los trabajos* III, 4.457)

This is a canonical – even medieval – rendering of the Fortune emblem, as she is often portrayed in an oceanic setting as a naked goddess who sports winged feet that tread upon spheres of breakable glass. According to Covarrubias, 'The mad sea and inconstant moon never have the same being and consistency, Fortune exceeds them both, changeable in her essence' [El mar insano, y la inconstante luna, / Jamas tienen un ser, y consistencia, / Con ellas haze tercio la Fortuna / Mas que las dos, mudable por esencia] (134) (figure 14).[24]

The image in Covarrubias's emblem visually conveys its religious intent by cradling the figure of Fortune in the hand of Providence, which helps reveal the nihilistic undertow of Auristela's use of the emblem, where Providence plays no part. The lesson we ought to take from Auristela's understanding of Fortune, which unveils her 'pagan' beliefs, becomes much clearer when seen in light of Alciato's *subscriptio* for this same emblem (figure 15): 'Art is a gift to counter Fortune,

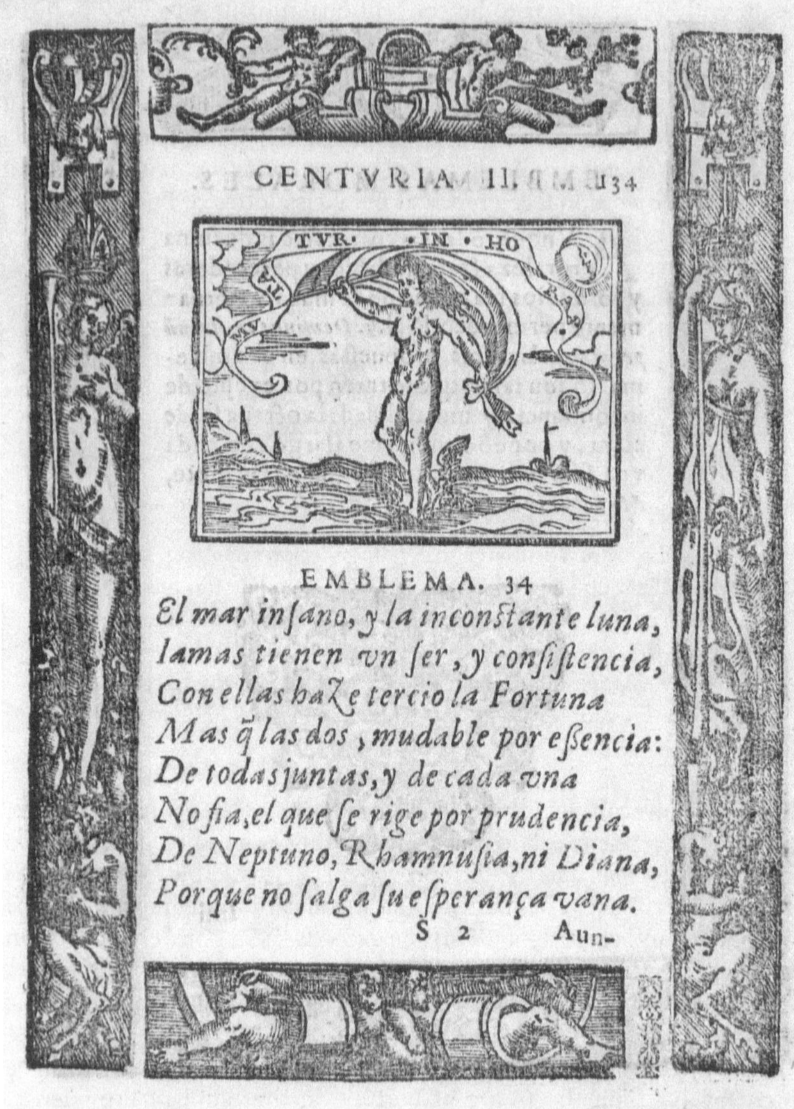

CENTVRIA III. 134

EMBLEMA. 34

El mar inſano, y la inconſtante luna,
Iamas tienen vn ſer, y conſiſtencia,
Con ellas haze tercio la Fortuna
Mas q̃ las dos, mudable por eſſencia:
De todas juntas, y de cada vna
No fia, el que ſe rige por prudencia,
De Neptuno, Rhamnuſia, ni Diana,
Porque no ſalga ſu eſperança vana.

S 2 Aun-

Figure 14 'Mutatur in horas,' in Sebastián de Covarrubias y Orozco, *Emblemas morales* (1610), 134

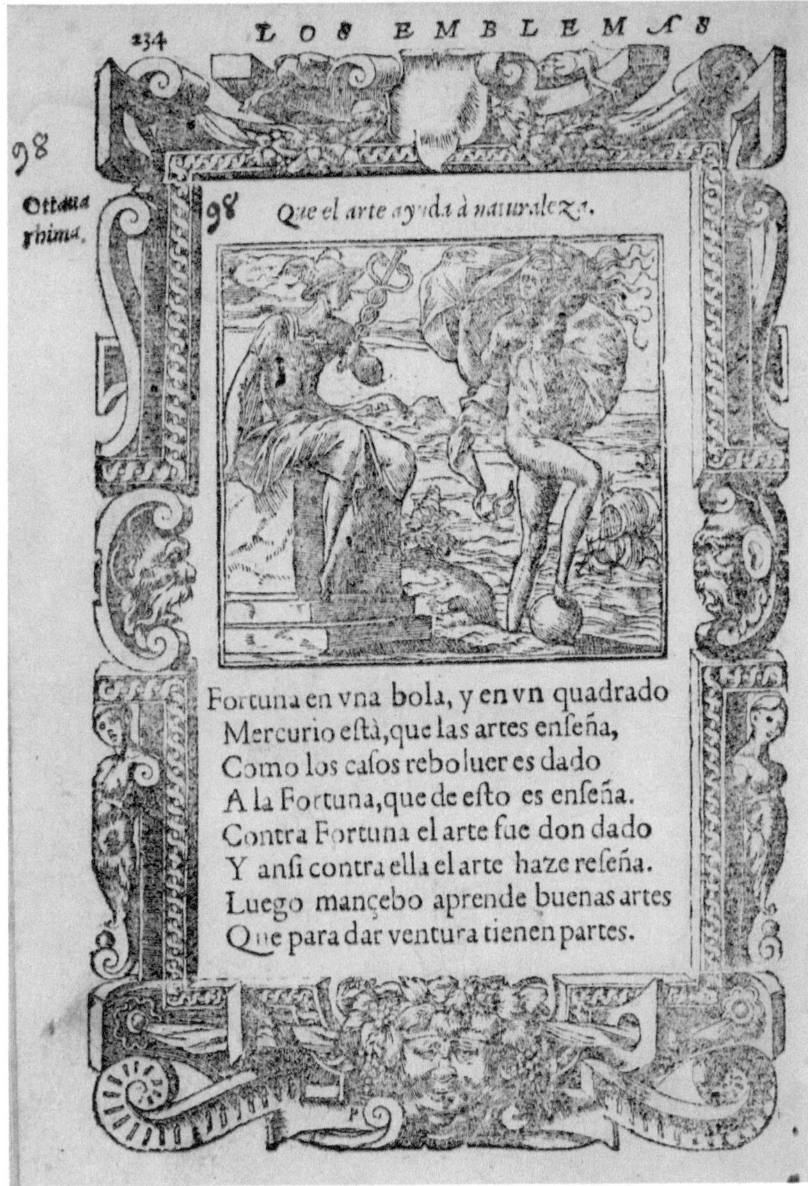

234 LOS EMBLEMAS

98

Ottaua rhima.

98 Que el arte ayuda à naturaleza.

Fortuna en vna bola, y en vn quadrado
Mercurio eſtà, que las artes enſeña,
Como los caſos reboluer es dado
A la Fortuna, que de eſto es enſeña.
Contra Fortuna el arte fue don dado
Y anſi contra ella el arte haze reſeña.
Luego mançebo aprende buenas artes
Que para dar ventura tienen partes.

Figure 15 'Que el arte ayuda à naturaleza,' in Alciato, *Emblemas* (1549), 234

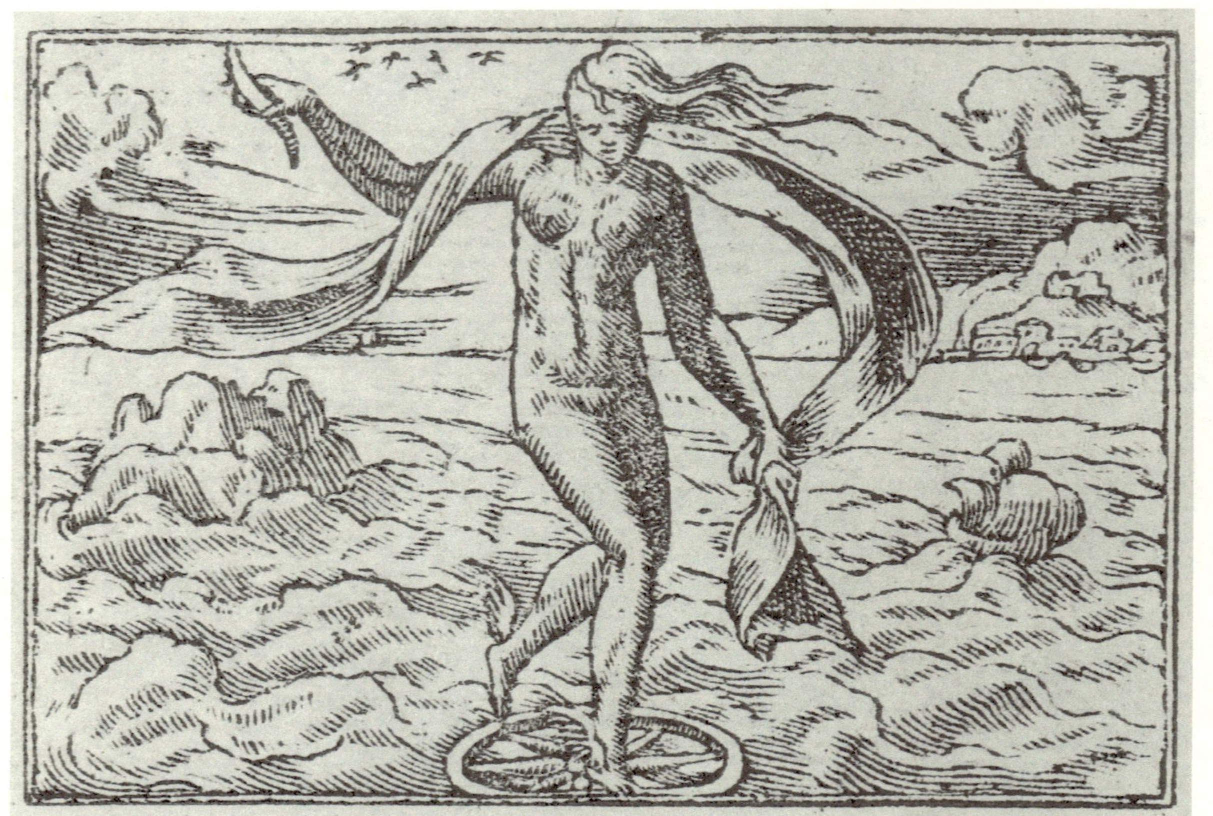

Figure 16 'La occasion,' in Alciato, *Emblemas* (1549), 36

and marches against her. So, young man, learn good arts, as they can bring you good fortune' [Contra Fortuna el arte fue don dado, / y ansí contra ella el arte haze reseña. / Luego, mancebo, aprende buenas artes / Que para dar ventura tienen partes] (234).

The exhortation to learn 'good arts' works well with Alciato's image of a blindfolded Fortune, as the inattentiveness of Fortune to man's trials offers up opportunities to navigate through her tempests, much as Gracián's *verdaderos sabios* demonstrate. Unlike the hopeless posture of Auristela, for Alciato there are ways to alter one's fortunes, which means taking responsibility for the event of one's coming into the world.

The most commonly cited emblematic motif in the *Persiles* is *la Ocasión*, an emblem that also appears in Alciato's *Emblemas* (figure 16). Much like Fortune, Occasion is portrayed as a naked woman with winged feet who stands on the wheel of fortune in the middle of the sea. Unlike Fortune, however, her long hair springs from the front of her head, and she holds a very large knife up in the air: 'So I can untie and cut as much as I can, I bring a knife of great sharpness [wit?]' [Y quánto desatar y cortar puedo, / Navaja traigo de gran agudeza] (36). As is well known, one must seize Occasion as soon as she appears, because once she is upon you it is too late: 'And so that whoever encounters me can grab hold of me, hair was placed on the front of my head. And if someone allows me to go by, he cannot take me from behind' [Y porque a quien topare pueda asirme / Cabello dio delante a mi cabeza. / Y por si alguno permitiere irme / No pueda por detrás después tomarme] (36). Turning our attention to the *figura*, it is noteworthy that Occasion does not seem to be subject to the constant movement of time but rather dances on Fortune's wheel, which has been toppled onto its side. Seizing an occasion in the event of its appearance, then, would seem to offer a way to control one's fortunes for those subjects willing and able to act in a timely manner. Whether or not this is the intended meaning is still impossible to determine, at least with respect to the author Alciato, since even by 1549 most evidence suggests that publishers and engravers (and even translators) exert more influence over the composition of the emblems than the author of the text (Rawles). Nevertheless, if we combine this emblem with Alciato's advice concerning artful ways to deal with one's fortunes, we arrive at a particularly Cervantine definition of aesthetic practice as a timely, which is to say, temporally constituted art. This understanding of aesthetic creativity is also at the heart of Gumbrecht's theory of material presence, which describes an encounter with artistically altered objects that challenges the reader-subject's understanding of what the world means or, what amounts to the same thing, what the metaphysical truth of the world is. Gumbrecht links this idea to the Bakhtinian notion of 'insularity,' which is a term Bakhtin uses to exemplify the ways in which the carnivalesque subverts one's hold on reality by violating the symbolic barriers – the insularity – between humanity as phenomenon and the processes of becoming of the human body. Insularity, or the Name of the Father, is what would otherwise shield Feliciana's consciousness of motherhood from the absolute Otherness represented by the physical presence, or thingness, of the *criatura*. What Cervantes stages here is not only the difference of the mother to the baby and her family, but, more importantly, the difference of the mother to herself. The infant stands in for the estrangement of the human subject from its own material manifestation, whose lack of meaning the honour code attempts to over-determine. What becomes present in the breaking of the 'natural' link between the body and its social interpellation, then, is the difference of the symbolic order to itself, which leads to an experience of presence saturated by a lack of meaning as opposed to the reduction of all life and history to the same meaning. Returning to the philological discussion at the beginning of this chapter, insularity is what fills the irrecoverable gap between the text and its idealized form and meaning, the text and the author, the author and himself, or the critic and his or her narrative concerning the relationship between the text and the author.

Is there a more appropriate figure to represent this concept of historicized presence than the emblematic figure of Occasion? If the subject does not recognize an opportunity to change the course of her life immediately and, moreover, grasp it in the event of its appearance, it is gone. The movement is so sudden that it becomes impossible to distinguish between appearance and recognition, which makes any temporal ordering of the relationship between the two completely arbitrary. Does Occasion's appearance precede one's recognition of it? Or is it the act of recognition that makes Occasion's appearance apparent? In either case, the recognition-appearance of an occasion holds the potential to change the entire course of a life and, more importantly, its meaning in a flash of insight which was inconceivable before the acknowledgment of its arrival. Occasion is literally the embodiment of time as change.

Contrary to the experience of presence of transubstantiated, metaphysical certitudes, Gumbrecht's scheme allows us to see how an occasional art privileges the affectively charged moment of 'aesthetic autonomy,' which is incommensurate with 'the institutional propagation of ethical norms' (*Production* 24). Similarly, by reaching back into the revolutionary possibilities offered by Alciato, Cervantes overturns the moralistic world of baroque aesthetics in favour of an autonomous potential to act otherwise. Rather than privilege the verisimilar pole of the binary of marvelous verisimilitude, he uses a carnivalesque anti-insularity, aesthetic intensity, and wonder to override the containment of the marvelous within meaning effects and an implied moral closure. This helps explain why Feliciana's story trumps Auristela's attempts to project moralizing norms on it and thereby erode 'the potential intensity' of the former (*Production* 102). It also explains Feliciana's preference for the Occasion figure in the narration of her love story: 'We often saw each other alone, for in such matters *occasion* never turns her back but rather offers us her forelock to grasp in the midst of impossibilities' [Vímonos muchas veces solos y juntos, que, para semejantes casos, nunca la ocasión vuelve las espaldas, antes, en la mitad de las imposibilidades, ofrece su guedeja] (III, 3.454; my emphasis). The use of this figure places the primary motivation for Feliciana's history, if not all of its effects and interpretations, in her own hands and connects it to her desire.

To understand the complexity of this figure, I would like to briefly comment on a number of examples in which Occasion offers her forelock in the *Persiles*. The characters who seize Occasion are most often associated with artistic, or artful talents, and not always in a positive way. It first appears in connection with the feminine wiles of Rosamunda, as satirically portrayed by the untrustworthy Clodio: 'When this woman was at the pinnacle of her luck and held fortune by the forelock, I was enraged and filled with desire to show the world how ill-used the wishes of my king and natural lord were' [Cuando ésta estaba en la cumbre de su rueda y tenía asida por la guedeja a la fortuna, vivía yo despechado y con deseos de mostrar al mundo cuán mal estaban empleados los de mi rey y señor natural] (I, 14.223). The reader will note a certain slippage in Clodio's use of the figure, as the normally impersonal and fatalistic Fortune is outfitted with a convenient handle by the conniving mistress of power. A more rigourous editor might chide Cervantes' careless use of emblems, but we might also read this chimerical emblem as an indication of Rosamunda's attempts to take personal control over the desire and fate of a head of state. According to Clodio, a poor model of upright behavior himself,

Rosamunda artfully manipulates the king's desire for her body, which empowers her to influence all sorts of political fortunes. Borja's mechanical rendering of the power of *ingenio* would work well in describing Rosamunda's veiled machinations, which emanate from the king's bed into the Court.

Occasion appears a second time on the island of Policarpo, when the Moorish enchantress Cenotia advises King Policarpo to use the accidental murder of Clodio to imprison the pilgrims on the island and thus carry out his desire to marry Auristela: 'Don't let this occasion, my lord, slip away from you and turn its bald spot towards you rather than its forelock' [No dejes, señor, que la ocasión que agora se te ofrece te vuelva la calva en lugar de la guedeja] (*The Trials* II, 11.148; *Los trabajos* II, 11.355). The artful one here is Cenotia, who seeks to exploit the occasion of Clodio's accidental death by manipulating the king's perverse desire for the young runaway in order to further her own desire for revenge. This is not unlike what we have seen with Rosamunda earlier, as in both cases the feminine figure empowers herself from a symbolically inferior position, reminding us of Bell's notions of ritual agency. We might also see the juxtaposition of these two uses of the emblem as a narrative progression, which moves from the more generalized political agenda of Rosamunda toward the very personal stake of Cenotia. What makes these two gestures of autonomy illegitimate is most likely the desire of both women to deceptively manipulate the desire and will of other subjects, which deprives the other of his sovereignty – not without the complicit and perverse desire of the royal 'victim,' I would add. The politically sovereign subjects of the king of England and King Policarpo are best read as exemplary figures in a much broader treatment of individual desires, rights, and social responsibility.

Although the examples in books III and IV are arguably more 'legitimate' than the ones we have just seen, their problematic relation to the symbolic order of Counter Reformation Spain is not so easily determined; indeed, the last example of book III can be seen as an emblem of Cervantes' understanding of Occasion and its relation to art. Here, Isabela Castrucho ingeniously parodies a ritual exorcism, which ends with her own marriage, the death of her uncle, and the baptism of her fiancé's baby brother. What is particularly original in this episode is that Isabela begins her story by portraying herself as an embodiment of Occasion. Similar to the plight of Feliciana (and Auristela), Isabela had been promised by her uncle to her cousin 'in order to keep the estate in the family' [porque la hacienda quedase en casa] (III, 20.615). In this case, however, the relation between the two religious sacraments that frame the episode is reversed. Where Feliciana begins her narration with her private, improvised marriage to Rosanio and ends with the public recognition of their son, Isabela's story begins during a public mass and ends with an improvised and very theatrical exorcism that becomes the occasion of her willful and deceptive marriage to Andrea Marulo. Note the allusion to the religious experience of transubstantiation in Isabela's description of the moment she realizes she is in love: 'his presence remained etched in my soul such that I could not remove it from my memory' [quedó su presencia tan impresa en mi alma, que no la podía apartar de mi memoria] (III, 20.615). Having little time to rewrite her quickly evolving life story, she writes to her beloved: 'I told him in no uncertain terms that occasion was offering her locks in my person: he should seize them' [díjele asimismo que la ocasión en mí le ofrecía sus cabellos: que los tomase] (III, 20.615). The industrious Isabela transforms herself into the figure of Occasion in order to fulfill her desires. In fact, there is no occasion without Isabela's actions, which corroborates my earlier statement concerning the impossibility of distinguishing between the event of an occasion and its recognition. The only question, really, is whether Andrea Marulo can be convinced to recognize it/her as such an occasion. To summarize, we have moved from an erotic experience of transubstantiation to a use of emblematic discourse that directly threatens the Name of the Father. This (sac)religious tone continues to the end of the episode when Isabela agrees to marry the well-played exorcist/priest (Andrea Marulo, of course) during the mock exorcism, which turns into a real wedding (and funeral and baptism!). What is more, in religious terms, the 'evil spirit' ejected from Isabela's body and then annihilated is none other than her own uncle, who stands in for her deceased father.[25] Her *inscriptio* for this anti-emblem is contained in her exclamation that all of this comes about 'Thanks to God and my diligence' [Gracias a Dios y a mi diligencia] (III, 21.618). According to Bell's notion of ritual structure, Isabela's artistic ingenuity is the material practice of a prodigious ritual agency, which attacks the conventional socio-religious and genealogical hiearchies of Counter Reformation Spain. The episode ends with the aforementioned marriage, funeral, and baptismal rites, with Isabela dressed for mourning on her wedding day: 'she dressed herself for mourning, Isabela, because this thing they call death mingles marriage beds with tombs and festive adornments with mourning clothes' [se puso luto, Isabela, porque esta que llaman muerte mezcla los tálamos con las sepulturas y las galas con los lutos] (III, 21.624). As Williamsen explains, there is really no way to untangle the Gordian knot of carnivalesque and non-carnivalesque motifs in this episode: 'even though the liberation from the official order proves ephemeral, the brief instant of hierarchical inversion may have lasting effects' (168).

Conclusion

My last example of Cervantes' use of Occasion comes not from the *Persiles* but from the Prologue to the *Novelas ejemplares*, in which the author apparently offers the reader a glimpse of his physical portrait and personal history: 'He is called Miguel de Cervantes Saavedra; he was a soldier for many years, and a captive for five and a half, where he learned to have patience in adversity; he lost in the naval battle of Lepanto his left hand to a harquebus shot, a wound that, although it seems ugly, he considers beautiful, for having earned it in the most memorable and high *occasion* that the last centuries have witnessed and that future ones may hope to see, battling under the triumphant banners of the son of that thunderbolt of war, Charles V, in fond memory' [[L]lámase Miguel de Cervantes Saavedra; fue soldado muchos años, y cinco y medio cautivo, donde aprendió a tener paciencia en las adversidades; perdió en la batalla naval de Lepanto la mano izquierda de un arcabuzazo, herida que, aunque parece fea, él la tiene por hermosa, por haberla cobrado en la más memorable y alta *ocasión* que vieron los pasados siglos ni esperan ver los venideros, militando debajo de las vencedoras banderas del hijo del rayo de la guerra, Carlos V, de feliz memoria] (cited in Rodríguez, *El escritor* 446; my emphasis). The elusive figure of Cervantes is apparently made present through a personal and inimitable history that combines a momentous occasion with the grotesquely scarred yet beautiful body of becoming. However, the split between the object of the description and the third person narrator refuses any complete closure around the identity of the author, who remains Other to this self-portrait. If the figure of Cervantes becomes suddenly present here, his farewell in the Prologue to the *Persiles* is equally precipitous, as he watches the young student with whom he had been conversing recede into the distance: 'I turned to embrace him, he likewise offered his arms to me, he spurred on his *burra* and left me as ill-disposed as he was well mounted on his *burra*, who had given my pen great *occasion* to write witticisms, but not all times are the same' [Tornéle a abrazar, volvióseme [a] ofrecer, picó a su burra y dejóme tan mal dispuesto como él iba caballero en su burra, a quién había dado gran *ocasión* a mi pluma para escribir donaires, pero no son todos los tiempos unos] (123; my emphasis).[26] In the first case, as J.C. Rodríguez explains, Cervantes answers the ad hominem insults hurled at him in the Prologue to Avellaneda's *Quijote;* and in the second, he is answering those critics who portray him as primarily a humorous writer. J.C. Rodríguez writes, 'if someone does not know how to "regard my wounds" it is because he does not know how to look (and in the end, as well, he does not know how to read), since a soldier's wounds are his true glory, his true stars' (*El escritor* 452). And so we move from the occasion of the writer's military greatness, symbolized by his scarred hand, to the missed occasion of Cervantes' critical acclaim, embodied by his last, 'greatest,' and scarred work, *El Persiles.* In both cases powerful truths concerning the writer and his art appear as suddenly as they fade into history. If there is an emblem that might stand in for an artistic practice that revels in the time-bound, materially based, and ever becoming grotesqueness of an authentically human condition, it could only be that of Occasion: an eternally young woman who offers her locks to those willing to wager on what Ortega y Gasset calls the 'eternity of the instant' (51).

Conclusion: Authorial Emblems

In the 2000 movie *Quills*, the Marquis de Sade, brilliantly played by Geoffrey Rush, smuggles his 'pornographic' novels out of the insane asylum where he is incarcerated by bundling them up in his soiled linens. This is not mere meta-phor-play on the part of the film's director, Philip Kaufman, as the trope of 'dirty laundry' establishes an intimate connection between the erotic and transgressive nature of the inmate's textual corpus and the repressive efforts of a self-consciously 'enlightened' society to separate itself from the embodied expressions of its most extreme, yet universal, currents of thought and behaviour. By focusing on the production, reception, and dissemination of the texts, rather than their content, which is consistently downplayed, Kaufman relocates the dramatic conflict outside of de Sade's texts themselves and points instead at their circulation as underground bestsellers. In this way the director begins to answer Foucault's question about what an author is: 'When Sade was not considered an author, what was the status of his papers? Were they simply rolls of paper onto which he ceaselessly uncoiled his fantasies during his imprisonment?' ('What Is an Author?' 227). As de Sade's novels become more popular outside of the hospital, *Quills* begins to explore their reception inside the asylum walls, thus forging an implicit connection between the diverse society of the asylum and society at large. The asylum walls play various roles in the exploration of these parallel spaces: on the one hand, they are meant to enclose de Sade's deviant art from polite society, a function that arguably serves to convert the novels into highly prized commodities, as the attempt to hide them makes them infinitely more desirable. On the other hand, the institutional enclosure protects the perversely violent actions of doctors and priests from the scrutiny of the outside world. The question of what is truly perverse about what Gutiérrez would call the macro-SADE is thus channeled towards the ideological sacred cows of the Enlightenment: commerce, science, reason, morality, and the material instrumentalities of those same ideals. One of the most striking features of this staging of the processes of artistic creation, dissemination, and, ultimately, containment is the wide range of readerly perspectives among the inmates and staff of the asylum, especially when they are juxtaposed to the reactionary postures of subjects who are supposedly more enlightened and, thus, reasonable. Many of the scenes in the movie display characters in the perverse act of enjoying de Sade's writing.

Kaufman starts with the hospital staff, some of which are erotically stimulated by de Sade's excessive sexual descriptions and begin to incorporate this curious manner of art into their sexual fantasies and social intercourse. For these subjects, art serves as a medium that creatively influences the sexual and emotional commerce of this microcosm of society. In the case of the maid Madeline, played by Kate Winslet, we encounter an 'innocent' mind that finds artistic and arguably political inspiration in the novels. It is she who sneaks the manuscripts out of the walled enclave and, in one case, transcribes the stories from the Marquis' stained bedsheets onto paper and thus converts them into a text. More striking still are the insistent parallels drawn between those inmates incarcerated due to their more destructive and potentially lethal pathologies – the inability to distinguish fiction and fantasy from truth and action – and the increasingly violent attempts of scientific, government, and religious authorities to arrest the quill of the comparatively rational de Sade. The circulation of de Sade's erotic fiction works to unveil the very real violence and unconscious fantasies of Enlightenment categories of thought, as the concrete actions of the authorities seem completely out of step with the fictional nature of the texts. The problem of course is that de Sade unveils the psychosexual and political unconscious of modernity through the excessive actions and thoughts of his characters. In symbolic terms, the critical attitude towards the novels embodies a combination of iconoclastic rejection and iconophilic phenomenalization of their ideas.

Sent by none other than Napoleon, the morally and scientifically upright Doctor Royen-Collard (Michael Caine) pressures the well-meaning if painfully naïve Abbot Coulmier (Joaquin Phoenix) to harness ever more tightly the 'privileges' of the institution's most intelligent and urbane if morally deviant inmate.[1] What begins with the confiscation of the Marquis' writing implements progresses to the ransacking of his quarters, after he improvises and writes a novel on his bedsheet with wine; the stripping of his body, after he uses his own blood to write a novel on the clothes he is wearing; and, finally, the bloody removal of his tongue, when he refuses to shut his mouth. As occurs so often in the *Persiles*, it is the authorities whose actions are seen to embody the barbarity of political oppression in their constant attacks on de Sade's person. Their absolute failure to bring down de Sade's project is an eloquent testament to one of the points I have attempted to make throughout this study: that the author and the text function on two distinct levels. The attempt to transduct and thus contain the power of literature by imprisoning, dismembering, and ultimately annihilating de Sade's body only serves to highlight the blindness of the authorities to their own excesses. In the end, they seem to accomplish precisely what they had hoped to avoid: the phenomenalization of some secret, ultimate, if monstrous, meaning to the texts, a meaning which cannot coexist with all of the diverse readings and uses to which the text is put.

The piecemeal and violent fragmentation of de Sade's social space and physical body reminds me of Borja's emblem on the *cynocephalo* (figure 3), the dog-headed 'animal from Ethiopia' who 'dies, bit by bit, one day dying a foot, another a hand, and thus his life ends' (390). Of course, rather than directing a critical light onto an increasingly violent institution of instrumental reason, as occurs in *Quills*, Borja's text reduces life to a small point, much as occurs in other emblems: 'Great are the benefits gained by the consideration of life's brevity, since it is so short, he will commit a great folly who truly considering it will not rein in his life, lasting so little time, it will seem a prolonged death rather than a long life which we live' [Grandes son los provechos, que se sacan de la consideracion de la brevedad de la vida, pues siendo ella tan corta, gran locura harà el que considerandolo de veras no refrenare su vida, haviendo de durar tan poco, que antes parece una muerte prolija, que vida larga la que vivimos] (390).

Bringing Borja's emblem to bear on the postmodern movie, and vice-versa, allows me to end this book by making a few comments about what emblematic literature – by which I mean most baroque literature – does and does not do in early modern Spain. A good place to start is R. de la Flor's aforementioned claim concerning the tendency of baroque literature to subvert itself, and thus all political and social institutions, in its recognition of the nothingness on which any earthly enterprise is founded: 'Something that could be defined by saying that the culture, symbolic constructions of art, and the discourses of the Hispanic Baroque carry within themselves the germs of their de authorization, the seeds of the their own *deconstruction*, and the elements of their disillusionment, intentionally showing themselves in a *trompe-l'oeil*, and revealing, with consummate persuasive and rhetorical skill, the fatal structure of an *illusio*, on which everything is founded. All of this demythifies and annuls the supposed exemplarity with which the imperial project promotes itself, placing the 'success' of its discursive strategy in doubt' (*Barroco* 22). I think it is clear from Borja's emblem that the *horror vacui* that both produces and is produced by baroque nihilism can be used for various ends, religious, social, political, artistic, etc. According to the world of the *Spiritual Exercises*, this terror of the void, of the absolute limitations on human reason and action, is deployed in the interests of a socially and politically conservative program of reader education. For the individual reader, the encounter with the void of human existence should produce an excessive self-discipline that checks one's desire for knowledge in this life and redirects it towards the inspection of one's own deviance. This is not to say that other uses of early modern melancholy emanating from the consciousness of inhabiting a fallen body in a fallen creation do not produce different kinds of readers. We have already seen in Gracián a more positive or affirmative manipulation of human limitations in the service of the courtly subject, but this subject only makes sense within the conservative ecosystem of the absolutist court, so we should not be too quickly convinced by R. de la Flor's radical thesis. For if earthly institutions become suspect under the annihilating gaze of the baroque artist, there is nothing more suspect, nothing more constitutively deviant, than the desire of the individual subject of representation, which brings me back to *Quills*.

There are two things from the movie that I would like to bring to bear on this study of the emblem, which I now bring to a close. The first has to do with Kaufman's metaphorical-visual choices, which allow us to allegorize what is happening to the Marquis. Beginning with the metaphor of the soiled linens and becoming more grotesquely corporeal as the movie progresses, with wine, blood, and finally excrement replacing writer's ink, de Sade, like the *cynocephalo*, is gradually dismembered of the technological instruments necessary for writing, even as his art exercises an increasingly forceful penetration into the social worlds around him. Yet these emblems of aesthetic practice give way to images that are much more difficult to abstract toward the level of meaning: the literal writing on the bed sheet with the metaphorical (sacramental?) wine; the inscription of the clothes with the writer's own blood; and the inability of the authorities to stop the flow of desire and words with anything less than a physical silencing and bloody removal of the tongue. Unlike the theoretical and practical dichotomy between *body* and *soul, sign* and *meaning*, which subtends the allegorical flexibility of the emblematic modes of representation, the carnivalesque body cannot be abstracted either from de Sade's writing or the movie's cry for artistic freedom.

In the spirit of cinematic suspense, I have saved the climactic example of Gumbrecht's 'aesthetics of *material presence*' for last: after having ordered the removal of the Marquis' tongue and preserved the quasi-religious relic in a jar of formaldehyde, the by-now pathologically violent Dr Royen-Collard is summoned to the dungeon, where de Sade has been chained by the neck in a circular bunker-like space, with a rag stuffed into his bleeding hole of a mouth. The reason for the summons is that the prisoner has erected yet another scandalous piece of writing on the circular walls of his prison, written by his own hand, which has been dipped in his own shit. The power of this image, which links state-sponsored violence, artistic freedom, and grotesque bodily matter, achieves the status of the sublime, as de Sade becomes an unwilling and unconscious martyr for an ideal that transcends his own act even as the act itself becomes literally embodied by his 'essence.' In Barthes's words, 'in precisely this way literature (it would be better from now on to say *writing*), by refusing to assign a "secret", an ultimate meaning, to the text (and to the world as text), liberates what may be called an anti-theological activity, an activity that is truly revolutionary since to refuse to fix meaning is, in the end, to refuse God and his hypostases – reason, science, law' (147).

In one of his many engagements with the German idealist Immanuel Kant, Jacques Lacan coins his own materialist metaphor for the Kantian sublime: the psychoanalyst's term for the sublime recompense that the Symbolic Order bestows upon the modern subject for his sacrifice to the categorical imperative of the law is 'a gift of shit' (268). According to Žižek's translation, 'Kant's transcendental object (his term for *a*) is … a kind of mirage which gives body to the inequality of the form to itself, not an index of the surplus of the material in-itself over form' (*Tarrying*

156). I take this to mean that the 'gift' that comes from the Symbolic Order is in no way commensurate with the sacrifice that is made in its name; the two, in fact, reside on different levels, and only a powerful transduction driven by desire can bring them together. Using John Huston's 1941 movie *The Maltese Falcon* as an example, Žižek notes that the falcon, supposedly fabricated by the Knights of Rhodes as a gift for Charles V of Spain, turns out to be a fake, which means that all of the intrigue and violence motivated by the incredible thirst for possessing the icon-like object has been for nothing (*Looking Awry*). This use of *nothing* in Žižek is specific to his theoretical structure for the real, which, as we have seen, arises from the contradictory, parallax perspectives in play around the object. The sublime nature of the object turns out to be an effect of the violent search for it. One can make a similar reading of *Quills* in that the State's prohibitions and censorship ultimately serve and justify de Sade's artistic enterprise, spurring on a reading public to acquire his novels in the same way that the author creates them: illegally. The perverse interest of the reading public is, in turn, constitutively related to the increasing weight of State-sponsored prohibitions, such that when the reader participates in the reception and dissemination of the novels, he or she fulfills the role that the State has created. This last turn of the screw then paves the way for the State to increase its violent repression of the Other, both inside and outside of the asylum. In the end, the actual content of the novels is beside the point, as their social meaning and function is actualized in markedly contradictory ways by different readers. This is precisely the point that R. de la Flor's radical thesis on the baroque misses. The constant evocation of the nothingness on which social institutions are founded does not necessarily work to subvert these institutions but rather increases the perceived necessity of their violent establishment and the increasingly aggressive nature of their defensive mechanisms. It is here where the difference between baroque theatre, for example, and Kaufman's movie can be noted, as it is not clear in a baroque honour play that the violence that subtends the honour code is excessive, or illegitimate. What is sublime, and perhaps subversive, about Kaufman's movie is not his questioning of the rational foundations of Enlightenment institutions but rather the surplus of desire and language over any attempt to contain them, a surplus that in this case is homologous to the surplus of consumption and digestion over the material need of the body for nourishment; a surplus of sexual energy in excess of any biological impulse for procreation; and a surplus of artistic production that threatens and subverts any social need for symbolic sublimation and libidinal compensation. In the end, the excessive violence of the State embodies this same surplus of institutional desire over the rational foundations on which it ostensibly rests.

The oblique, or anamorphic, truths that de Sade's story discovers become lost if we look too hard at the figure of the author himself. The power of Kaufman's statement emanates from the matrix of social relations from which de Sade's art springs: according to Gutiérrez's scheme, on the level of the micro-Sade, it is apparent that the artist is not in complete control of his artistic drive, as the increasing pressure put on his incarceration is in large part responsible for his frenetic and self-destructive output; on the other, by perceiving how the macro-SADE is caught in an institutionalized dialectic of guilt and punishment (these are residual religious terms, of course), the spectator/reader sees how his art is able to speak powerfully to the moral contradictions embedded in an enlightened scientism. Through this process, Kaufman dismembers and annihilates de Sade's body, not in the interest of punishing the transgressor, but rather to show how the transgression itself is to be found in the relationship between bodies and discourses in which subjects are caught, and not in the bodies and discourses themselves. As with the astonishing birth of the unnamed child of Feliciana de la Voz, the dismemberment of de Sade reveals the Otherness of the subject to himself. Kaufman quite literally isolates and then annihilates the form of the author in order to inspect the material structure of de Sade's strategic practice as a conflictive medium, *emblem*, for the violent negotiation of social and political forces.

Benjamin, Read, Egginton, and especially Bakhtin have shown that in early modernity the body was thought to somehow exceed or limit a sign's potential to coincide completely with its ideal form. In the emblem's transduction of the world of bodies into the world of souls, images into meaning, we recognize that signs themselves exhibit an analogous otherness with respect to meaning due to a material presence and incorrigibility that simultaneously exceeds and contributes to the mystification of a knowledge whose reality comes about through a ritual process of selection, assemblage, and framing. For Bell, it is the sense that symbolic authority proceeds from an Other place that makes ritualization so powerful. It should be clear by now how this works in the emblem; but how is this related to the form of the author? Throughout this study I have endeavored to construct a dialogue of sorts between two seemingly antagonistic forms of emblematic practice: the *empresa* and the *emblema*. As Juan de Horozco y Covarrubias stresses, these two forms represent two distinct modes of authorial as well as readerly activity. The *empresa* partakes of what we might call the myth of the individual artist, as a main goal of this structure is to foreground and display the independent creativity of the *impresario*. If there is a constitutive Otherness to this authorial structure, it is channeled towards individual genius, or the transcendental inspiration of the *vate*. The emblem, on the other hand, situates the author according to a traditional structure of discursive authority in which his practice is both legitimized and shielded within a strategic and institutionally conservative deployment of what Foucault has called the archive (*Archeology*). In both cases, a cult of genius arises, one of the most powerful effects of which is the channeling of critical and interpretative energies into the problematic (I would say 'empty') space of authorial intent, the main question most often being: 'What did the author ultimately intend?' We can readily recognize this form in the individualistic *empresa*, but it is no less present and influential in the enterprises of Borja and Horozco. In every case, the author points a light at his own activity in the hope that the reader will recognize his genius and his legitimacy.

When Calderón brackets off theatrical form from liturgical content, he creates objects of scrutiny at the same time as he constructs a reception structure for the reader; when Crespo separates his violent actions from their allegorical rationalization he does the same thing. In Žižek's words, 'Parallax means that *the bracketing itself produces its object*' (*Parallax* 56). What this means for the emblem is that the humanist subject is from the very beginning implicated in the object of his quest. So, too, is his reader, who, due to the form of the emblem, perceives reality as a nut to be cracked, a handle to grab or avoid, a vessel to be touched and inspected: in other words, an enigma. In light of Kaufman's treatment of the relationship between de Sade's mythical figure as AUTHOR and his circulation, it would be more correct to start with the social recognition of genius and move (backwards) towards the creative act, rather than the traditional order for coupling the two levels or moments of creation. In Egginton's words, 'the subject who is thus figured as holder of original and immediate intention is revealed to be the sort of afterimage of the very process of utterance that expresses that ostensible intention' (*Philosopher's Desire* 84). In other words, we would do well to consider the author as another emblematic, discursive form, historical in nature, rather than a phenomenon or transcendental essence.

By retreating from the 'profound' meaning of emblematic enigmas toward the emblematic form, as I have endeavored to do in this study, what I hope to have accomplished is to show how the meaning of the emblem, and allegorical meaning in general, is not so much communicated by the form as produced by it. This is what Žižek means when he talks about the parallax relationship of ideology and material relations of production: 'The key trap [sic] is not to be blinded by form, but to reduce form to a "mere form," that is, [not] to overlook how the secret of essence *needs* this form, how the form itself is essential' (*Parallax* 55). Taking the problematic *causa* of Cervantes as a case in point, the movement from the contradictory nature of Cervantes' texts to the essence of his ostensible authorial intent is the basic form on which philological certitude has traditionally been based. By declaring that he is the stepfather and not the father of *Don Quixote I*, Cervantes recognizes the irony that arises from the fact that texts and authors function at different levels, much like signs and meaning are stuck on different sides of language. Any attempt to reduce the space between these two phenomena by invoking an authorial presence moves textual criticism into the realm of ritual practice, thus unearthing, once again, the dynamic of ironic self-betrayal that María Alberta Sacchetti analyses so productively in her study of the *Persiles*. Complicating the matter even more is the fact that early modern writers consciously don authorial masks, often with several competing objectives in mind. Nerlich is correct to say that an authorial mask is one way to protect oneself against persecution from authorities, but this is not the only reason for staging one's artistic activity. As we have seen in Gracián and Cervantes, the mask underlines the basic fact that no author is able to completely control the effects of his artistic utterance because the nature of language is such that no subject can completely control what is not his or hers to control to begin with. In similar fashion, the incongruity created by positing an authorial essence in order to substantiate a scientific form is the basic truth and irony of authorial form. I would argue that to seek the meaning of the text by searching for an elusive authorial intent is proscribed by that same text, which constantly and often unconsciously subverts the form of authorial discourse as an illusory form of discursive power. What the critic would do well to avoid, in the end, is the creation of authorial emblems.

Notes

Introduction

1 Unless otherwise indicated, all translations into English are my own.
2 Conrad Peutinger served both the Emperor Maximilian and Charles V, after Maximilian's death. He is a fascinating figure who was a respected humanist and antiquarian. Among his more interesting projects was a series of elaborate woodcuts he designed to accompany lavish editions of poems by Maximilian, as well as a collection of ancient Roman inscriptions he published, again, at the suggestion of Maximilian. It is hard not to consider the possibility that Peutinger's role in the creation of *the emblem* eclipses Alciato's. Remy, Arthur F.J. 'Conrad Peutinger.' *The Catholic Encyclopedia.* Vol. 11. New York: Robert Appleton Company, 1911. 3 Apr. 2009 http://www.newadvent.org/cathen/11784d.htm.
3 In Foucault's words, 'In short, it is a matter of depriving the subject (or its substitute) of its role as originator, and of analyzing the subject as a variable and complex function of discourse' ('What Is an Author?' 229).
4 Daly settles on this broad definition in an attempt to embrace the many forms and expressions of what is, in fact, an incredibly diverse collection of literary, artistic, and architectural discourses. In doing so he follows the pioneering theoretical work of Dietrich Jöns. Where Albrecht Schöne 'insists on the "potential facticity" and inherent thing-meaning relationships as *the* characteristic of the emblem … Jöns … emphasizes that with its allegorical roots in the Middle Ages the emblem is an instrument of knowledge, a way of interpreting reality, the basis of which is the Christian medieval belief in the significance of the qualities of things (cf p 56)' (*Literature in Light of the Emblem* 52).
5 I have taken the phrase 'materialities of communication' from the volume

by the same title edited by Gumbrecht and K. Ludwig Pfeiffer. Gumbrecht writes, '"Materialities of communication" represents the desire for a theory that integrates these three tendencies – toward less anthropocentric (less spiritual), less antitechnological, and less transcendental forms of human self-reference ... the totality of phenomena contributing to the constitution of meaning without being meaning themselves' ('A Farewell to Interpretation' 392, 398).

6 See Giuseppina Ledda, *Contributo allo studio della letteratura emblematica in Spagna (1559–1613)*, especially chapters 2, 4, 6.

7 See María Jesús Díez Garretas, 'Divisas, motes y momos durante el reinado de los Reyes Católicos.'

8 For a discussion of how literature becomes the primary social practice of the modern courtly subject, see Francisco Sánchez, *An Early Bourgeois Literature in Golden Age Spain.*

9 See William Egginton, *How the World Became a Stage: Presence, Theatricality, and the Question of Modernity*, chapters 1 and 2.

10 This discussion follows Santiago Sebastián's Introduction to the recent edition of Daza's translation, 19–26.

11 Michel Foucault writes: 'In writing, the point is not to manifest or exalt the act of writing, nor is it to pin a subject within language; it is, rather, a question of creating a space into which the writing subject constantly disappears' ('What Is an Author?' 225).

12 Russell is actually referring to early modern emblem theorists when he writes: 'So it would appear that emblems actually influenced the perception of hieroglyphics more than hieroglyphics influenced the creation of the emblems' (*Emblematic Structures* 117).

13 Karen Pinkus and Fernando R. de la Flor are two important exceptions to the more traditional philological/iconological approach to the emblem.

14 See Daly, 'Digitizing'; Antonio Bernat Vistarini and John T. Cull, 'On the Trail of Hispanic Emblem Studies'; and Rafael García Mahíques, 'La emblemática y el problema de la interpretación icónica: el caso de la "vanitas."'

15 For a rigorous critique of Maravall's concept of baroque guided culture, see Hilaire Kallendorf, '¿Qué he de hacer?: The *Comedia* as Casuistry.'

16 On Velázquez, see José Ortega y Gasset, *Papeles sobre Velázquez y Goya* 22–5; On Lope de Vega, see Rodríguez, *El escritor* 50.

1 Emblem Theory

1 As the reader has no doubt noticed, I have *emblematically* lifted the heading for this chapter from Bell's *Ritual Theory, Ritual Practice.*

2 The first critic to note the Spanish turn towards a more religiously informed and institutionally framed theory and practice of the emblem is Giuseppina Ledda, *Contributto*. For a more complete picture of the Spanish emblem book scene, see especially Pedro F. Campa, *Emblemata Hispanica: An Annotated Bibliography of Spanish Emblem Literature to the Year 1700*.

3 For an explanation of this dialectical movement from In-itself to For-itself in Hegelian terms, see Slavoj Žižek, *The Sublime Object of Ideology* 176–7.

4 See García Mahíques, *Empresas morales* for a detailed history of Borja's genealogy, diplomatic career, and artistic program.

5 These debates continue into the present day, as evidenced by Daly's study of the German scholars Dietrich Jöns and Albrecht Schöne: 'If Heckscher and Wirth stress the element of wit and enigma in the emblem, Schöne plays down these aspects, insisting on the necessary relationship between word (i.e., meaning) and picture, which derives from the tradition of medieval bestiaries and hieroglyphics, a tradition in which objects are intended to convey inherent meanings (pp. 26–30, 45–50). Jöns emphasizes the tradition of religious exegesis in the emblem as a mode of thought ('Denkform'), while insisting on the neutrality of the form in the Alciatus type of emblem as an artistic form ('Kunstform')' (*Literature* 6).

6 Mahíques, *Empresas*; Campa, 'The Space between Heraldry and the Emblem: The Case in Spain' 53.

7 Daly writes, 'The *impresa* represents the "principle of individuation" (Sulzer, p 35): it was used by one person only "as the expression of a personal aim" (Schöne, p 45). The word itself comes from the Italian for "undertaking," which underlines the functional purpose of the *impresa*. The emblem, on the other hand, is addressed to a larger audience, its message is general, and it fulfills a didactic, decorative, or entertaining function, or any combination of these' (*Literature* 23). J.J. García Arranz and F.J. Pizarro Gómez elaborate on some of the former's functions: 'the *device*, due to its double mission to show a personal intention or quality – be it the "expression of an honest and praiseworthy desire," a "concept or thought concerning good works," "a proposal for obtaining honour and praise through actions," a "sign of a virtuous and noble soul," or a "sign of a concept that is found in the soul" – as well as to stimulate the intellect of whoever interprets it at the same time, requires a level of elegance and dignity formed through a conceptual and visual perfection which demanded the aforementioned regulation' ('La visión' 192). Robert Clements finds yet another definition that validates Borja's objections: 'In the prologue to his *Empresas espirituales y morales*, Juan Francisco de

Villava legislates that *imprese* are formed from historical truth while emblems are products of imagination, citing as the distinction the concepts of tree-on-skull and skull-on-tree found in Covarrubias. Later, Ménestrier was to rephrase the distinction as one between the pictorial and the mystical senses' (111).

8 The 1726 *Diccionario de Autoridades* defines *beneplácito* as the 'approval, permission, or assent given to the judgment and taste of the person, normally superior, for the execution of some work' [aprobación, permisso, ò assenso dado al arbitrio y gusto de persona, regularmente superior, para la execución de alguna obra] (*RAE* online).

9 R. de la Flor cites the characterization of the *Ejercicios Espirituales* by Georges Bataille in *La experiencia interior*: 'It is an error to assign the *Exercises* of St. Ignatius to the discursive method: it inscribes itself within a discourse that regulates everything but in a dramatic way. The discourse exhorts: represent yourself, say to yourself, the place, the characters of the drama, and remain there like one of them; it dissipates – tensing your will in order to do it – the torpor, the absence towards which the words lead' (*Emblemas* 204).

10 Covarrubias's *Tesoro de la lengua castellana o española* lists very similar definitions. However, it does not include the connotations taken from St. Teresa, which were the most relevant for my reading of Borja's text.

11 All entries are taken from the *RAE* online.

12 Although the *Empresas morales* was first published in 1580, the more common text to cite is the 1680 edition due to the fact that it contains all of the emblems from the first part plus a second part with 100 additional emblems. I have indicated from which part of the expanded edition the illustrations have been taken.

13 See Garcilaso de la Vega, Sonnet XXIII, and translation, in Elias L. Rivers, 37.

14 In the words of Bell, 'with regard to objects as sacred symbols, their sacrality is the way in which the object is more than the mere sum of its parts and points to something beyond itself, thereby evoking and expressing values and attitudes associated with larger, more abstract, and relatively transcendent ideas' (*Ritual Theory* 157).

2 Anamorphosis and Theoretical Depth of Meaning

1 Pedro Mexía's *Silva de varia leción* contains a similar interpretation of TAV: 'From the sign and figure of the cross; as before Christ suffered on it, it was revered and esteemed by the Arabs and Egyptians, since it is the

perfect figure' [De la señal y figura de la cruz; como antes que Cristo padeciese en ella fue acatada y preciada por los árabes y egipcios, y como ella de sí es perfectísima figura] (cited by Selig, *Studies* 66).

2 The historical linguist Mark Hale provides a more straightforward explanation when he writes, 'transduction involves the mapping of an entity in one form onto a distinct form,' which provides a clearer concept for understanding my claim that the author and the text (and the reader) function on different linguistic and material levels (55).

3 See also Maravall, *Culture*, 19–56.

4 Panofsky writes, 'The particular form of this unity once again finds its theoretical analogue in the view of space of contemporary philosophy: in the metaphysics of light of pagan and Christian neoplatonism. "Space is nothing other than the finest light," according to Proclus; here, just as in art, the world is conceived for the first time as continuum. It is also robbed of its solidity and rationality: space has been transformed into a homogeneous and, so to speak, homogenizing fluid, immeasurable and indeed dimensionless' (*Perspective* 49).

5 See also Christine Buci-Gluscksmann, *Baroque Reason: The Aesthetics of Modernity*.

6 See particularly *Culture* and *El mundo social de la Celestina*.

7 Maravall, 'Teatro, fiesta e ideología en el barroco' 183. Maravall's notions are taken up and problematized in Godzich and Spadaccini's essay 'Popular Culture and Spanish Literary History.' The authors differentiate between an 'uncritical' or 'inattentive' reception, linked to the uneducated reader/listener who uncritically consumes the fragmented if regulated production of early mass-produced texts, chapbooks in this case; an 'elite' reception of educated or cultured readers who recognize the manipulative nature of mass culture and perhaps even identify with the manipulators (Horozco's cultured reader); and, finally, the totalizing view of the modern novel, both the most ideologically hegemonic and potentially subversive for the nascent absolutist State, 54–60.

8 Praz transcribes the five rules of Giovio for the construction of an *impresa*: '1) that the device should have a just proportion between the body (that is, the picture) and the soul (the motto); 2) that it should not be so obscure as to need the Sibyl for its interpreter, nor so transparent that every mean mechanic might understand it; 3) that above all it should make a fine show, that is, represent things pleasing to the eye, such as stars, fire, water, trees, instruments, fantastic animals and birds; 4) that the human figure should not appear therein; 5) that the motto which is its soul should be in a different language from that of the author of the

device, so that the sentiments should be somewhat more concealed, and that the motto should be brief but no so much so as to be obscure and misleading' (63).

3 Lope de Vega's Emblematic *Indios*

1 See also Aurora Egido, *La fábrica*, and Pablo Restrepo-Gautier.

2 I use both terms here because although the plot structure and the division of the play into three acts argue for its categorization among Lope's historical comedies, the cosmological vision, the primordial importance of the symbol of the cross, and the inclusion of a Catholic mass move the work toward a religious classification. For further discussions of the generic classification of the play, see Brotherton, 'Lope de Vega's *El nuevo mundo descubierto por Cristóbal Colón*: Convention and Ideology'; Case, 'El indio en las comedias de Lope de Vega'; Moisés R. Castillo, 'Lope de Vega, Inventor de América: *El nuevo mundo descubierto por Cristóbal Colón*'; and Dille, 'El descubrimiento y la conquista de América en la comedia del Siglo de Oro.'

3 On the 'invention of America,' see Edmundo O'Gorman, *La invención de América*, 16–17.

4 In the introduction to his bilingual edition of the play, Shannon places the writing of the play in the year 1600, basing his argument on Lope's sojourn at the palace of the Duke of Lerma and the access that Lope would have had to the high ranking aristocrat's library, where he would have found the chronicles from which Shannon and others have gleaned a partial catalogue of the playwright's historical sources. In spite of Shannon's well argued thesis concerning the date of the play, I would place its composition in the years 1606–9, for two main reasons. First, the play contains an ironic reference to windmills in 2.1009-13: 'Pinzón: "He created a world without foundation in his singular imagination like a windmill, and this is the world for which he searches"' [Hizo un mundo sin cimiento / en su ingenio singular / como molino de viento, / y este mundo va a buscar]. With *ingenio* and *molino*, the Cervantine resonance is hard to miss. Second, the play is rich in both Moorish characters and allusions to the conflict between Christians and 'Moors' (more often than not, Moor and Morisco are conflated, which is to say misconstrued, by Golden Age authors), placing it within the growing anti-Morisco sentiment in Madrid, which culminates in 1609 with their expulsion from Castile.

5 Entrambasaguas cites Barry: 'at the precise moment when Spain is going

to rapidly fall from its greatness of the sixteenth century, [Lope] celebrated the two events that had most contributed to making her a leader of nations' (X). Henry Kamen points out that in the years 1585–1605, the English sent two hundred voyages and the Dutch sent one hundred to the Carribean and South America to exploit Spain's inability to defend its overseas possessions. Furthermore, in a period of ten years Spain signed peace treaties with France (1598), England (1604), and Holland (1609): 'The conclusion of peace between France and Spain in 1598, the year of the death of Philip II, was a momentous event that appeared to many Spaniards to be a humiliating retreat' (311).

6 In her study on the *Plus Ultra* legend, Sandra Sider points out that 'Charles first displayed the device in 1516, when the Order of the Golden Fleece assembled in Brussels.' Later on, she cites the work of Earl Rosenthal, who 'has also demonstrated that the motto "Non Plus Ultra" supposedly inscribed on the Columns of Hercules during ancient times may actually have been contrived during the sixteenth century as a mythopoetic response to Charles V's "Plus Ultra"' (257–8).

7 Octavio Paz writes: 'Another and even stranger syncretist emblem: that cross, in the form of the letter *tau,* is none other than the so-called Egyptian cross that according to tradition was found in the temple of Serapis. An Egyptian emblem converted into a *sign* of the Christian prefigurations of hermeticism' (173).

8 See Steinberg, *The Sexuality of Christ in Renaissance Art and Modern Oblivion.*

9 Case is actually referring to Act 1, where the 'reconquest' of Granada foreshadows the conquest of Paradise: 'Thus, the "minidrama" metadramatically presages the christian enterprise in America as predestined and as a continuation of the war against the muslims in Spain and conflicts between idolatry and the Devil' (15).

10 For an extended discussion of Lope's use of the plot structure of the honour play in *El nuevo mundo,* see M. Castillo, 'Lope de Vega.'

11 Brotherton points out that Lope's use of American history is quite eclectic, yet another emblematic quality of the play: 'The name Tacuana evidently derives from a text describing an expedition in Brazil; Alvar Nuñez Cabeza de Vaca provides the origin of both Dulcanquellín and Tapirazú, but in texts referring to Florida and Brazil respectively. The god of these people is Ongol, a name found in a text detailing the religious beliefs of the Araucanians of Chile' (37).

12 The same dynamic comes into play when Dulcanquellín talks about the mysterious prophecies his parents had recounted to him concerning the

future arrival of some foreign visitors to their land, as well as the challenge, either epic or pastoral (I am thinking of Juan del Encina's eclogues), that Tapirazú throws in his rival's face to see who can hold a wooden beam on his shoulders, or lift a boulder, both images that allude to the central symbols of Christianity.

13 Moisés Castillo's *Indios en escena: La representación del amerindio en el teatro del Siglo de Oro* was just coming to press when I was editing this manuscript.

14 The actual agent of the seduction is ambiguous, although I would argue that the barbarian woman is the active partner in this failed attempt at miscegenation.

15 Shannon writes: 'Lope implies that even the simplest of *Indios*, the *gracioso*, is capable of grasping the concepts of Christianity' (6); while M. Castillo calls them 'semi-adoctrinado[s]' ('Lope de Vega' 59).

16 John T. Cull has determined that these 'appearances' are the most emblematic moments in Golden Age theatre: 'The combination of striking visual motifs (*pictura*) in the form of dramatic dialogue (*subscriptio*) imitated the structure of the emblem ... These scenes, designed to provoke *admiratio* in the spectators, often embodied the play's central message, or moral' ('Hablan poco' 620).

17 The allusion to the Centaurs also serves to reintroduce the Herculean motifs associated with the Hapsburg device 'Plus Ultra,' which in the baroque serves to unite Roman imperial rituals and Christological symbols. Sider writes, 'Hercules playes an important role in Roman imperial ritual. During the reign of Diocletian and Maximian, the latter was celebrated as a Hercules figure, which raised the emperor to the status of a demi-god ... Charles' association with the ancient Roman emperors was strengthened, moreover, by his Spanish heritage. He was considered by his contemporaries to be the culmination of the tradition in which Spain had provided imperial leadership in the persons of Trajan, Hadrian, and Theodosius ... Hadrian's mother was from Cadiz, whose coat-of-arms incorporates *Plus Ultra*.' Finally, '[d]uring the late Renaissance, the labors of Hercules became associated with the agonies of Christ' (260–1).

18 See Weiner's thesis in 'La guerra y la paz en tres comedias de Lope de Vega.'

19 Sor Juana Inés de la Cruz picks up on this theme of the unknown god in her Loa for *El divino Narciso*. In the case of the Mexican nun, however, the expected hierarchical subrogation of the 'Dios de las semillas' to Christ the Savior never takes place, as the two religions become historically dif-

ferent if equally valid manifestations, or masks, of the same unnamed and unknowable god.

20 How a barbarian chieftain knows what the phoenix is, or represents, is a problem of another order altogether, best considered alongside the proto-*gongorista castellano* spoken by the *indios*.

21 Once again, the similarities of the cross to the victory palm are hard to miss, as pointed out by Galera Andreu, who cites Gellio: 'I have here why Plutarch says, in battle, the palm branch has changed into a symbol of Victory, because it is natural for this wood to never cede to the force that presses on and oppresses it' (64). Later on he cites Juan de Mal Lara, who writes: 'At the tables of great men the fruit of this illustrious plant brings honour, it encourages the young to win victory, as the soul only honours constancy, and whosoever tries such sweet fruit will thereafter reach a glorious life' [En las mesas de grandes tiene honra / La fruta que esta planta ilustre lleva, / Alienta joven gana la victoria / Que sola la constancia el alma honra / Y quien de tan suave fruto prueva / Alcancara [sic] después de Vida Gloria] (64).

22 See particularly Entrambasaguas; Shannon; Weiner, 'La guerra'; and Teresa J. Kirschner, 'Exposición y subversión del discurso hegemónico en pro de la conquista en *El nuevo mundo de Lope de Vega*.'

23 See Entrambasaguas.

4 From Hieroglyphic Presence to Representational Sign

1 Cited in the Appendix of Hans Belting's monumental study of religious imagery *Likeness and Presence: A History of the Image Before the Era of Art*.

2 Carroll B. Johnson writes, 'Calderón's *auto* uneasily straddles a space where social theory and practice and Counter-reformation theology approach and interact with theatrical tradition and the socio-ideological dimension of secular theatre. The points of intersection are where the internal tensions of Calderón's society and his dramatic practice become visible' (247).

3 Arellano notes that Calderón limits his dramatic production to courtly festivals and sacramental drama once he is ordained in 1651. Later, his nomination as chaplain of the Reyes Nuevos of the cathedral in Toledo is delayed due to the objections of the head chaplain concerning Calderón's dramatic activities. Social acceptance, let alone respectability, was a constant struggle for poets, directors, and actors in early modernity (*Calderón* 18).

4 See Gumbrecht, *Production*; Egginton, *How the World*.

5 See William A. Christian, *Local Religion in Sixteenth-Century Spain*; and Sarah T. Nalle, *God in La Mancha: Religious Reform and the People of Cuenca, 1500–1650.*
6 In Egginton's scheme, *dramatization* implies the perfect imitation of the original primordial event, which becomes intrahistorically 'present' through the dramatic performance; while *theatricality* implies a self-conscious representation of fictional situations in which the difference between the actor and his or her role can never be completely closed.
7 See Nalle, *Mad for God; God in La Mancha.*
8 Arellano and Duarte reproduce the *disposition* from Calderón's *El sacro Parnaso,* which includes the following description: 'The drawings of the painted [nymphs] should be dressed like Sibyls and they should all have in their places some cards *whose mottos* will be given in time' (75; my emphasis).
9 Dutton's transcription of this poem and its heading inserts letters that are missing in the source document. Thus, 'cima' is shorthand for *cimera* and 'lre' is shorthand for *letra*. The reader will note that the rest of the 'Spanish' is equally archaic.
10 See Díaz Balsera.
11 See also Wardopper, who writes, 'imagination is at the same time the *creative* faculty of poets and the *treasonous* faculty of the characters imagined by them' ('La imaginación' 925).
12 For a discussion of a self-parodying example of Calderón's self-representation in the context of the *comedia nueva,* see Margaret R. Greer, '"La vida es sueño o ¿risa?" Calderón Parodies the *auto*.'
13 In his book *Looking Awry*, Slavoj Žižek connects the 'other' anamorphic gaze with the subversion of ideological fantasies of historical necessity and transcendence. See also David R. Castillo, *(A)wry Views*.
14 It is interesting to note that the differences between Luther and the Council of Trent are not nearly as vast as the rhetorical bombast of the arguments would lead one to believe. As Antonio Regalado states, 'The issue that provoked the Council was the lutheran doctrine of consubstantiation or "breading," that Christ and the bread existed together' (*Calderón* 2:33).
15 Calderón's contemporary, René Descartes, attempts an analogous marriage of mathematics to transubstantiation in a bid to legitimize his new science, but he is ultimately unsuccessful. See Tomaso Cavallo, 'Real Accidents, Surfaces and Digestions: Descartes and the "very easily explained" Transubstantiation.'
16 See Nalle, *Mad for God.*

17 I have borrowed the phrase 'hyberbolic and universal solidity' from my earlier citation from Egginton, in which he characterizes the full space of medieval ritual dramatization.

5 Calderón's *El alcalde de Zalamea*

1 By informing his protagonist of the king's imminent arrival at the same time he is told of his election as mayor of Zalamea, Calderón leaves no doubt as to the premature and premeditated nature of Crespo's actions.

2 Charles Aubrun concludes, 'the juridical foundation of Calderón's thesis is debatable, and even fallacious' (171).

3 If one takes into consideration the historical events that coincide with the accepted date of the composition of the play (1642–51 in Díez Borque's edition), it becomes clear that political fragmentation on the peninsula is by most accounts more than just a theatrical concern, as had arguably been the case in the somewhat apocalyptic writings of the *arbitristas* earlier in the century. As we have seen with Horozco y Covarrubias and Lope de Vega, it is precisely in these moments of high crisis in which the idea of the State seems most able to articulate its unity and its hopes for future restoration.

4 Pratt distinguishes between an ethnographic discourse 'in which European metropolitan subjects represent to themselves their others (usually their conquered others)' and 'an *autoethnographic* text, by which I mean a text in which people undertake to describe themselves in ways that engage with representations others have made of them' ('Arts' 585). Mendo's discourse is autoethnographical, and the irony with which Calderón treats him underlines both the 'knight's' subjugated status and the illegitimacy of his enterprise as far as the status quo is concerned.

5 Alciato has an emblem that underlines Crespo's illegitimate stance with respect to his bucolic wealth. The image shows a cloud of locusts decimating a wheat field, and the motto reads, 'Nihil reliqui,' or 'I have left nothing behind' [No he dejado nada atrás]. The commentary indicates that it is pointless to attempt to avoid disaster by turning inward; rather, 'There is no hope except in God' [No hay en qué esperar sino en Dios] (*Alciato: Emblemas*, emblem CXXVII. 167).

6 The point is debatable, as the status of the peasant, even a wealthy peasant, is not clearly articulated in the Spanish baroque. The necessity of the peasant's material wealth, however, is generally recognized, which is what necessitates his interpellation into the monarchical-seigniorial project, albeit at a lower rung on the hierarchical ladder. Carolyn Morrow

juxtaposes these contrasting views of honour in the seventeenth century: the more commonly held view, at least in the Court, was that 'peasants have no more honour than their life, nor more concerns than to play the game of whoever lives wins' (189). But this notion stands in contrast to a reminder that López Bravo gives his readers in 1616: 'we have already talked about the different classes of farmers and that the duties of field-hands and shepherds are very dignified' [hemos hablado ya de las distintas clases de agricultores y de que el oficio de los labradores y de los pastores es de gran dignidad] (cited in Morrow 141).

7 See also Charles Ganelin, 'Calderón Incorporated: Hands and Speech in *Las tres justicias en una* and *El postrer duelo de España.*'

8 Bell cites Radcliffe-Brown, who believes that ritual not only alleviates anxiety but, more importantly, creates it. The role of such anxiety would be to increase the dependency of ritual participants on the forms and structures of ritual activities: 'I suggest to you that what makes and keeps man a social animal is not some herd instinct, but the sense of dependence in the innumerable forms that it takes' (*Ritual Perspectives* 28).

9 'CUNNING: The deceit that one ingeniously uses on another, using ambiguous terms and dubious and equivocal words' [CAUTELA. El engaño que uno hace a otro ingeniosamente, usando de términos ambiguos y de palabras dudosas y equívocas] (Covarrubias Orozco, *Tesoro* 287).

10 Both Cull and Egginton cite John J. Allen's study of the theatrical use of discoveries, or *appareo*. I cite Egginton: 'Of the five functions Allen lists for *apariencias*, the first on the list is "demonstrate results of violence"' (*How the World* 111). See also José María Ruano de la Haza, *La puesta en escena en los teatros comerciales del Siglo de Oro*, 223–70.

11 See A.A. Parker, *The Approach to the Spanish Drama of the Golden Age*. Lest we become swayed by Calderón's representation of the monarchy and lose sight of its written policy concerning rebellious peasants, Noël Salomon recounts the reaction of Charles I to the execution of Juan Palafox in Monreal: 'Under the reign of Charles I the [townspeople] killed Juan Palafox, their master, with a crossbow, in the town of Monreal. The response of the king was to send an armed force, commanded by the governor of Aragón, to the town of Monreal, which was set ablaze and almost completely destroyed, while some of the inhabitants received an exemplary punishment' (720). Salomon provides similar examples involving Felipe II, including the town of Ariza (721). In sum, there are marked contradictions between the edicts cited by Díez Borque concerning the behavior of the king's troops and the monarchy's violent

reaction to attempts by rural inhabitants to take matters into their own hands after having suffered abuse by the royal troops (Introducción).

12 See Salomon's discussion of examples of how provincial *alcaldes* exploited their economic superiority to take advantage of the *hidalgo* class (707).

6 A Ritual Practice for Modernity

1 See R. de la Flor, *La peninsula metafísica: Arte, literatura y pensamiento en la España de la Contrarreforma*.

2 See Sagrario López, 'La emblemática en *El Criticón* de Baltasar Gracián' (353); see also Campa, 'La génesis.'

3 Selig has compiled all of the references to Alciato in the *Agudeza* in his article 'Gracián and Alciato's *Emblemata*' (1–11).

4 All translations from the Spanish in this chapter are my own.

5 This relationship between taste and spiritual substance is also present in the writings of San Francisco de Borja: 'before beginning the meditation, he will look at the image and in particular he will notice what is there to see; because the function of the image is much like adding spice to the morsel, which must be eaten, such that nothing remains but to eat it' [antes de comenzar la meditación, mirará la imagen y particularmente advertirá lo que en ella hay que advertir, para considerarlo en la meditación mejor y para sacar mayor provecho de ella; porque el oficio que hace la imagen es como dar guisado al manjar, que se ha de comer, de manera que no queda sino comerlo] (cited in García Mahíques, Introducción 39).

6 For a Kantian take on Gracián, see especially Egginton, 'Gracián'; and Cascardi, 'Gracián and the Authority of Taste.'

7 Current criticism is returning to the mind-body connection with compelling results. See especially Catherine Connor (Swietlicki), 'Bridging the Performance Gap: The Body, Cognitive Theory, and *Comedia* Studies.' Batllori and Peralta underline the problematic nature of these diagnoses even as they cite them for the perusal of the reader: 'We should also take note of how the undulations of his psychosomatic profile coincide only in part, during his life, with his state of health: in 1633 (Lérida) the bilious and sanguine complexion corresponds to his strong physical state, similar, but not identical, to that which was noticed in 1625; and it continues this way in 1636 (Gandía) and 1639 (Huesca); the reports from 1642 (Zaragoza) are missing, but the ones from 1645 (Valencia) return to his bilious and melancholic humour … When the tension and discontent

grow, in 1655, while still in Zaragoza, the choleric and melancholic temperament reappears, which is to say, gloomy, without the impetuousness of those who are bilious' (59–60).

8 See Domingo Ynduráin, 'En torno al *Examen de ingenios* de Huarte de San Juan.'

9 Huarte writes, 'And if we were to pass these four drops of humours to the tongue and give them a pitcher of water to drink, one would say it was sweet, the other bitter, the other salty, and the other metallic' [Y si estas cuatro gotas de humores las pasásemos a la lengua y les diésemos a beber un jarro de agua, el uno diría que era dulce, el otro amarga, el otro salada y el otro acero] (*Examen de ingenios para las ciencias* 173).

10 '[T]he understanding has the natural virtue and strengths to produce and give birth inside itself to a child, which the natural philosophers call *knowledge* or a *concept*, which is the language of the mind' [[E]l entendimiento tiene virtud y fuerzas naturales de producir y parir dentro de sí un hijo, al cual llaman los filósofos naturales *noticia* o *concepto*, que es *verbum mentis*] (Huarte 188).

11 '[The] name *ingenio*, which descends from the root *ingenero*, which means to engender within itself a complete and true figure which directly represents the nature of the subject whose science one learns' [[El] nombre *ingenio*, el cual desciende de este verbo *ingenere*, que quiere decir engendrar dentro de sí una figura entera y verdadera que representa al vivo la naturaleza del sujeto cuya es la ciencia que se aprende] (Huarte 193).

12 In the *Criticón*, Gracián elaborates on why truth is so unpalatable to human nature. The reason is that the most basic truths are man's fallen nature and his perverse desires, thus truth tends to deconstruct any power, knowledge, or truth that the human subject constructs by reminding him that it is all, in the end, *lodo*.

13 Gracián gives us the following description of *engaño* in *El Criticón*: 'note that face, which at first glance seems true, and is not human but rather that of a fox; the top half is a serpent; its body is so twisted and its entrails so confused that it is enough to turn them all around; it has the backbone of a camel and even the nose is bent; at its tail it is a siren, and, what is worse, such are its fruits. It cannot go straight; can you not see how the neck twists around?; it walks bent over, and not well inclined. The hands are all gnarled, the feet are crooked, its sight is crossed. And with all of this, it speaks in falsetto, in order not to proceed correctly in anything' [nota aquel rostro, que a primera vista parece verdadero, y no es de hombre, sino de vulpeja; de medio arriba es serpiente; tan torcido tiene el cuerpo y sus entrañas tan revueltas, que basta a revolverlas; el

espinazo tiene de camello y hasta la nariz tiene corcova; el remate es de sirena, y aun peor, tales son sus dexos. No puede ir derecho; ¿no ves como tuerce el cuello?; anda acorvado, y no de bien inclinado. Las manos tiene gafas, los pies tuertos, la vista atravessada. Y a todo esto, habla en falsete, para no hablar ni proceder bien en cosa alguna] (I, 8.182–3).

14 In *El Criticón*, one of the strongest indications of this ritual transformation is the movement from material to immaterial organs, exemplified most strikingly in the transformation of the mammalian breast into the reservoir of the memory: 'Thus I believed that the savage who fed me at her breasts (pechos) was my mother' [Assí yo ... creía madre la que me alimentaba fiera de sus pechos] (I, 1.71), gives way to 'knowledge was food to her and noble novelties her sustenance; such that she took things from the breast of her memory and passed them to her understanding' [el saber era su comer y las nobles noticias su alimento; que fuesse sacando de los senos de la memoria las cosas y passándolas al entendimiento] (III, 6.655).

15 See David R. Castillo, 'Gracián and the Art of Public Representation'; and Nicholas Spadaccini and Jenaro Talens, 'Introduction: The Practice of Worldly Wisdom: Rereading Gracián and the New World Order.'

16 Huarte writes, 'They call inventive geniuses in the Tuscan language *capricious*, due to their likeness to a goat in walking and grazing. The latter never takes pleasure in the easy path; she always prefers walking alone through the crags and heights, looming over the great depths; whereby she never follows any path nor wants to travel in company' [A los ingenios inventivos llaman en lengua Toscana *caprichosos*, por semejanza que tienen con la cabra en el andar y pacer. Esta jamás huelga por lo llano; siempre es amiga de andar a sus solas por los riscos y alturas, y asomarse a grandes profundidades; por donde no sigue vereda ninguna ni quiere caminar con compañía] (344–5). Calderón's privileging of the difficult and mountainous journey of *Buen Genio* is apt here, and reminds us of the eucharistic origins of taste. We can also take note of the negative withdrawal of the *ingenio*, as it gazes from the heights of inspiration into the abyss of nonidentity represented by the *vulgo* (see Read, *Visions*).

17 See Egginton's application of the Heideggerian model of subjectitivity in *How the World*, 135.

18 I owe this last observation to an email exchange with David R. Castillo.

7 Bodies and Corpses, Voices and Silence

1 For a fascinating treatment of 'late style' as an aesthetic phenomenon, see Edward Said's *On Late Style: Music and Literature against the Grain.*

2 William Childers has noted this same turn in Forcione's criticism of the novel (48–9).
3 All translations are my own, except where otherwise indicated.
4 Whinnom writes, 'Despite the success of a limited number of imaginative works, Golden-Age printing in Spanish is dominated by prose non-fiction, by devotional, moralizing, and historical works' (194).
5 See R.L. Kagan, *Students and Society in Early Modern Spain*.
6 Antonio Bernat Vistarini provides a summary of emblematic approaches to Cervantes in 'Algunos motives emblemáticos en la poesía de Cervantes' (83n1).
7 See Cull, 'Emblem Motifs in *Persiles y Sigismunda*.'
8 See Egido, 'Los silencios del *Persiles*' and 'Poesía y peregrinación en el *Persiles*. El templo de la Virgen de Guadalupe.'
9 See Frederick A. De Armas, 'A Banquet of the Senses: The Mythological Structure of *Persiles y Sigismunda, III*.'
10 See Selig, '*Persiles y Sigismunda*: Notes on Pictures, Portraits, and Portraiture.'
11 See Mary Gaylord Randal, 'Ending and Meaning in Cervantes' *Persiles y Sigismunda*.'
12 This is not the only example of foreshadowing that involves hands in Book I. When Bradamiro takes Auristela and Periandro's hands in his bid to abscond with the beautiful pair of slaves, he foreshadows similar scenes in which Auristela 'arranges' the marriage of the mismatched fishermen, and in which Maximino gives Sigismunda's hand to Persiles.
13 For an ironic representation of the symbolic power of hands, see Juan Ruiz's uproarious episode in which the uncultured Romans usurp the symbolic superiority of the conquered Greeks in a public contest of hand signals (*El libro de buen amor* 21–7).
14 Maestro is particularly virulent on this point when he states, 'Literature is the only discourse that never ages; it is prior to all theoretical form or activity … it is … uncompromising and superior to any aesthetic precept and any formulation of moral law … Literature always outlives its interpretations. And thanks to them as well. There is no greater irony' (21–3). See also Cesáreo Bandera, *La mímesis conflictiva*.
15 *Orchesta* appears in the emblematic genealogy assembled in the prologue to Horozco's *Emblemas morales*, and it means a 'silent exposition [of] hands that dance' [exposición callada [de] manos que dançan] (B5).
16 I am reminded of Achilles' attempt to avoid serving in the Greek army. In his case, of course, the removal of his disguise leads to his inscription.
17 It is worth noting that the barbaric ritual, in which the barbarian who

successfully drinks the ashes from the immolated heart of the sacrificial victim will be named king, is reminiscent of the story of the golden calf in Exodus 32. When Moses returns from the mountain, where he received the Ten Commandments, he finds the Isrealites dancing and worshipping the golden idol. In his anger, he has the idol incinerated, and he takes the ashes and throws them on the water and then commands the idolaters to drink the purgative.

18 Daly underlines this emblematic operation by citing Monroy's argument in which the latter points out that the emblematic object does not possess a meaning in and of itself: '[Monroy] argues that meaning is not inherent in the object pictured in the emblem, but "is artificially derived from it, imposed on it. It [the meaning] does not lie in the object, is not discovered, but rather invented. The emblem has an inventor; it is the personal, ingenious ["unverbindlich"] aperçu of an author"' (*Literature* 81).

19 See Casalduero; Avalle-Arce, '*Persiles* and Allegory'; and Forcione, *Cervantes' Christian Romance*.

20 This characterization of a temporarily fallen character returns in the last book when Persiles flees to the countryside upon Auristela's declaration of her intention to enter a convent: 'He settled in behind a tree, in such a way that he and the tree formed the same shade' [Acomodóse detrás de un árbol, de tal forma que él y el árbol hacían una misma sombra] (IV, 12.698).

21 See Nalle's *God in La Mancha* for examples of how difficult it was to disseminate the doctrine of the immaculate conception in rural Castile.

22 Diana De Armas Wilson suggests that Cervantes' decision to use the Virgin of Guadalupe arises from the importance he gives to mother-figures, and women in general, in the *Persiles*: 'It may be argued that Feliciana involves herself in the pilgrimmage to the Black Madonna of Guadalupe as a mother-quest, since Black Madonnas – those hermetic wonder-workers who preside over sex, pregnancy, and childbirth in Catholic countries – are especially venerated as the maternal aspect of Mary' (*Allegories* 211).

23 See also Frederick De Armas.

24 Compiled and cited in the *Enciclopedia Akal de Emblemas Españoles Ilustrados* (692).

25 The text establishes this analogy between Satan and Isabela's uncle in the following way: 'In the middle of this, which did not seem that anyone other than Satan had ordered it, Isabela's uncle entered showing signs of great happiness' [Estando en esto, que no parece sino que el mismo Satanás lo ordenaba, entró el tío con muestras de grandísima alegría] (III, 21.620).

26 I could find no satisfactory English translation for *burra*. Since Cervantes has stressed the female gender of the beast twice, I have left it there in the attempt to preserve the not-so-hidden irony of the noble student mounted on a less than aristocratic beast of burden.

Conclusion

1 One of the most interesting aspects of Kaufman's de Sade is that the writer himself seems comparatively disinterested, if not physically impotent, in the sexual act itself. His driving interest in Madeline, which seems at first to be erotic in nature, reveals itself to be an instance of his more general fascination with the dialectic of pleasure and guilt, *jouissance* and revulsion. His deviance is limited to the imaginative and artistic spheres of activity, while those around him, with the exception of Madeline, are spurred on to ever greater acts of perversion and violence.

Works Cited

Alciati, Andrea. *Los emblemas. Traducidos en rhimas españolas*. Ed. and trans. Bernardino Daza Pinciano. Lyon: G. Rovillio, 1549.

Alciato: Emblemas. Ed. Santiago Sebastián, intro. Aurora Egido, trans. of emblems Pilar Pedraza. Madrid: Ediciones Akal, 1993.

Altschul, Nadia. *La literatura, el autor y la crítica textual*. Madrid: Editorial Pliegos, 2005.

Andrews, Lew. *Story and Space in Renaissance Art. The Rebirth of Continuous Narrative*. Cambridge, UK: Cambridge UP, 1995.

Arellano, Ignacio. *Calderón y su escuela dramática*. Madrid: Laberinto, 2001.

Arellano, Ignacio, and J. Enrique Duarte. *El auto sacramental*. Madrid: Laberinto, 2003.

Armas, Frederick A. De. 'A Banquet of the Senses: The Mythological Structure of *Persiles y Sigismunda, III*.' *Bulletin of Hispanic Studies* 70 (1993): 403–14.

Assmann, Jan. 'Ancient Egypt and the Materiality of the Sign.' *Materialities of Communication*. Ed. Hans Ulrich Gumbrecht and K. Ludwig Pfeiffer, trans. W. Whobrey. Stanford: Stanford UP, 1994. 15–31.

Aubrun, Charles. '*El Alcalde de Zalamea*. Ilusión cómica e ilusiones políticas y sociales.' *Hacia Calderón. Séptimo Coloquio Anglogermano, Cambridge, 1984*. Ed. Hans Flasche. Stuttgart: Franz Steiner, 1985. 169–75.

Avalle-Arce, Juan Bautista. '*Persiles* and Allegory.' *Cervantes* 10.1 (1990): 7–13.

Avilés, Luis F. 'To the Frontier and Back: The Centrifugal and the Centripetal in Cervantes' *Persiles y Sigismunda* and Gracián's *El Criticón*.' *Symposium* 50 (1996): 141–63.

Baena, Julio. *El círculo y la flecha: principio y fin, triunfo y fracaso del* Persiles. Chapel Hill: U of North Carolina P, 1996.

– *Discordancias cervantinas*. Newark, DE: Juan de la Cuesta, 2003.

Bakhtin, Mikhail M. *Rabelais and His World*. Trans. Helene Iswolsky. Cambridge, MA: MIT P, 1968.

Baltrusaitis, Jurgis. *Anamorphic Art*. Trans. W.J. Strachan. New York: Harry N. Abrams, 1969.

Bandera, Cesáreo. *La mímesis conflictiva*. Prologue by Réne Girard. Madrid: Gredos, 1975.

Bataillon, Marcel. 'Ensayo de explicación del "auto sacramental."' *Varia lección de clásicos españoles*. Madrid: Gredos, 1964. 183–205.

Batllori, Miguel, and Ceferino Peralta, eds. *Baltasar Gracián en su vida y en sus obras*. Zaragoza: Institución Fernando el Católico, 1969.

Battistini, Andrea. 'The Telescope in the Baroque Imagination.' *Reason and Its Others: Italy, Spain, and the New World*. Ed. David R. Castillo and Massimo Lollini. Hispanic Issues 32. Nashville: Vanderbilt UP, 2006. 3–38.

Bell, Catherine. *Ritual Perspectives and Dimensions*. Oxford: Oxford UP, 1997.

– *Ritual Theory, Ritual Practice*. Oxford: Oxford UP, 1992.

Belting, Hans. *Likeness and Presence: a History of the Image before the Era of Art*. Trans. E. Jephcott. Chicago: U of Chicago P, 1994.

Benjamin, Walter. *The Origins of German Tragic Drama*. Trans. John Osborne. London: NCB, 1977.

Bennet, Tony. *Outside Literature*. New York: Routledge, 1990.

Bernat Vistarini, Antonio. 'Algunos motivos emblemáticos en la poesía de Cervantes.' *Actas del II Congreso Internacional de la Asociación de Cervantistas 1995*. Ed. Giuseppe Grilli. Napoli, 1995. 83–95.

Bernat Vistarini, Antonio, and John T. Cull. 'On the Trail of Hispanic Emblem Studies.' *Emblem Scholarship: Directions and Developments. A Tribute to Gabriel Hornstein*. Ed. Peter M. Daly. Turnhout: Brepols Publishers, 2005. 25–50.

Bhabha, Homi. *The Location of Culture*. Rev. ed. New York: Routledge, 2004.

Blanco, Mercedes. 'Literatura e ironía en *Los trabajos de Persiles y Sigismunda*.' *Actas del II Congreso Internacional de la Asociación de Cervantistas*. Ed. Giuseppe Grilli. Napoli: Instituto Universitario Orientale, 1995. 625–35.

Blue, William R. 'Peribáñez and Economics.' *Texto y espectáculo: Selected Proceedings of the Symposium on Spanish Golden Age Theater. Mar. 11, 12, 13, 1987, University of Texas at El Paso*. Ed. Barbara Mujica. Lanham: UP of America, 1989. 47–52.

Borja, Francisco de. *Tratados espirituales*. Intro. and ed. by C. de Dalmeses. Ed. Juan Flores. Barcelona: Espirituales Españoles, 1964.

Borja, Juan de. *Empresas Morales*. Brussels: F. Foppens, 1680.

– *Empresas morales*. Ed. and intro. Carmen Bravo-Villasante. Madrid: Fundación Universitaria Española, 1981.

Bourdieu, Pierre. *The Field of Cultural Production: Essays on Art and Literature*. Ed. and intro. R. Johnson. New York: Columbia UP, 1993.

– *Outline of a Theory of Practice*. Cambridge, UK: Cambridge UP, 1977.

Bouza, Fernando. *Communication, Knowledge, and Memory in Early Modern Spain*. Trans. S. López and M. Agnew, foreword R. Chartier. Philadelphia: U of Pennsylvania P, 2004.

Bouzy, Christian. 'Dios como arquetipo actancial en los *Emblemas Morales* de Juan de Horozco (Segovia, 1589): retórica y resorte dramatúrgico del emblema-predicación.' *Studea Aurea. Actas del III Congreso de la AISO*. Ed. Ignacio Arellano et al. Pamplona-Toulouse: GRISO-LEMSO, 1996. 151–68.

– 'La poètique de l'emblème au siècle d'Or: Juan de Horozco, théoricien du symbole.' *Hommage des Hispanistes Français a Henry Bonneville*. Ed. Michel Moner and J.-P. Clément. Poitiers: Société des Hispanistes Français de l'Enseignement Supérieur, 1996. 75–110.

Brotherton, John. 'Lope de Vega's *El nuevo mundo descubierto por Cristóbal Colón*: Convention and Ideology.' *Bulletin of the Comediantes* 46 (1994): 33–47.

Buci-Glucksmann, Christine. *Baroque Reason: The Aesthetics of Modernity*. Trans. Patrick Camiller, intro. Bryan S. Turner. London: Sage Publications, 1994.

Buck-Morss, Susan. *The Dialectics of Seeing: Walter Benjamin and the Arcades Project*. Cambridge, MA: MIT P, 1995.

Bynum, Caroline Walker. *The Resurrection of the Body in Western Christianity, 200–1336*. New York: Columbia UP, 1995.

Calabrese, Omar. *Neo-Baroque*. Trans. Charles Lambert, foreword Umberto Eco. Princeton: Princeton UP, 1992.

Calderón de la Barca, Pedro. *El Alcalde de Zalamea*. Ed. J.M. Díez Borque. Madrid: Castalia, 1976.

– *El gran teatro del mundo. El gran mercado del mundo*. Ed. Eugenio Frutos Cortés. Madrid: Cátedra, 1991.

– *La vida es sueño*. Ed. Ciriaco Morón. Madrid: Cátedra, 1989.

Campa, Pedro F. *Emblemata Hispanica: An Annotated Bibliography of Spanish Emblem Literature to the Year 1700*. Durham: Duke UP, 1990.

– 'La génesis del libro de emblemas jesuita. *Literatura emblemática hispánica. Actas del I Simposio Internacional (La Coruña, 14–17 de septiembre, 1994)*. Ed. Sagrario López Poza. La Coruña: Universidade da Coruña, 1996. 43–60.

– 'The Space between Heraldry and the Emblem: The Case in Spain.' *Emblem Scholarship: Directions and Developments. A Tribute to Gabriel Hornstein*. Ed. Peter M. Daly. Turnhout: Brepols Publishers, 2005. 51–82.

Carey-Webb, Allen. 'Other-Fashioning: The Discourse of Empire and Nation in Lope de Vega's *El nuevo mundo descubierto por Cristóbal Colón.' Amerindian Images and the Legacy of Columbus*. Ed. Rene Jara and Nicholas Spadaccini. Hispanic Issues 9. Minneapolis: U of Minnesota P, 1992. 425–51.

Cartagena Calderón, José R. *Masculinidades en obras: El drama de la hombría en la España imperial*. Newark, DE: Juan de la Cuesta, 2008.

Casalduero, Joaquín. *Sentido y forma de "Los trabajos de Persiles y Sigismunda"*. Madrid: Gredos, 1975.

Cascardi, Anthony. 'Gracián and the Authority of Taste.' *Rhetoric and Politics. Baltasar Gracián and the New World Order*. Ed. Nicholas Spadaccini and Jenaro Talens. Minneapolis: U of Minnesota P, 1997. 255–86.

Case, Thomas E. 'El indio en las comedias de Lope de Vega.' *Looking at the Comedia in the Year of the Quincentennial*. Proceedings of the 1992 Symposium on Golden Age Drama at the University of Texas, El Paso, March 18–21. Ed. Barbara Mujica and Sharon D. Voros. Lanham, MD: UP of America, 1993. 13–21.

Castillo, David R. *(A)wry Views: Anamorphosis, Cervantes, and the Early Picaresque*. West Lafayette, IN: Purdue UP, 2001.

– 'Gracián and the Art of Public Representation.' *Rhetoric and Politics. Baltasar Gracián and the New World Order*. Ed. Nicholas Spadaccini and Jenaro Talens. Minneapolis: U of Minnesota P, 1997. 191–208.

Castillo, David R., and Nicholas Spadaccini. 'El antiutopismo en *Los trabajos de Persiles y Sigismunda*: Cervantes y el cervantismo actual.' *Cervantes* 20.1 (2000): 115–31.

Castillo, Moisés R. *Indios en escena: La representación del amerindio en el teatro del Siglo de Oro*. West Lafayette, IN: Purdue UP, 2009.

– 'Lope de Vega, inventor de América: *El nuevo mundo descubierto por Cristóbal Colón*.' *Bulletin of the Comediantes* 54.1 (2002): 57–90.

– 'El secreto de Vitoria y sus silencios.' *Romance Languages Annual VIII* (1997): 397–403.

Castro, Américo. *El pensamiento de Cervantes*. Notas de Julio Rodríguez-Puértolas. Madrid: Editorial Noguer. 1972.

Cavallo, Tomaso. 'Real Accidents, Surfaces and Digestions: Descartes and the "very easily explained" Transubstantiation.' *The Poetics of Transubstantiation: From Theology to Metaphor*. Ed. D. Burnham and E. Giaccherini. Aldershot, Hants, England; Burlington, VT: Ashgate, 2005. 11–25.

Cervantes, Miguel de. *Don Quixote*. Trans. J.M. Cohen. London: Penguin Books, 1950.

– *Don Quixote de la Mancha I y II*. Ed. and notes Tom Lathrop. Newark, Delaware: Juan de la Cuesta, 1998.

– *Los trabajos de Persiles y Sigismunda*. Ed. Carlos Romero Muñoz. Madrid: Cátedra, 2002.

– *The Trials of Persiles and Sigismunda: A Northern Story*. Trans. Celia Richmond Weller and Clark A. Colahan. Berkeley: U of California P, 1989.

Checa, Jorge. 'Alegoría, verdad y verosimilitud en *El Criticón*.' *Documentos A* 5 (1993): 116–26.

Childers, William. *Transnational Cervantes*. Toronto: U of Toronto P, 2006.

Christian, William A. *Local Religion in Sixteenth-Century Spain*. Princeton: Princeton UP, 1981.

Clements, Robert J. *PICTA POESIS. Literary and Humanistic Theory in Renaissance Emblem Books*. Roma: Edizioni di Storia e Letteratura, 1960.

Connor (Swietlicki), Catherine. 'Bridging the Performance Gap: The Body, Cognitive Theory, and *Comedia* Studies.' *Bulletin of the Comediantes* 55.2 (2003): 11–54.

Contreras, Jaime. 'Family Patronage: The Judeo-Converso Minority in Spain.' *Cultural Encounters: The Impact of the Inquisition in Spain and the New World*. Ed. Anne J. Cruz and Mary Elizabeth Perry. Berkeley: U of California P, 1991. 127–45.

Correa Calderón, E. *Baltasar Gracián: su vida y su obra*. Madrid: Gredos, 1961.

Covarrubias Orozco, Sebastián. *Emblemas morales*. Madrid: Luis Sánchez, 1610.

– *Tesoro de la lengua castellana o española*. 2nd ed. Ed. Felipe C.R. Maldonado, revised by Manuel Camarero. Madrid: Editorial Castalia, 1995.

Cruz, Sor Juana Inés de la. *Obras Completas*. México: Porrúa, 1987.

Cull, John T. 'Emblem Motifs in *Persiles y Sigismunda*.' *Romance Notes* 32.3 (1992): 199–208.

– 'Emblematics in Calderón's *El médico de su honra*.' *Bulletin of the Comediantes* 44.1 (1992): 113–30.

– '"Hablan poco y dicen mucho": The Function of Discovery Scenes in the Drama of Tirso de Molina.' *The Modern Language Review* 91 (1996): 619–34.

Daly, Peter M. 'Digitizing the European Emblem: Issues, Problems and Prospects.' *Florilegio de estudios de emblemática. Actas del VI Congreso Internacional de Emblemática de The Society for Emblem Studies, A Coruña 2002*. Ed. Sagrario López Poza. La Coruña: Sociedad de Cultura Valle Inclán, 2004. 49–64.

– *Literature in Light of the Emblem. Structural Parallels between the Emblem and Literature in the Sixteenth and Seventeenth Centuries*. Toronto: U of Toronto P, 1979.

Daza Pinciano, Bernardino. *Emblemas*. Lyon: Mathia Bonhomme, 1549.

Deleuze, Gilles. *The Fold: Leibniz and the Baroque*. Trans. and foreword Tom Conley. Minneapolis: U of Minnesota P, 1993.

– and Félix Guatarri. *A Thousand Plateaus: Capitalism and Schizophrenia*. Trans. and foreword Brian Massumi. Minneapolis: U of Minnesota P, 1987.

de Man, Paul. *The Resistance to Theory*. Theory and History of Literature, 33. Minneapolis: U. of Minnesota P, 1986.

Derrida, Jacques. 'Différance.' *Margins of Philosophy*. Trans. Alan Bass. Chicago: U of Chicago P, 1982.

Díaz Balsera, Viviana. *Calderón y las quimeras de la culpa: Alegoría, seducción y resistencia en cinco autos sacramentales*. West Lafayette: Purdue UP, 1997.

Dietz, Donald. *The Auto Sacramental and the Parable in Golden Age Literature*. Chapel Hill, NC: U of North Carolina P, 1973.

Díez Borque, José María. Introducción. *El Alcalde de Zalamea*. By Pedro Calderón de la Barca. Ed. J.M. Díez Borque. Madrid: Castalia, 1976. 7–100.

– 'El auto sacramental calderoniano y su público: funciones del texto cantado.' *Calderón and the Baroque Tradition*. Ed. K. Levy, J. Ara, and G. Hughes. Waterloo, ON: Wilfrid Laurier UP, 1985. 49–67.

Díez Garretas, María Jesús. 'Divisas, motes y momos durante el reinado de los Reyes Católicos.' *Isabel la Católica: los libros de la reina*. Burgos: Instituto Castellano y Leonés de la Lengua Caja Burgos, 2004. 29–46.

Dille, Glen F. 'El descubrimiento y la conquista de América en la comedia del Siglo de Oro.' *Hispania* 71 (1988): 492–502.

Dunn, Peter N. 'Honour and the Christian Background in Calderón.' *Bulletin of Hispanic Studies* 37 (1960): 75–105.

Dutton, Brian, ed. *El Cancionero del siglo XV, c. 1360–1520*. Salamanca: U de Salamanca, 1990–1.

Echeverría, Bolívar. 'La Compañía de Jesús y la primera modernidad en América Latina.' *Barrocos y modernos: Nuevos caminos en la investigación del Barroco iberoamericano*. Ed. Petra Schumm. Frankfurt; Madrid: Vervuert; Ibero-Americana, 1998. 49–65.

– *La modernidad de lo Barroco*. Mexico, D.F.: UNAM, 1998.

Egginton, William. 'Gracián and the Emergence of the Modern Subject.' *Rhetoric and Politics. Baltasar Gracián and the New World Order*. Ed. Nicholas Spadaccini and Jenaro Talens. Minneapolis: U of Minnesota P, 1997. 151–69.

– *How the World Became a Stage: Presence, Theatricality, and the Question of Modernity*. Albany: State U of New York P, 2003.

– *The Philospher's Desire: Psychoanalysis, Interpretation and Truth*. Stanford: Stanford UP, 2007.

Egido, Aurora. *La fábrica de un auto sacramental: Los encantos de la culpa*. Salamanca: U de Salamanca, 1982.

– 'Poesía y peregrinación en el *Persiles*. El templo de la Virgen de Guadalupe.' *Actas del Tercer Congreso Internacional de la Asociación de Cervantistas*.

Ed. Antonio Bernat Vistarini. Palma: Universitat de les Illes Balears, 1998. 1–41.

– 'Los silencios del *Persiles.*' *On Cervantes: Essays for L.A. Murillo.* Ed. James A. Parr. Newark, DE: Juan de la Cuesta, 1991. 21–46.

Enciclopedia Akal de Emblemas Españoles Ilustrados. Compiled and ed. by Antonio Bernat Vistarini and John T. Cull, classical sources and motto translations by Rev. Edward J. Vodoklys, presentation by Peter M. Daly and Sagrario López Poza. Madrid: Akal, 1999.

Entrambasaguas, Joaquín de. Prólogo. *El nuevo mundo descubierto por Cristóbal Colón.* By Lope de Vega. Ed. J. de Entrambasaguas. 2nd ed. Madrid: Instituto de Cultura Hispánica, 1963.

Fernández López, José. 'Retórica y emblemática en España: Los emblemas 181 y 182 de Alciato y sus comentaristas.' *Florilegio de estudios de emblemática. Actas del IV Congreso Internacional de Emblemática de The Society for Emblem Studies, A Coruña 2002.* Ed. Sagario López Poza. La Coruña: Sociedad de Cultura Valle-Inclán, 2004. 347–58.

Flecniakowska, J.L. '¿Auto sacramental o comedia devota?' *Historia y Crítica de la Literatura Española.* Vol. 3. Ed. Aurora Egido. Barcelona: Edición Crítica, 1983. 248–53.

Forcione, Alban. 'At the Threshold of Modernity: Gracián's *El Criticón.*' *Rhetoric and Politics. Baltasar Gracián and the New World Order.* Ed. Nicholas Spadaccini and Jenaro Talens. Minneapolis: U of Minnesota P, 1997. 3–70.

– *Cervantes, Aristotle and the 'Persiles'.* Princeton: Princeton UP, 1970.

– *Cervantes' Christian Romance: A Study of 'Persiles y Sigismunda.'* Princeton: Princeton UP, 1972.

Foucault, Michel. *The Archeology of Knowledge.* Trans. A.M. Sheridan Smith. London: Tavistock, 1972.

– *The Order of Things. An Archaeology of the Human Sciences.* Translation of *Les Mots et les choses.* New York: Random House, 1994.

– 'What Is an Author?' *The Book History Reader.* Ed. David Finkelstein and Alistair McCleery. New York: Routledge, 2002.

Friedman, Edward H. 'Resisting Theory: Rhetoric and Reason in Lope de Vega's *Arte Nuevo.*' *Neophilologus* 75 (1991): 86–93.

Frutos, Eugenio. 'La filosofía del Barroco y el pensamiento de Calderón.' *Revista de la Universidad de Buenos Aires* 9 (1951): 173–230.

Gadamer, Hans-Georg. *Truth and Method.* New York: Continuum, 1975.

Galera Andreu, Pedro A. 'La Palmera, Arbor Victoriae: Reflexiones sobre un tema emblemático.' *Goya* 187–8 (1985): 63–7.

Gállego, Julián. *Visión y símbolos en la pintura española del Siglo de Oro.* Madrid: Cátedra, 1987.

Ganelin, Charles. 'Calderón Incorporated: Hands and Speech in *Las tres justicias en una* and *El postrer duelo de España*.' *Bulletin of the Comediantes* 53.1 (2001): 179–95.

García Arranz, José Julio, and Francisco Javier Pizarro Gómez. 'La visión de la naturaleza en los emblemistas españoles del siglo XVII.' *Literatura emblemática hispánica. Actas del I Simposio internacional*. Ed. Sagrario López Poza. Teruel: Instituto de Estudios Turolenses, 1994. 221–44.

García Mahíques, Rafael. 'La emblemática y el problema de la interpretación icónica: el caso de la "vanitas."' *Actas del I Simposio Internacional de Emblemática*. Ed. Sagrario López Poza. Teruel: Instituto de Estudios Turolenses, 1994. 59–91.

– Introducción. *Empresas morales de Juan de Borja: Imagen y palabra para una iconología*. Ed. García Mahíques. Valencia: Ajuntament de Valencia, 1998. 17–51.

García Mahíques, Rafael, ed. *Empresas morales de Juan de Borja: Imagen y palabra para una iconología*. Valencia: Ajuntament de Valencia, 1998.

Gaylord Randal, Mary. 'Ending and Meaning in Cervantes' *Persiles y Sigismunda*.' *Romanic Review* 74.2 (1983): 152–69.

Godzich, Wlad. *The Culture of Literacy*. Cambridge, MA: Harvard UP, 1994.

– 'Language, Images, and the Postmodern Predicament.' *Materialities of Communication*. Ed. Hans Ulrich Gumbrecht and K. Ludwig Pfeiffer. Trans. W. Whobrey. Stanford: Stanford UP, 1994. 355–70.

Godzich, Wlad, and Nicholas Spadaccini. 'Popular Culture and Spanish Literary History.' *Literature among Discourses: the Spanish Golden Age*. Ed. and intro. Wlad Godzich and Nicholas Spadaccini. Minneapolis: U of Minnesota P, 1986. 41–61.

Gombrich, E.H. *Symbolic Images: Studies in the Art of the Renaissance*. Chicago: U of Chicago P, 1972.

González de Zárate, Jesús María. *Método iconográfico*. Vitoria: Ephialte, 1991.

Gracián, Baltasar. *Agudeza y arte de ingenio*. Ed. Gilberto Prado Galán. México: UNAM, 1996.

– *Arte de ingenio, tratado de la agudeza*. Ed. Emilio Blanco. Madrid: Cátedra, 1998.

– *El comulgatorio*. Ed. and intro. E. Correa Calderón. Madrid: Espasa-Calpe, 1977.

– *El Criticón*. Ed. Santos Alonso. Madrid: Cátedra, 1993.

– *El Héroe y El Discreto*. Ed. Aurora Egido. Madrid: Alianza Editorial, 1997.

– *Oráculo manual y arte de prudencia*. Ed. Emilio Blanco. Madrid: Cátedra, 1997.

Greenberg, Mitchell. *Canonical States, Canonical Stages. Oedipus, Othering, and Seventeenth-Century Drama.* Minneapolis: U of Minnesota P, 1994.

Greer, Margaret R. '"La vida es sueño ¿o risa?" Calderón Parodies the *auto.*' *Bulletin of Hispanic Studies* 72 (1995): 313–25.

Gumbrecht, Hans Ulrich. 'A Farewell to Interpretation.' *Materialities of Communication.* Ed. Hans Ulrich Gumbrecht and K. Ludwig Pfeiffer. Trans. William Whobrey. Stanford: Stanford UP, 1994. 389–402.

– *Making Sense in Life and Literature.* Trans. Glen Burns, foreword Wlad Godzich. Minneapolis: U of Minnesota P, 1992.

– *The Powers of Philology.* Urbana-Champaign: U of Illinois P, 2003.

– *Production of Presence: What Meaning Cannot Convey.* Stanford: Stanford UP, 2004.

Gurd, Sean. Iphigenias at Aulis: *Textual Multiplicity, Radical Philology.* Ithaca and London: Cornell UP, 2005.

Gutiérrez, Carlos M. *La espada, el rayo y la pluma.* West Lafayette, IN: Purdue UP, 2005.

Hale, Mark. *Historical Linguistics: Theory and Method.* Oxford: Blackwell Publishing, 2007.

Harrison, Stephen. *La composición de* Los trabajos de Persiles y Sigismunda. Madrid: Editorial Pliegos, 1993.

Hoffmann, Konrad. 'Alciato and the Historical Situation of Emblematics.' *Emblematic Variants: Literary Echoes of Alciati's Term Emblema: A Vocabulary Drawn from the Title Pages of Emblem Books.* Ed. William S. Hecksher and Agnes B. Sherman. New York: AMS, 1995. 1–45.

Holy Bible. New International Version. Grand Rapids, MI: Zondervan, 1984.

Horozco y Covarrubias, Juan de. *Emblemas morales.* Çaragoça: Alonso Rodrigues y Juan de Bonilla, 1603.

Huarte de San Juan, Juan. *Examen de ingenios para las ciencias.* Ed. G. Serés. Madrid: Cátedra, 1989.

Huston, John. *The Maltese Falcon.* Perf. Humphrey Bogart and Mary Astor. Warner Brothers Studios, 1941.

Iser, Wolfgang. *The Art of Reading: A Theory of Aesthetic Response.* Baltimore and London: The Johns Hopkins UP, 1978.

Jay, Martin. 'Scopic Regimes of Modernity.' *Force Fields: Between Intellectual History and Cultural Critique.* New York: Routledge, 1993. 114–33.

Johnson, Carroll B. 'Social Roles and Ideology, Dramatic Roles and Theatrical Convention in *El gran teatro del mundo.*' *Bulletin of the Comediantes* 49 (1997): 247–72.

Kagan, Richard. 'Politics, Prophecy, and the Inquisition in Late Sixteenth-Century Spain.' *Cultural Encounters: The Impact of the Inquisition in Spain and the New World*. Ed. Anne J. Cruz and Mary Elizabeth Perry. Berkeley: U of California P, 1991. 105–26.

– *Students and Society in Early Modern Spain*. Baltimore: Johns Hopkins UP, 1974.

Kallendorf, Hilaire. 'Dressed to the Sevens, or Sin in Style: Fashion Statements by the Deadly Vices in Spanish Baroque *Autos Sacramentales*.' *The Seven Deadly Sins: From Communities to Individuals*. Ed. Richard Newhauser. Leiden: Brill, 2007. 145–84.

– '¿Qué he de hacer? The *Comedia* as Casuistry.' *The Romanic Review* 95.3: 327–59.

Kamen, Henry. *Empire: How Spain Became a World Power, 1492–1763*. New York: Penguin, 2002.

Kaufman, Philip, dir. *Quills*. Perf. Geoffrey Rush, Kate Winslet, Joaquin Phoenix, and Michael Caine. 20th Century Fox, 2000.

Kirschner, Teresa J. 'Exposición y subversión del discurso hegemónico en pro de la conquista en *El nuevo mundo de Lope de Vega*.' *El escritor y la escena*. Ed. Ysla Campbell. Ciudad Juárez: Universidad Autónoma de Ciudad Juárez, 1993. 45–58.

Lacan, Jacques. *The Four Fundamental Concepts of Psychoanalysis (The Seminar of Jacques Lacan, Book 11)*. Ed. Jacques-Alain Miller. New York: Norton, 1998.

Lauer, A. Robert. '*El Alcalde de Zalamea* y la comedia de villanos.' *El escritor y la escena III: Estudios en honor de Francisco Ruiz Ramón. Actas del III Congreso de la Asociación Internacional de Teatro Español y novohispano de los Siglos de Oro (9–12 de marzo de 1994, Ciudad Juárez)*. Ed. Ysla Campbell. Ciudad Juárez: Universidad Autónoma de Ciudad Juárez, 1995. 162–74.

Ledda, Giuseppina. *Contributo allo studio della letteratura emblematica in Spagna (1559–1613)*. Pisa: Pisa UP, 1970.

Lezra, Jacques. *Unspeakable Subjects: The Genealogy of the Event in Early Modern Europe*. Stanford: Stanford UP, 1997.

López, Sagrario. 'La emblemática en *El Criticón* de Baltasar Gracián.' *Los días del Alción. Emblemas, Literatura y Arte del Siglo de Oro*. Ed. Antonio Bernat Vistarini and John T. Cull. Palma de Mallorca: José J. de Olañeta, Universitat de les Illes Balears & College of the Holy Cross, 2002. 353–73.

– Introducción. *Empresas políticas*. By Diego Saavedra Fajardo. Ed. Sagrario López. Madrid: Cátedra, 1999. 11–134.

– 'Los libros de emblemas y la imprenta.' *Lectura y signo* 1 (2006): 177–99.

Maestro, Jesús G. *El mito de la interpretación literaria: Rojas, Cervantes y Calderón: La ética de la literatura y sus dogmas*. Madrid; Frankfurt: Iberoamericana; Vervuert, 2004.

Maravall, José Antonio. *The Culture of the Baroque. Analysis of a Historical Structure*. Trans. Terry Cochran. Minneapolis: U of Minnesota P, 1986.

– *Estado moderno y mentalidad social (siglos XV–XVII)*. Primera Edición en *Revista de occidente*, 1972. Madrid: Alianza Editorial, 1986.

– 'La literatura de emblemas en el contexto de la sociedad barroca.' *Teatro y literatura en la sociedad barroca*. Madrid: Seminarios y Ediciones, 1972. 149–88.

– *El mundo social de la Celestina*. Madrid: Gredos, 1986.

– *Poder, honor y élites en el siglo XVII*. Madrid: Siglo XXI, 1979.

– 'Teatro, fiesta e ideología en el barroco.' *Teatro y literatura en la sociedad barroca*. Madrid: Seminarios y Ediciones, 1972. 71–96.

– *Teoría del saber histórico*. 3rd.edition. Madrid: Revista de Occidente, 1967.

– *Velázquez y el espíritu de la modernidad*. Madrid: Ministerio de Educación y Centro de Estudios Políticos y Constitucionales, 1999.

Marin, Louis. *Portrait of the King*. Foreword by Tom Conley. Minneapolis: U of Minnesota P, 1988.

Martin, Vincent. *El concepto de 'representación' en los autos sacramentales de Calderón*. Intro. Fernando R. de la Flor. Kassel/Pamplona: Edition Reichenberger/U de Pamplona, 2002.

Martín-Estudillo, Luis, and Nicholas Spadaccini. 'Afterword: Reasoning the Other.' *Reason and Its Others: Italy, Spain, and the New World*. Ed. David R. Castillo and Massimo Lollini. Hispanic Issues 32. Nashville: Vanderbilt UP, 2006. 331–40.

Massey, Lyle. 'Anamorphosis through Descartes or Perspective Gone Awry.' *Renaissance Quarterly* 50.4 (1997): 1148–89.

McCarthy, Cormac. *The Road*. New York: Alfred A. Knopf, 2006.

McCready, Warren T. '*Empresas* in Lope de Vega's Works.' *Hispanic Review* 25 (1957): 79–104.

Menéndez Pelayo, Marcelino. *Calderón y su Teatro*. Madrid: Murillo, 1881.

Micozzi, Patrizia. 'Imágenes metafóricas en la canción a la Virgen de Guadalupe.' *Actas del II Congreso Internacional de la Asociación de Cervantistas*. Ed. Giuseppe Grilli. Naples: Instituto Universitario Orientale, 1995. 711–23.

Mitchell, W.J.T. *Iconology: Text, Image, Ideology*. Chicago: U of Chicago P, 1986.

– *What Do Pictures Want? The Lives and Loves of Images*. Chicago: U of Chicago P, 2005.

Morrow, Carolyn. 'Discourse and Class in *El alcalde de Zalamea*.' *Bulletin of the Comediantes* 44.1 (1992): 133–47.

Nalle, Sara Tilghman. *God in La Mancha: Religious Reform and the People of Cuenca, 1500-1650*. Baltimore: Johns Hopkins UP, 1992.

– 'Literacy and Culture in Early Modern Castile.' *Past and Present* 125 (1989): 65–96.

– *Mad for God: Bartolomé Sánchez, the Secret Messiah of Cardenete*. Charlottesville/London: U of Virginia P, 2001.

Nancy, Jean-Luc. *Au fond des images*. Paris: Galilée, 2003.

Nebrija, Antonio de. *Gramática de la lengua castellana*. Ed. A. Quilis. Madrid: Editora Nacional, 1980.

Nerlich, Michael. *El* Persiles *descodificado, o La 'Divina Comedia' de Cervantes*. Trans. J. Munárriz. Madrid: Hiperión, 2005.

O'Gorman, Edmundo. *La invención de América*. México and Buenos Aires: Fondo de Cultura Económica, 1958.

Ortega y Gasset, José. *Papeles sobre Velázquez y Goya*. Ed. Paulino Garagorri. Madrid: Revista de Occidente en Alianza Editorial, 1987.

Panofsky, Erwin. *Meaning in the Visual Arts*. Garden City, NY: Doubleday Anchor Books, 1955.

– *Perspective as Symbolic Form*. Trans. Christopher S. Wood. New York: Zone Books, 1991.

Parker, A.A. *The Allegorical Drama of Calderón*. London: Dolphin Book Shop, 1943.

– *The Approach to the Spanish Drama of the Golden Age*. London: The Hispanic and Luso-Brazilian Councils, 1957.

– 'The Father-Son Conflict in the Drama of Calderón.' *Forum for Modern Language Studies* 2 (1966): 99–113.

Paz, Octavio. *Sor Juana or, The Traps of Faith*. Trans. Margaret Sayers Peden. Cambridge, MA: Harvard UP, 1988.

Pelegrin, Benito. *Ethique et esthétique du Baroque: L'Espace jésuitique de Baltasar Gracián*. Arles: Actes Sud, 1985.

Pfeiffer, Karl Ludwig. 'Dimensions of Literature.' *Materialities of Communication*. Ed. Hans Ulrich Gumbrecht and K. Ludwig Pfeiffer. Trans. William Whobrey. Stanford: Stanford UP, 1994. 45–62.

Phillips, Jerry. 'Cannibalism qua capitalism: the metaphorics of accumulation in Marx, Conrad, Shakespeare and Marlowe.' *Cannibalism and the Colonial World*. Ed. Francis Barker, Peter Hulme, and Margaret Iverson. Cambridge, UK: Cambridge UP, 1998. 183–203.

Pinkus, Karen. *Picturing Silence. Emblem, Language, Counter-Reformation Materiality*. Ann Arbor: U of Michigan P, 1996.

Poppenberg, Gerhard. 'Religión y política en algunos autos sacramentales de Calderón.' *Calderón: protagonista eminente del barroco europeo*. Ed. Kurt and Theo Reichenberger. Vol 1. Kassel: Edition Reichenberger, 2000. 87–115.

Popper, Karl. *The Open Society and Its Enemies*. Volume II. New York: Harper and Row, 1962.

Pratt, Mary Louise. 'Arts of the Contact Zone' *Ways of Reading: An Anthology for Writers*. Ed. David Bartholomae and Anthony Petrosky. Boston; New York: Bedford; St Martin's, 1999. 582–96.

– *Imperial Eyes: Travel Writing and Transculturation*. London and New York: Routledge, 1992.

Praz, Mario. *Studies in Seventeenth-Century Imagery*. Roma: Edizioni di Storia e Letteratura, 1964.

R. de la Flor, Fernando. *Barroco: Representación e ideología en el mundo hispánico (1580–1680)*. Madrid: Cátedra, 2002.

– *Emblemas: Lecturas de la imagen simbólica*. Madrid: Alianza Editorial, 1995.

– *La peninsula metafísica: Arte, literatura y pensamiento en la España de la Contrarreforma*. Madrid: Biblioteca nueva, 1999.

– Prólogo. *El concepto de 'representación' en los autos sacramentales de Calderón*. By Vincent Martin. Kassel/Pamplona: Edition Reichenberger/U of Pamplona, 2002. 7–16.

– 'Sacrificial Politics in the Spanish Colonies.' *Reason and Its Others: Italy, Spain, and the New World*. Ed. David R. Castillo and Massimo Lollini. Hispanic Issues 32. Nashville: Vanderbilt UP, 2006. 243–58.

– 'La sombra del *Eclesiastés* es alargada. "Vanitas" y deconstrucción de la idea de mundo en la emblemática española hacia 1580.' *Emblemata aurea. La emblemática en el arte y la literatura del siglo de oro*. Ed. R. Zafra and J.J. Azanza. Madrid: Ediciones Akal, 2000. 337–52.

RAE: Real Academia Española; Diccionario de la lengua castellana. 1726. http://www.rae.es/rae.html.

Rappaport, Roy A. *Ecology and Meaning, and Religion*. Richmond, CA: North Atlantic Books, 1979.

Rawles, Stephen. 'Layout, Typography and Chronology in Chrètien Wechel's Editions of Alciato.' *An Interregnum of the Sign. The Emblematic Age in France*. Ed. David Graham. Glasgow: Glasgow Emblem Studies, 2001. 49–71.

Read, Malcolm. *Juan Huarte de San Juan*. Boston: Twayne Publishers, 1981.

– 'The Modernity of the Subject: Anthony Cascardi and Juan Carlos Rodríguez.' *Revista Canadiense de Estudios Hispánicos* 30.3 (2006): 471–96.

– *Visions in Exile: the Body in Spanish Literature and Linguistics*. Amsterdam: J. Benjamins, 1990.

Regalado, Antonio. *Calderón: Los orígenes de la modernidad en la España del Siglo De Oro*. 2 volumes. Barcelona: Destino, 1995.

Restrepo-Gautier, Pablo. *La imaginación emblemática en Tirso de Molina*. Newark, DE: Juan de la Cuesta, 2001.

Rivers, Elias L., ed. and trans. *Renaissance and baroque poetry of Spain, with English prose translations*. New York: Dell Publishing Co., 1966.

Rodríguez, Juan Carlos. *El escritor que compró su propio libro: para leer el* Quijote. Barcelona: Random House Mondadori, 2003.

– *Theory and History of Ideological Production. The First Bourgeois Literatures (the 16th Century).* Trans. Malcolm K. Read. Newark, DE: U of Delaware P, 2002.

Romero Muñoz, Carlos. Introducción. *Los trabajos de Persiles y Sigismunda.* By Miguel de Cervantes. Ed. Carlos Romero Muñoz. Madrid: Cátedra, 2002. 11–60.

Ruano de la Haza, José María. *La puesta en escena en los teatros comerciales del Siglo de Oro.* Madrid: Castalia, 2000.

Ruiz, Juan, Arcipreste de Hita. *Libro de buen amor.* Ed. Alberto Blecua. Madrid: Cátedra, 2001.

Russell, Daniel. *Emblematic Structures in Renaissance French Culture.* Toronto: U of Toronto P, 1995.

Saavedra Fajardo, Diego de. *Idea de un príncipe político cristiano representada en cien empresas.* Ed. Sagrario López. Madrid: Cátedra, 1999.

Sacchetti, Maria Alberta. *Cervantes'* Los Trabajos de Persiles y Sigismunda. *A Study of Genre.* London: Tamesis, 2001.

Said, Edward. *On Late Style: Music and Literature Against the Grain.* New York: Pantheon Books, 2006.

– *Orientalism.* New York: Random House, 1978.

Salomon, Noël. *Lo villano en el teatro del Siglo de Oro.* Madrid: Editorial Castalia, 1985.

Sánchez, Francisco. 'Cultura y persona en Gracián.' *RLit* 122 (1999): 375–88.

– *An Early Bourgeois Literature in Golden Age Spain.* Chapel Hill: U of North Carolina P, 2003.

Sebastián, Santiago. *Emblemática e historia del arte.* Madrid: Cátedra, 1995.

– 'Influencias e interferencias en los orígenes de la Emblemática española.' *Actas del I Simposio Internacional de Emblemática, Teruel, 1–1 de octubre de 1991.* Ed. Sagrario López. Teruel: Instituto de Estudios Turolenses, 1994. 445–53.

– Introduction. *Alciato: Emblemas.* Ed. Santiago Sebastián. Madrid: Akal, 1985. 19–26.

Selig, Karl Ludwig. 'Gracián and Alciato's *Emblemata.*' *Comparative Literature* 8 (1956): 1–11.

– '*Persiles y Sigismunda*: Notes on Pictures, Portraits, and Portraiture.' *Hispanic Review* 41 (1973): 305–12.

– *Studies on Alciato in Spain.* New York and London: Garland, 1990.

Shannon, Robert M. Introduction. *El nuevo mundo descubierto por Cristóbal Colón. Una edición crítica y bilingüe.* By Lope de Vega. Ed. Robert M. Shannon. New York: Peter Lang, 2001. 1–69.

Sider, Sandra. 'Transcendent Symbols for the Hapsburgs: Plus Ultra and the Columns of Hercules.' *Emblematica: An Interdisciplinary Journal of Emblem Studies* 4.2 (1989): 257–72.

Silverman, Joseph. 'On Knowing Other People's Lives, Inquisitorially and Artistically.' *Cultural Encounters: the Impact of the Inquisition in Spain and the New World*. Ed. Anne J. Cruz and Mary Elizabeth Perry. Berkeley: U of California P, 1991. 157–75.

Spadaccini, Nicholas, and Jenaro Talens. 'Introduction: The Practice of Worldly Wisdom: Rereading Gracián and the New World Order.' *Rhetoric and Politics. Baltasar Gracián and the New World Order*. Ed. Nicholas Spadaccini and Jenaro Talens. Minneapolis: U of Minnesota P, 1997. ix–xxxii.

Steinberg, Leo. *The Sexuality of Christ in Renaissance Art and Modern Oblivion*. 2nd ed. Chicago: U of Chicago P, 1996.

Sullivan, Henry. 'Imaginaria comerciante y diabólica en el auto *El gran mercado del mundo*.' *Hacia Calderón. Décimo Coloquio Anglogermano, Passau 1993*. Ed. H. Flasche. Stuttgart: Franz Steiner, 1994. 165–74.

Turner, Victor. *The Ritual Process: Structure and Anti-Structure*. Foreword by R. D. Abrahams. New York: Aldine de Gruyter, 1969.

Wardropper, Bruce W. 'La imaginación en el metateatro calderoniano.' *Actas del Tercer Congreso Internacional de Hispanistas*. Ed. C.H. Magis. México: Colegio de México, 1970. 923–30.

– *Introducción al teatro religioso del Siglo de Oro. La evolución del auto sacramental 1500–1648*. Madrid: Revista de Occidente, 1953.

Weiner, Jack. *En busca de la justicia social: Estudios sobre el teatro epsañol del Siglo de Oro*. Washington, DC: Scripta Humanistica, 1984.

– 'La guerra y la paz en tres comedias de Lope de Vega.' *Revista de Estudios Hispánicos* 17.1 (1983): 65–79.

Whinnom, Keith. 'The Problem of the "Best-Seller" in Spanish Golden-Age Literature.' *Bulletin of Hispanic Studies* 57.3 (1980): 189–98.

White, Hayden. *Tropics of Discourse: Essays from Cultural Criticism*. Baltimore: Johns Hopkins UP, 1978.

Williamsen, Amy C. *Cosmic Chaos: Exploring* Los trabajos de Persiles y Sigismunda. Newark, DE: Juan de la Cuesta, 1994.

Wilson, Diana De Armas. *Allegories of Love. Cervantes's* Persiles y Sigismunda. Princeton: Princeton UP, 1991.

Ynduráin, Domingo. '*El alcalde de Zalamea*, historia, ideología, literatura.' *Edad de Oro* 5 (1986): 299–311.

– 'En torno al *Examen de ingenios* de Huarte de San Juan.' *Boletín de la Real Academia Española* 79 (Jan.–April 1999): 7–54.

Žižek, Slavoj. 'The Cartesian Subject versus the Cartesian Theater.' *Cogito and the Unconscious*. Ed. Slavoj Žižek. Durham, NC: Duke UP, 1998. 247–74.

– *Looking Awry: an Introduction to Jacques Lacan through Popular Culture*. Cambridge, MA: MIT Press, 1991.
– *Organs without Bodies: On Deleuze and Consequences*. New York: Routledge, 2004.
– *The Parallax View*. Cambridge, MA: MIT Press, 2006.
– *The Sublime Object of Ideology*. New York: Verso, 1989.
– *Tarrying with the Negative: Kant, Hegel, and the Critique of Ideology*. Durham, NC: Duke UP, 1993.

Index

www.ingramcontent.com/pod-product-compliance
Lightning Source LLC
LaVergne TN
LVHW090805070826
844660LV00022B/1089

* 9 7 8 1 4 8 7 5 2 6 2 1 4 *